A RELIGIOUS FOUNDATION OF HUMAN RELATIONS

A RELIGIOUS FOUNDATION OF HUMAN RELATIONS: BEYOND GAMES

by George Henderson

Norman
University of Oklahoma Press

By George Henderson

Foundations of American Education (with William B. Ragan) (New York, 1970)
Teachers Should Care (with Robert F. Bibens) (New York, 1970)
America's Other Children: Public Schools Outside Suburbia (editor) (Norman, 1971)
To Live in Freedom: Human Relations Today and Tomorrow (Norman, 1972)
Education for Peace: Focus on Mankind (editor) (Washington, D.C., 1973)
Human Relations: From Theory to Practice (Norman, 1974)
Human Relations in the Military: Problems and Programs (Chicago, 1975)
A Religious Foundation of Human Relations: Beyond Games (Norman, 1977)

Library of Congress Cataloging in Publication Data

Henderson, George, 1932–
  A religious foundation of human relations.

  Includes bibliographical references and index.
  1. Church and social problems.   2. Sociology, Christian.   I. Title.
       HN31.H43   261.8'3   76-62510

Copyright 1977 by the University of Oklahoma Press, Publishing Division of the University. Manufactured in the U.S.A.

To my wife, Barbara, and our children

PREFACE

EACH year, a growing number of people have come to realize that no amount of behavioral-science theory will allow us to produce a humane society if such theory is devoid of a humane foundation. And belatedly these same people have come to realize that Christianity *is* a humane foundation for human relations. Each year, millions of Americans spend billions of dollars and countless hours trying to find peace with themselves and with God. In retrospect, it is clear to me that an excellent starting point is an enlightened study of Scripture.

In an effort to bridge the gap between behavioral-science theories and Judaeo-Christian doctrines, I have elected to focus on the works of ancient and contemporary writers. Although my selection of writers is limited, I believe my point is made: there is much in the Bible that supports our efforts to build a truly humane nation. Indeed, some of the most sophisticated new scientific pronouncements are merely variations of old Judaeo-Christian themes. Of course, a similar case could be made for other religions—Islam, Hinduism, Buddhism, Shintoism, Taoism, and Confucianism—as they relate to human relationships.

A Religious Foundation of Human Relations

I am aware that racial segregation, sexism, poverty, and war have been supported by individual and group interpretations of Scripture. With this in mind, I am not encouraging an analysis of religious tenets in order to disrupt human relationships. Instead, this book is written for students and teachers, lay persons, clergy—anyone interested in improving interpersonal and intergroup relationships.

I am indebted to many persons for their encouragement and counsel. My gratitude goes to Kenneth Beaver, George Brennen, Dorothy Dittmar, Nancy Freebairn, Patrick Furfari, Robert Hailey, Evans Moore, John Shaw, and Donald Wiggins for their excellent suggestions. Special thanks go to Norma Banks and Ellen Blyden for their contribution to Chapter 1.

It is my hope that I have contributed to bridging the gap between academe and community practices. Above all else, I encourage you to improve upon this small volume.

George Henderson

CONTENTS

			Page
Preface			vii
Chapter 1	Toward Religious Identity		3
	The Quest for Ultimate Value		4
	Early Religious Influences		6
	Contemporary Issues and Programs		12
	Judaeo-Christian Perspectives		29
	A Final Caution		33
Chapter 2	Brotherhood		35
	Four Theorists		36
	Passive Resistance		42
	Nonviolence		49
	Toward an Open Society		55
	Individual Initiative		60
Chapter 3	Love		66
	Philosophical Perspectives		67
	Psychological Perspectives		75
	Theological Perspectives		83
	Homosexuality		89

A Religious Foundation of Human Relations

Chapter 4	Marriage	97
	Adjusting to Marriage	98
	Open Marriage	109
	Divorce	111
	Additional Biblical Insight	115
Chapter 5	Education	118
	Progressive Education	119
	Beyond Basic Needs	128
	Equal Educational Opportunity	135
	Human Relations in Higher Education	141
Chapter 6	Justice	147
	Platonic Justice	148
	Conscience and Justice	154
	Civil Rights	157
	Democratic Justice	165
Chapter 7	Control	173
	Environment	174
	Population	177
	Spatial Control	187
	Abortion	189
	Euthanasia	198
	And Women, Too	205
Chapter 8	The Helping Relationship	212
	I-Thou	213
	The Self-Actualized Person	217
	The Nature of the Helping Relationship	223
	Drug Addiction	230
	The Search for Balance	237
Chapter 9	The Future	242
	Looking Ahead	243
	Higher Education	249
	Correctional Institutions	255

Contents

	Poverty	262
	Racism	270
	Computers	274
Notes		281
Index		299

A RELIGIOUS FOUNDATION
OF
HUMAN RELATIONS

1
TOWARD RELIGIOUS IDENTITY

ROBERT N. BELLAH has pointed out quite succinctly the nature of an elaborate and well-institutionalized civil religion in America:

Let us look more closely at what [President John F.] Kennedy actually said. First, he said, "I have sworn before you and Almighty God the same solemn oath our forebears prescribed nearly a century and three quarters ago." The oath is the oath of office, including the acceptance of the obligation to uphold the Constitution. He swears it before the people (you) and God. Beyond the Constitution, then, the president's obligation extends not only to the people but to God. In American political theory, sovereignty rests, of course, with the people, but implicitly, and often explicitly, the ultimate sovereignty has been attributed to God.[1]

Kennedy's 1961 inaugural address is but one of several examples I could cite to show religion's impact on American political ideology. Needless to say, politics spills over into almost every aspect of our lives. It is important to note that although the civil religion of America is very much an outgrowth of biblical archetypes—Exodus, Chosen People, Promised Land, and so forth—this religion is not itself Christianity. None of the presidents has mentioned Christ in his inaugural address, but each of them has mentioned God.

While steeped in ancient history, the civil religion of America readily accommodates modern prophets: politicians, religious leaders, philosophers, and behavioral scientists. Few people would question the presence of religion in the moral fiber of our society. Many writers have, however, questioned the value of religion, especially Christianity, as a positive force in our history.

THE QUEST FOR ULTIMATE VALUE

The collective attempt of the human race to understand its own history is a classical study in frustration. This frustration notwithstanding, human beings have tried continually to understand their present by extracting significance from their past and even by imposing upon their present a social order which is shaped by their expectations of the future. Despite the time gaps inherent in the juxtaposition of such words as *past, present,* and *future,* the life of an individual—as well as the human race—testifies to a mind-boggling oneness between time, however distant, and human experiences, however disparate. This condition prompted artist-philosopher Samuel Beckett to observe in *Proust* that "yesterday is not a milestone that has been pased but a daystone on the beaten track of the years, and irremediably a part of us, within us, heavy and dangerous."[2]

The human race has always been concerned with the need for structuring universal reality, not only temporarily, but ultimately. In this regard, perhaps the oldest area of human activity is religion. No other pursuit reveals more of the paradoxical nature of the human make-up than religion, which consists in "man's concern for his ultimate value and how to

Toward Religious Identity

attain it, preserve it, and enjoy it."[3] Despite differences of opinion regarding our ultimate value and despite elaborate and conflicting schemes for determining and systematizing values, history attests to the ever present problem of relating in practical terms to this concern. This problem, Archie J. Bahm concluded, is fundamental to religion.[4]

It is certainly understandable that attempts to define and relate practically to our existence are difficult. More likely than not, our confrontations with the universe arouse complex emotions within us. That is, most people are puzzled by the cyclic patterns of the seasons, the unerring polarities of days and nights, the conflict between our own reason and emotion, the glorious process of birth, and the inevitable call of death. We are mentally shaken when we consider the idea of infinite time and compare it to our limited consciousness of a single moment. Yes, we are terrified when we realize our smallness in comparison to the magnitude of the universe. But if, on the one hand, we are forced to submit to the unknown "powers that be," we become, on the other hand, significant by the growing realization that we are unique pieces of the universal picture of life. In short, human life seems to have a complexity beyond our powers of comprehension.

Historically, religion is one of the institutions men and women have perpetuated in an attempt to work out the meaning of existence. Thus religion is both a catalyst to understanding basic elements of our make-up and a philosophic border within which we have sought to give at least a semblance of order to these elements. Because the varieties of religious beliefs and practices are almost unlimited, students of human relations are faced with the tremendous problem, Bahm points out, of selecting "representative perspectives that will do justice to the numerous complexities and at the same time provide insights into the authentic vision of each major religious movement."[5] Given the magnitude of the task, I have elected to focus on the religious contributions of Western cultures and the forces which shaped them. Only recently have we begun to realize that there is much to be gained from a study of Eastern religious thought. More time is needed before the contributions of Eastern religions to human relations in the Western world can be evaluated adequately.

EARLY RELIGIOUS INFLUENCES

Religion contributes to human relations because it offers what is perhaps our most comprehensive evidence of the basic nature of human beings, evidence which can affect significantly the theory and practice of effective human relations. This is borne out in a brief glance at the religious orientation of primitive peoples, specifically the societies of ancient Egypt and Mesopotamia, where Western religions originated (the word *primitive* is used here in the sense of *ancient*, not with the negative or culturally prejudiced connotations it has acquired over the years).

The religious beliefs and practices of primitive societies were animistic and reflected preoccupation with mana, a term adopted by anthropologists to designate the force or forces which primitive man believed to pervade the world.[6] Therefore, mana is indicative of a mentality which gave rise to early religious beliefs and practices that have influenced some of the religious attitudes of modern man.

Mana encapsulates the primitive belief in a powerful, invisible, all-pervading force at work in the universe. The primitive influence on modern consciousness is obvious: today, many people still believe in invisible powers that affect their lives. In fact, our entire scientific, industrial, and commercial way of life depends on our belief in electrons, that is, in invisible powers. Mana also encompasses the ancient belief in one total, universal Energy, for primitive people felt little necessity to give consistent answers regarding the number of manas. Even this attitutde is deeply embedded in the modern temperament: "We still do not know whether existing power is all one or whether it is distributed among dispersed parts."[7] The implications are far reaching in terms of the primitive life-

Toward Religious Identity

style; "from it developed polytheisms pantheons interrelating gods . . . trinities, duotheisms, hierarchical systems of gods of their incarnations, as well as varieties of monotheisms, pantheisms and panentheisms."[8]

Since mana's effects on us may be good or evil, we, like primitive people, cannot help experimenting with ways of controlling it. Manas which manifest themselves in the wind, sun, thunder, and time seem beyond our power to influence. Other manas, such as those in rocks, animals, and persons, are frequently within our power. It should be clear by now that knowledge of primitive religious beliefs can provide a basis for grasping the nature of religion in general, especially as it has evolved into modern ritualistic practices. Christian Holy Communion services, for example, involving "eating the Body and drinking the Blood of Christ," signify the Christian's need for partaking of the substance of divinity, for attaining more mana; recognition of its possession provides the believer with a feeling of confidence and attainment, even immortality. But the chief contribution of the religious nature of primitive man as he related to his gods lies in his attempt to act out his belief in mana and to explain his participation in the process of life.

A sense of paradoxical unanimity and complexity is primitive religion's most lasting contribution to human relations. Despite the later polytheistic entities which primitive people accepted as the embodiments and causes of mana, they were well aware of the commonality of the human predicament. In modern times, this awareness is still a prime motivation for human-relations programs.

We can now focus on the genesis of Western religion, specifically Egypt and Mesopotamia, where animism influenced a complex polytheism which, in turn, gave way dramatically to a belief in one supreme God, Yahweh.[9] From Yahweh, Moses eventually received the Ten Commandments, a contract or covenant under which Yahweh was to protect the Hebrews. In return, the Hebrews were to serve Yahweh forever by living out the terms of the contract. Thus two contributions to human relations are apparent: (1) monotheism, a theological reference point which not only articulates our relationship to the question of ultimacy but also suggests the ideal relationship between humans (our relationship to people in the Western world depends to a large extent on our view of God and on the relationship between God and man), and (2) the existence of a contract which spells out our responsibilities to God and man.

Academic human-relations training began in the field of business management, and the idea of the contract still prevails.[10] Perhaps even more crucial to the nature of Judaism's contribution to human relations is the fact that the modern contracts which govern areas of personal and professional human relations often attempt to embody the spirit of the Ten Commandments, at least in the idea of equality of regard between people. The spirit of neighborly equality and love permeates the last five of the Ten Commandments: "Six days shalt thou labour and do all thy work.... Honour thy father and thy mother.... Thou shalt not kill. Thou shalt not commit adultery. Thou shalt not steal." Obviously, the social impact of these five commandments is immeasurable; they deal with crucial aspects of communal living, including attitudes toward work, family, marriage, and crime.

Furthermore, Judaism's contribution to human relations includes its aggressive and theistic tone, as well as its body of literature.[11] The documented religious history of the Jews as recorded in the Old Testament of the Bible provides us with a picturesque look at many facets of human relations—alternative ways in which religion can be used to affect both personal and community behavior. Although organized religion is no longer the center of culture (as it generally was in the early days of Judaism), churches still exercise great influence over their members. For good or ill, organized religion's influence on the life-style of nations is not to be dismissed.

The impact of primitive Greek religions on Western society is seen in our nation's philosophic, rational, and scientific characteristics. Edith Hamilton maintains that the Greeks' religious beliefs and practices make us aware that we are their descendants, intellectually, artistically, politically. "Nothing we learn about them," she writes, "is alien to ourselves."[12]

With the advent of Homer's Greece about 1,000 B.C., humankind became the center of the universe, the most important thing in it. It was in Greece that "man first realized what mankind was."[13] Reflecting this ideological revolution, the Greeks created gods in their own image:

Until then, gods had no semblance of reality. They were unlike all living things. In Egypt, a towering colossus, immobile, beyond the power of the imagination to endow with movement, as fixed in the stone as the tremendous temple columns, a representation of the human shape deliberately made unhuman. Or a rigid figure, a woman with a cat's head suggesting inflexible, inhuman cruelty. Or a monstrous mysterious sphinx, aloof from all that lives. In Mesopotamia, bas-reliefs of bestial shapes unlike any beast ever known, men with birds' heads and lions with bulls' heads and both with eagles' wings, creations of artists who were intent upon producing something never seen except in their own minds, the very consummation of unreality. . . .

These and their like were what the pre-Greek world worshipped. One need only place beside them in imagination any Greek statue of a god, so normal and natural with all its beauty, to perceive what a new idea had come into the world. With its coming the universe became rational.[14]

The effect of this egocentrism and rationality on human relations is prodigious. All of the Western world's modern institutions—universities, churches, governments, banks, and so forth—accept rationality as one of the cohesive elements of their programs. But there was more than idle rationality in the Greek religious approach; the Greeks used rationality to confront and come to terms with the intangibilities and mysteries of human existence. When Paul says in the Bible that the invisible must be understood by the visible, he was borrowing the idea from the Greeks.

In the Greeks' relationship to their gods we see the first attempt to free people from the paralyzing fear of the omnipotent, omnipresent Unknown. Magic, a powerful force in the world before this period, was significantly downgraded. It is true that often the Greek gods were only slight improvements upon their worshippers and that there were beast gods, but the rationality of Greek mythology is astonishing.

Although Greek mythology is not, of course, a religion in the true sense of the word, religious elements are present. The degree to which the Greek myths enlighten us about what human beings needed in their gods and what they got from their gods reflects the degree to which the Greeks were religious. From Homer through the tragedians (and even later), most Greek literature revealed a deep realization of the dependency relationship between man and the gods. Zeus, in fact, is similar in many ways to the Christian God: "Our Zeus, the giver of every good gift, the common father, and saviour and guardian of mankind."[15]

This brief review of Greek mythology and religious beliefs and practices clearly reveals their several distinct contributions to the helping professions: the accent on human life, the concern with the psychological well-being of people as reflected in the nature and quality of their activities, and the quest for excellence in human affairs.

Finally, it is important that we examine the contributions of Christianity as one of the major influences on the helping professions. The most obvious contributions evolve around the teachings of Christ. The essence of Christ's wisdom is contained in the Sermon on the Mount, the Lord's Prayer, and the parables. Although two thousand years of conflicting interpretations leave most investigators unsure of their views, some of the historical interpretations have become quite influential and are generally recognized as part of the Christian doctrine.

The foremost Christian contribution to human relations is the concept of love. The Greeks emphasized self-love and the Old Testament portrayed Yahweh as a God of fear and justice, but Jesus said, "God is love." This simple idea was new. Thus Jesus commanded: "Thou shalt love the Lord thy God with all

Toward Religious Identity

thy heart, and with all thy soul, and with all thy strength, and with all thy mind."

Faith in the power of love has deeply affected the Western world, but the effect has not been totally positive. Wars, racism, poverty, and sexism are a few negative conditions that have been supported under the guise of love. To deny that human relations are not sometimes motivated by values less humane than love is to deny the obvious. And yet the love which Christ described as being God and consequently recommended for human beings has become a challenge and guide for millions of persons. It has become the yardstick by which many people measure the humaneness of their relationships. Christ's love ethic has ample room for justice and forgiveness; he urged that we forgive "seventy times seven." The clash between ancient and modern Christian temperaments is clearly portrayed in the conflict of love versus justice. The distorted view that a society cannot have both seems to be especially pronounced in our technological twentieth century.

Jesus the psychiatrist was concerned with the healing of souls, and he taught psychological principles, many of which are embodied in twentieth-century approaches to psychological health. "The Kingdom of Heaven," he said, "is within you, and whosoever shall know himself shall find it." He also urged his followers to "take no care for tomorrow." Application of the present rather than anxious concern for the future is highly recommended by various professions in modern society.

As debate over the merits of religion continues, it is indisputable that the Christian church still wields much influence over millions of minds. For this reason, the life of Christ continues to be a source of considerable interest. Admittedly, there are some points of controversy within the Bible; there are discrepancies, for example, between what Christ taught and what Paul recommended. And, of course, Protestant and Catholic organizations have at times used Christian dogma to achieve horrifying ends. But such details are not the major foci for our discussion of Christianity's contributions to human relations and the other helping professions, such as social work, education, and psychology. One fact is inescapable: Christianity has directly affected the entire modern ethos.

CONTEMPORARY ISSUES AND PROGRAMS [16]

The past decade has been a time of great stress for the peoples of the world. This is especially true in America, where the mood of our culture has shifted, as Langdon Gilkey observed in 1968, toward external social problems. His comment on the role of the churches is crisp:

Reflecting this shift, the secular subjects intriguing to theologians have also changed: Christian ethics is currently less interested in problems of neurosis and self-acceptance than it is in those of the relation of affluence to the Protestant ethic of work; of automation to the Christian responsibility for full employment; of delinquency to the ideals of order and self-expression; and of the slums to the question of human dignity; not to mention issues raised by the "sexual revolution" and LSD. Overshadowing all these current social crises has been the civil rights movement—of enormous concern to the leadership of the churches and of vast significance in the deep reappraisal of the failures and the new tasks of American religion. [17]

To this list I would add the issues of environmental control, war, and penal reform.

The secular nature of American theology is attested, as Gilkey stated, by the fact that "Marxist concepts, Freudian images, and sociological structures appear on the surface, lying on the page next to biblical and traditional notions, or replacing them by some mode of translation."[18] These and other forces have sparked the desire within some persons for America to become truly a religiously pluralistic society.

A religiously pluralistic society is not unlike the political and social pluralism civil rights advocates have sought. In such a society, the principal religious groups claim freedom for themselves and equal freedom for others, whatever their beliefs may be.[19] Crucial to the concept are understanding and

Toward Religious Identity

acceptance of differences; thus the need for cooperation is implicit. Areas of cooperation are as varied as the imagination. For instance, Franklin H. Littell has suggested that Protestants, Catholics, Jews, and other religious groups can cooperate in "fair-housing practices, equal employment possibilities, 'shared-time' programs between public and private schools, 'cluster programs' in higher education, improved schooling and Head Start programs, [and] equal justice for all at law."[20]

However, cooperation often becomes nothing more than an abortive effort to promote religious charity. "The do-good activities which the churches facilitate," Bryan Wilson observes, "and which some theologians deplore, are indeed often ways of going through the motions, and often only the monetary motions at that."[21] When this happens, the concept of brotherhood becomes as shallow as it was in the nineteenth century when Thomas Carlyle told the following story:

A poor Irish widow, her husband having died in one of the lanes of Edinburgh, went forth with her three children, base of all resource, to solicit help from the Charitable Establishments of that city. At this Charitable Establishment, and then at that she was refused; refused from one to the other, helped by none;—till she had exhausted them all; till her strength and her heart failed her; she sank down in typhus-fever; died, and infected her lane with fever, so that "seventeen other persons" died of fever there in consequence. The humane Physician asks thereupon, as with a heart too full for speaking; would it not have been economy *to help the poor widow? She took typhus-fever, and killed seventeen of you!—very curious. The forlorn Irish widow applies to her fellow-creatures, as if saying, "Behold, I am sinking, bare of help; ye must help me!" They answer, "No, impossible; thou art no sister of ours." But she proves her sisterhood; her typhus-fever* kills *them: they were actually her brothers, though denying it! Had human creature ever to go lower for a proof?*[22]

Such social blindness and deafness cause and perpetuate the social ills people claim to deplore. The words of Karl Menninger are appropriate here: "If we do not live for pleasure, we shall

A Religious Foundation of Human Relations

soon find ourselves living for pain. If we do not regard as sacred our own joys and the joys of others, we open the door and let into life the ugliest attribute of the human race, which is cruelty — the root of all other vices."[23] Nothing is immune to such ugliness, not even the family.

During the two decades since World War II, the United States has enjoyed a family boom. This boom in domesticity almost certainly fed the postwar religiosity that reached its peak in the late fifties. A remarkably high marriage rate led quickly to a high rate of family formation, and new families locating in the suburbs swelled church membership rolls and caused hundreds of new churches to be built. In such a milieu, "family life" naturally became attractive to the churches. Family-life agencies prospered, drawing on the skills of psychiatrists, psychologists, educators, sociologists, and lawyers. A considerable family-life journalism flourished. Premarital counseling took on a new self-consciousness. Pastors, rabbis, and priests affiliated with colleges enjoyed heavy business. Husbands, wives, and husbands-and-wives could attend special conferences, belong to special clubs, and go on special retreats.[24]

Along with change has come new emphasis on human-relations training in churches. *T-group, encounter group, simulation game,* and *transactional analysis* have become common terms in activities among many religious groups. In some instances, the activities enjoy a fervor associated with Holy Communion. Thus in a few instances human-relations training has become a kind of social communion through which the participants seek redemption for their human-relations sins. And the new priests have become facilitators or trainers.

When a trout rising to a fly gets hooked on a line and finds himself unable to swim about freely, he begins with a fight which results in struggles and splashes and sometimes an escape. Often, of course, the situation is too tough for him. Sometimes he masters his difficulties; sometimes they are too much for him. His struggles are all that the world sees and it

Toward Religious Identity

naturally misunderstands them. It is hard for a free fish to understand what is happening to a hooked one.[25]

Precisely this understanding is sought in the helping relationship—that is, for the well-balanced, healthy, psychologically mature human being to counsel, love, care for, or administer therapy to another human being in conflict or feeling uncomfortable with himself, with other persons, with his environment, or with all of these.

The concept of the helping relationship can be imagined as extending on a continuum, if you will, from person/higher power on one end to client/professional therapist on the other, neither being mutually exclusive; in between are all others in the helping professions, self-help groups, pastoral counseling, and everyday encounters wherein problems arise and advice is solicited or offered.

The remainder of this section is a compilation of research divided into arbitrary categories which seem to have emerged as different aspects or components of the helping relationship. Nevertheless, an attempt has been made to tie together and label those contributions among which was seen some connection of theory or line of thinking; others are included because they seem to speak to the inquiry, even though they seem to defy categorization. Consequently, some of the citations may appear to have been left dangling.

Human Relationships. Human beings seem so peculiar and ambivalent at times in their struggle to deal both with their need to be individuals possessing unique qualities and with their need to be social. Paul Tournier relates the dynamics of such dualism in this fashion:

Always one is divided between showing oneself and hiding.... I am reminded of a remark made by one of my patients: "Life is a universal game of hide-and-seek in which we just pretend to hide." And yet I do desire his personal contact. It is even a thing that I am particularly greedy for; it is one of the things that I value most in life. The obstacle to contact is not only in the external circumstances of the modern world . . . ; nor is it only in our uncertainty about what we really are. It is much bigger. It is a positive force, an instinct that prompts us to run away in order to avoid the dialogue. As my friend Jean de Rougemont has remarked, "man seeks man and flees from him."[26]

We often are full of mistrust and misunderstanding when we dare to enter into human relationships.

In daily life it happens all the time that we presume that the psychology of other people is the same as ours. We suppose that what is pleasing or desirable to us is the same to others and that what seems bad to us must also seem bad to them. It is only recently that our courts of law have nerved themselves to admit the psychological relativity of guilt in pronouncing sentence. The tenet quod licet Jovi non licet bovi *still rankles in the minds of all unsophisticated people; equality before the law is still a precious achievement. And we still attribute to the other fellow all the evil and inferior qualities that we do not like to recognize in ourselves, and therefore have to criticize and attack him, when all that has happened is that an inferior "soul" has emigrated from one person to another. The world is still full of* bêtes noires *and scapegoats, just as it formerly teemed with witches and werewolves.*[27]

Nevertheless, we are all involved in interpersonal relationships by virtue of our humanity, and these relationships, one of which is the helping relationship, are not inherently unpleasant and unhealthy; indeed, they can lead to the enhancement of those involved. Anthony Storr argues for maturity in interpersonal relationships by first describing what the immature relationship is like:

To incorporate another person is to swallow him up, to overwhelm him, and to destroy him; and thus to treat him ultimately as less than a whole person. To identify with another person is to lose oneself, to submerge one's own identity in that of the other, to be overwhelmed, and hence to treat oneself ultimately as less than a whole person. To pass judgment, in

Jung's sense, is to place oneself in an attitude of superiority; to agree offhandedly is to place oneself in an attitude of inferiority . . . the personality can cease to exist in two ways— either by destroying the other, or being absorbed by the other— and maturity in interpersonal relationships demands that neither oneself nor the other shall disappear, but that each shall contribute to the affirmation and realization of the other's personality.[28]

Carl G. Jung warns against taking a dichotomous view of human beings. Although Jung's personal and scholarly biases seem to emphasize the uniqueness of the individual, he nevertheless acknowledges the specieshood of mankind as well:

There is and can be no self-knowledge based on theoretical assumptions, for the object of self-knowledge is an individual— a relative exception and an irregular phenomenon. Hence it is not the universal and the regular that characterize the individual, but rather the unique. He is not to be understood as a recurrent unit but as something unique and singular. . . . At the same time man, as member of a species, can and must be described as a statistical unit; otherwise nothing general could be said about him. . . . This results in a universally valid anthropology or psychology . . . with an abstract picture of man as an average unit from which all individual features have been removed. But it is precisely these features which are of paramount importance for understanding *man . . . understanding the individual obliges me to commit* lèse majesté, *so to speak, to turn a blind eye to scientific knowledge. . . . This conflict cannot be solved by an either-or but only by a kind of two-way thinking; doing one thing while not losing sight of the other. . . . The individual, however, as an irrational datum, is the true and authentic carrier of reality, the* concrete *man as opposed to the unreal ideal or normal man to whom the scientific statements refer.*[29]

It is of crucial importance that those involved in the helping relationship keep always in mind the distinction Jung made in an effort to avoid labeling, stereotyping, generalizing,

A Religious Foundation of Human Relations

categorizing, and rationalizing the unique human being who defies reduction and simplification. Scientific theory certainly has its place and has provided us with varied and invaluable heuristic tools to use in our roles as helpers, but let us be willing and prepared to discard these theoretical devices when they do not fit or when they cease to lend understanding of the individual or group with whom we are in contact.

Jung succinctly connects the secular and sacred aspects of the human relationship:

It is, unfortunately, only too clear that if the individual is not truly regenerated in spirit, society cannot be either for society is the sum total of individuals in need of redemption. I can therefore see it only as a delusion when the Churches try—as they apparently do—to rope the individual into a social organization and reduce him to a condition of diminished responsibility, instead of raising him out of the torpid, mindless mass and making clear to him that he is the one important factor and that the salvation of the world consists in the salvation of the individual soul.[30]

As has been clearly demonstrated, not everyone involved in the helping relationship, either as professionals or nonprofessionals, chooses to acknowledge the spiritual dimension in man. Nevertheless, the spiritual or religious reality of individuals cannot be wished away. In one way or another, the helping persons will have to confront this problem for themselves and their own reality in order to help others in the event that their realities include the spiritual dimension. Martin Buber took on as the cornerstone of his philosophy Ludwig A. Feuerbach's conception of dialogue. "True dialectic," Feuerbach wrote, "is not a monologue of the solitary thinker within himself, it is a dialogue between *I* and *Thou*."[31] Robert W. Miller says of Feuerbach:

His "essence of Christianity" is precisely this dialogue: "Man with man—the unity of I *and* Thou—*is God." This is the meaning of the incarnation, that Jesus stood in this relation, and whoever obeys his command, "Love one another as I have loved you," also enters into it. "Christ is the consciousness of our unity. Therefore, whoever loves man for the sake of man . . . is a Christian; he is Christ himself."*[32]

Self-Knowledge. M. Esther Harding was correct: "We cannot change anyone else; we can change only ourselves, and then usually only when the elements that are in need of reform have become conscious through their reflection in someone else."[33] Abraham H. Maslow, Carl R. Rogers, Carl Jung, Theodore Roszak, and Jess Lair are but a few in a long list of persons who are convinced that we must be in touch with and have a grasp of what is going on within our own selves before we can begin to help another. Maurice Nicoll, Scottish psychologist, theologian, and student of Jung, wrote of self-knowledge as it applies to the helping relationship:

No one as he is mechanically—that is, as formed by life and its influences—can enter into and understand another, and, from that, give help, unless he already knows from his own self-observation, self-study and insight and work on himself, what is in the other person. Only through self-knowledge is knowledge of others practically possible. . . . One of the greatest evils of human relationships is that people make no attempt to enter into one another's position but merely criticize one another without any restraint and do not possess any inner check to this mechanical criticism owing to the absence of any insight into themselves and their own glaring crudities, faults and shortcomings. . . . This lack of psychological responsibility, both to oneself and to others, is perhaps especially characteristic of modern times and is the source of one part of the widespread modern unhappiness that marks the present age, in which, amongst other things, there is a decline in even ordinary human kindness, with a resulting hardness which is among the most dangerous factors in regard to the future, and which effectually stops all possibility of the right development of the emotional life.[34]

Love. Can we participate in a helping relationship without love? Perhaps, the word *love* is too nebulous because its referent is an exceedingly wide range of behavior, relationships, and feelings. We could say that in the helping relationship the word *love* means "to value the humanness of one another." "The question of human relationship and of the inner cohesion of our society is an urgent one in view of the atomization of the pent-up mass man, whose personal relationships are undermined by general mistrust," wrote Jung. "To counter this danger, the free society needs a bond of an affective nature, a principle of a kind like *caritas*, the Christian love of your neighbor. . . . Where love stops, power begins, and violence, and terror."[35]

In his book *Intimate Behavior*, Desmond Morris discusses love and touching. According to Morris, loving means touching and body contact. We spend much time talking about the way we talk and we frequently try to see the way we see, but seldom do we touch on the way we touch. Perhaps touch (referred to by some writers as the mother of senses) is such a basic response that we take it for granted. Whatever the reasons, Morris believes we have gradually become less and less touchful and more and more distant and that physical untouchability has been accompanied by emotional remoteness.[36] In explaining how the human animal, who has a great need for it, responds to the lack of love, he paints this pathetic picture of contemporary humanity:

In our crowded urban world, we have battled on in this way, further and further from a state of loving, personal intimacy, until the cracks have begun to show. Then, sucking our metaphorical thumbs and mouthing sophisticated philosophies to convince ourselves that all is well, we try to sit it out. We laugh at educated adults who pay large sums to go and play childish games of touch and hug in scientific institutes, and we fail to see the signs. How much easier it would all be if we could accept the fact that tender loving is not a weakly thing, only for infants and young lovers. If we could release our feelings, and indulge ourselves in an occasional, and magical, return to intimacy.[37]

Toward Religious Identity

What professional helpers can do to meet the intimate needs, especially those of touching, of persons who seek their help is questionable. It is abundantly clear, however, that such needs are being left unfulfilled in countless numbers of people in pain and that a return to emphasis on the simple yet complex power of love, in both physical and emotional expressions, is of paramount concern to anyone involved in a helping relationship. In a discussion of unselfish love's powers, Pitirim A. Sorokin, a renowned sociologist, stated that "unselfish creative love can stop aggressive inter-individual and inter-group strife and can transform inimical relationships between persons and groups into amicable ones; that love begets love, and hate begets hate."[38]

Making Choices. Whether we are involved in a helping relationship as professionals or as friends and confidantes, it is inevitable that at some point in the relationship the problem of making choices will arise. Kurt Goldstein believes the right kind of choosing is essential to bringing about a change in an individual or encouraging personal growth and development:

Certainly we always try to eliminate suffering and especially pain. But it is not the task of therapy merely to reduce mental and physical suffering. One may be inclined to do this because one assumes that the elimination of suffering is an essential or even the essential drive of man, as psychoanalysis proclaims in the form of the pleasure principle. But placing this in the foreground would often not help the patient. The idea of the pleasure principle, particularly when applied to normal life, overlooks the enormous significance of tension for self-realization in its highest forms. Pleasure, in the sense of relief from tension, may be a necessary state of respite. But it is a phenomenon of "stand-still."... One can achieve the right attitude toward the problem of the elimination of suffering in patients and in normal individuals only if one considers its significance for self-realization and its relationship to the value of health. If the patient is able to make the choice we have mentioned, he may still suffer but may no longer feel sick; i.e., though some-

what disordered and stricken by a certain anxiety, he is able to realize his essential capacities at least to a considerable degree. . . . The central aim of "therapy"—in cases in which full restitution is not possible—appears to achieve transformation of the patient's personality in such a manner as to enable him to make the right choice; this choice must be capable of bringing about a new orientation, an orientation which is adequate enough to his nature to make life appear to be worth living again.[39]

Helping relationships in which choosing is being continually delayed or postponed by the helper and avoided or procrastinated by the client should be seriously questioned. All too often the helper is meeting his or her own needs by being too protective and not allowing the client to experience the pain and discomfort which generally accompany choosing. Growth or change is stymied by this unhealthy, dependent situation.

Rollo May sees the choosing of values as the central concern and goal toward which a person must move if he or she is to grow and eventually become integrated as a human being. "The Human Being not only *can* make such choices of values and goals," May writes, "but he is the animal who *must* do so if he is to attain integration. For the value—the goal he moves toward—serves him as a psychological center, a kind of core of integration which draws together his powers as the core of a magnet draws the magnet's lines of force together."[40] Knowing what one wants is simply the foundation of what in the maturing person is the ability to choose one's own values. The mark of mature persons is that their living is integrated into self-chosen goals: they know what they want.

Religion. In his easygoing, colloquial manner of expressing thoughts which, when written more eloquently and with a more sophisticated style might be considered profundities, Jess Lair shares this point about religion and people:

To me, religion is epitomized by a statement which I think was made by Tillich, the Protestant theologian. In any situa-

tion, the moral response is that response which is most loving in that situation. Tillich is talking about response because he doesn't care about thinking, he's only concerned about your doing what your hand turns to. . . . One way to read Christianity is a protest against legalism and against a foolish belief in laws alone. Even the Commandments aren't paramount. When asked which Commandment was greatest, Christ said none of them but to love thy neighbor as thyself. So the only law is the law of love, and how are we to know how to love our neighbor? Simple. We look at him as he is at the moment and do for him what he needs rather than doing what we want to do or ignoring him.[41]

Perhaps referring to the same underlying idea, W. Gordon Ross, a religious philosopher, says two important components of religion are religion as caring and religion as relationship: "Those in whom religion has taken hold cannot say, 'I don't care.'. . . Caring is not a garment which can be doffed or donned at will. It is an achievement, and in its best form, it is an unlimited concern. Perhaps some people can more easily or readily achieve this condition than others."[42] There is a belief that empathy—and perhaps, along with it, caring—is something that some individuals have and others do not, or at least have to a lesser degree. Although this is debatable, it does seem that some persons are more willing (or for them it is easier to express this gift) to care for others.

"Relationship," Ross says, "is indispensable for adequate communication. . . . When communication breaks down, human associations are riven as with an axe."[43] The helping relationship is only one type of relationship which keeps open the lines of communication between individuals and makes viable human associations.

Søren Kierkegaard, the father of contemporary existentialist philosophy, describes the task of the helping person in this manner: "The highest one human being can do for another is to make the other free, to help him stand on his own feet— alone . . . when a person has overcome all, precisely then is he perhaps closest to losing everything . . . no longer can he fight against something or someone else . . . now he must stand alone."[44]

Values. The clarification of values is an indispensable component of the helping relationship. Of concern in this section are the values of the helper. Expression of them may be honest and noninterfering or manipulative, depending on how willing the helper is to take a look at where he or she "is coming from" and to take steps to avoid forcing his or her personal value orientation on the person being helped. Transactional analyst Claude Steiner focuses on the issue in this manner:

The issue of manipulation will be dealt with. . . . It has long been suspected, and it is now generally accepted, that no therapist can hope to avoid imposing his system of values upon his patient. The issue of manipulation has now become simply a question of whether a therapist, consciously and overtly, is willing to expose his patient to his values or whether he prefers to do it without his own and his patient's awareness. To the transactional analyst, the therapeutic contract makes it clear that the patient wants the therapist to use whatever technique he feels will cure him of his condition, and it is the treatment contract that gives the transactional analyst permission to apply pressures based on his value system. On the other hand, the patient is justified in expecting the therapist to limit the application of his judgments to the confines established by the contract.[45]

Goldstein elaborates further on the crucial reasons for allowing the client to establish and clarify his own values: "It would not be helpful if the new orientation of the patient were determined by the values of the therapist. The patient must find his own values, i.e., come to an ordered condition which permits his self-realization to the extent that satisfies him. The degree of self-realization he attains will depend upon the extent to which he is able to make the choice. This depends upon his previous personality and his mental capacities."[46] An old adage is appropriate here: Let the buyer beware.

Types of Therapy. One approach to the helping relationship is reality therapy as proposed by William Glasser. In essence, Glasser's therapy depends on what might be called a "Psychiatric version of the three R's, namely, *reality, responsibility,* and *right* and *wrong.*"[47] He feels that the people who occupy prisons, mental hospitals, clinics, and offices have not learned to fulfill their basic human needs. For Glasser, the basic human needs are relatedness and respect, and they are satisfied by doing what is realistic, responsible, and right.

Glasser feels that fulfillment of basic physiological needs is not the concern of the helper; rather, the helper must be concerned with two basic psychological needs: the need to love and be loved and the need to feel that we are worthwhile to ourselves and others.[48] If these are not fulfilled, pain and suffering will result. We all have these needs, regardless of age; however, we vary in our ability to fulfill them.

The helper, then, is concerned "with those who have not learned or who have lost the ability to fulfill their needs."[49] Glasser avoids labeling people, preferring to view labels only as descriptions of irresponsibility. He does, however, label behavior, substituting *responsible* for *mental health* and *irresponsible* for *mental illness.* According to this theory, the helper's job is to aid the client in becoming more responsible so that he can meet his basic needs himself. Glasser's concept of reality is crucial to understanding this approach. Perhaps it is best described in the following statement:

In their unsuccessful effort to fulfill their needs, no matter what behavior they choose, all patients have a common characteristic: They all deny the reality of the world around them. Some break the law, denying the rules of society; some claim their neighbors are plotting against them, denying the improbability of such behavior. Some are afraid of crowded places, close quarters, airplanes, or elevators, yet they freely admit the irrationality of their fears. Millions drink to blot out the inadequacy they feel but that need not exist if they could learn to be different; and far too many people choose suicide rather than face the reality that they could solve their problems by more responsible behavior. Whether it is partial denial or the total blotting out of all reality of the chronic back-ward patient in the state hospital, the denial of some or all of reality is common to all patients. Therapy will be successful when they are able to give up denying the world and to recognize that reality not only exists but that they must fulfill their needs within its framework.... A therapy that leads all patients toward reality, toward grappling successfully with the tangible and intangible aspects of the real world, might accurately be called a therapy toward reality.[50]

In this theory, the helper assumes an active role in teaching the patient responsible behavior. Glasser takes the existentialist point of view, as is demonstrated in his conviction that the patient is responsible for his own life and actions. The therapy is concerned with the here-and-now and not with delving into the past. Reality therapy does not search for insights into the causes of a patient's behavior and through an understanding of it assume the individual will learn better ways of behaving by himself or from others. Rather, the therapist takes every opportunity to teach patients better ways to fulfill their present needs. That is, the therapist examines the patient's daily activities and suggests better ways for him to behave, solve problems, or approach people. In the words of Glasser: "Once involvement is gained and reality is faced, therapy becomes a special kind of education, a learning to live more effectively."[51]

One other type of therapy will be mentioned briefly: transactional analysis. Without going into the foundation of the transactional theory of personality, it is important to discuss games, one of three major concepts on which it is based (the other two are ego states and scripts):

A game is an ongoing series of complementary ulterior transactions progressing to a well-defined, predictable outcome. Descriptively it is a recurring set of transactions, often repetitious, superficially plausible, with a concealed motivation; or, more colloquially, a series of moves with a snare, or "gimmick."

Toward Religious Identity

> *Games are clearly differentiated from procedures, rituals, and pastimes by two chief characteristics: (1) their ulterior quality, and (2) the payoff. . . . Every game . . . is basically dishonest, and the outcome has a dramatic, as distinct from merely exciting, quality.*[52]

If skilled intervention is applied by the therapist working with both the covert motives and the payoffs involved in the game playing of a particular individual, game-dependent behavior may be dismantled effectively in exchange for healthier kinds of transactions. "Fortunately," Eric Berne, concludes, "the rewards of game-free intimacy, which is or should be the most perfect form of human living, are so great that even precariously balanced personalities can safely and joyfully relinquish their games if an appropriate partner can be found for the better relationship."[53]

In biting cynicism as well as alarming realism, Theodore Roszak described many therapies as merely attempts to ease the patient or client or person being helped into adjusting to what are seemingly the most impossible situations:

> *Moreover, there will be improved therapies of adjustment and many "future shock absorbers" to ease the pain. In June, 1968, as part of a British Broadcasting Corporation documentary film a leading member of the National Health Service spoke of the growing need for a "Ministry of Well-Being" (he did not wince to quote from Orwell), whose task it would be to adjust the recalcitrant to an ever more demanding social reality.*[54]

Social Casework. Material on the casework relationship tends to be the most explicit, tangible, goal oriented, and clearly delineated. For example, Naomi Brill defines the helping relationship as "a dynamic interaction between two or more individuals. This interaction begins when communication first takes place and is a continuous and ongoing process throughout the lifetime of the relationship. It is a reciprocal process, cumulative in nature, in which, once initiated, each successive response tends to be made in terms of those which have preceded it."[55] Felix P. Biestek described casework as a way to "help a person meet a problem, fill a need, receive a service. The means to his purpose are the mobilization of dormant capacities in the individual, or the mobilization of appropriate community resources, or both, depending upon the needs of each client."[56] The core material of the casework relationship is interaction of the basic attitudes and emotions of the caseworker and client. These may be listed as follows: to be treated as an individual, to be allowed to express feelings, to receive sympathetic response to problems, to be recognized as a person of worth and dignity, to be judged fairly, to be allowed to make choices and decisions, and to be able to keep secrets.[57] All seven are found in training groups (T-groups), encounter groups, and organizational development (OD).

Self-Help Groups. Self-help groups, such as Alcoholics Anonymous, Gamblers Anonymous, Synanon, Recovery, Weight Watchers, and countless others springing up all over the country, are fascinating and in many instances highly successful in treating individuals who, for one reason or another, have turned to lay persons, rather than professionals, for help. The spirit of commitment and fellowship seems to be very high in many of the organizations; under no circumstances should they as a group be discounted in importance or effectiveness. For certain individuals, they are important and effective. The following excerpt from the book *Alcoholics Anonymous* conveys the strength and cohesion of at least one type of self-help group:

We are average Americans. All sections of this country and many of its occupations are represented, as well as many political, economic, social, and religious backgrounds. We are people who normally would not mix. But there exists among us a fellowship, a friendliness, and an understanding which is indescribably wonderful. We are like the passengers of a great liner the moment after rescue from shipwreck when camaraderie, joyousness and democracy pervade the vessel from steerage to Captain's table. Unlike the feelings of the ship's passengers, however, our joy in escape from disaster does not subside as we go our individual ways. The feeling of

Toward Religious Identity

having shared in a common peril is one element in the powerful cement which binds us. But that in itself would never have held us together as we are now joined. . . . The tremendous fact for every one of us is that we have discovered a common solution. We have a way out on which we can absolutely agree, and upon which we can join in brotherly and harmonious action. This is the great news this book carries to those who suffer from alcoholism.[58]

If there is any feeling that sums up what I am trying to convey, it is expressed by these lines:

> *I feel so much better — less hopeless and guilty*
> *Since I found out that*
> *I was not chosen to be God.*[59]

JUDAEO-CHRISTIAN PERSPECTIVES

Social conflicts of the mid–twentieth century have sent many supporters of religious morality back to theological foundations in an attempt to accommodate Judaeo-Christian traditions to the current ethical problems that characterize contemporary society. This is the age of scientific exploration of outer space, psychological probing of inner space, and sociological delineation of personal space. Consequently, religious leaders have become increasingly hard pressed to make relevant interpretations of standard religious doctrine which are applicable to such controversial subjects as abortion, racism, women's liberation, homosexuality, drug abuse, poverty, and euthanasia. In order to explore current theological perspectives in relation to these and other subjects, I will review briefly the basic values undergirding the Judaeo-Christian heritage, which is accepted as the moral rule of thumb for much of Western civilization.

Discussing precepts that Christians assert are the foundations of morality, George C. McCauley defines values as "the kinds of things that a man is willing to pay a price for, things which are considered worth his energetic effort. They are areas in which he concentrates even at personal cost. There is an element of wanting and desiring, plus a determination to carry through."[60] If religion is to intervene in secular affairs successfully, it is not enough merely to define values; if they are to be understood, the means by which religious values are acquired also must be examined. Concerning the acquisition of values, McCauley writes: "If Jesus has values, it would follow that he gets them the normal way people get values, from family, from reflection, from abrasive or convincing incidents, from a person he has grown to respect or love, from watching and weighing, from arguments and prayer, from disappointments and conversations."[61] Values, then, are acquired through a variety of human experiences.

When in the first century a pagan asked Rabbi Hillel, a contemporary of Jesus, to instruct him concerning the values of the entire Torah while standing on one foot, the rabbi replied: "That which is hateful to you, do not inflict on your fellow beings. All the rest is commentary."[62] This particular example of Jewish perspective is cited to mark the similarity between the values of early Jewish thought and the Christian admonition "Do unto others as you would have them do unto you." Concerning such commonality of perspective with Catholicism, Eva Fleishner wrote: "The Roman Catholic and Jewish communities possess both universal and national religious-ethnic dimensions, and in this sense they have very much in common. They are not simply creedal fellowships, but have rich social substance in which the religious and moral ideals and values are incorporated in the very lives of their people."[63]

Although on some issues, such as abortion, the variance between Judaism and some elements of the Christian skein of Western religious thought is readily apparent, we should not ignore Judaism's substantial contribution to Christianity: "Judaism brought forth at the moment of its greatest crises, new and viable forms of life and worship, the creativity of which Christian scholars have only recently begun to acknowledge, even to admire."[64]

If one significant difference between the Jewish and Christian perspectives is to be singled out, many authorities would agree that it lies in the Christian focus on mercy or compassion as opposed to the Jewish esteem for judgment or justice:

The New Testament itself has trouble bringing together in the same breath the themes of judgment and forgiveness. Of the two, Jesus' emphasis seems to fall on the latter. . . . The forgiveness of sins seems to be a capsule summary of his mission, as he deals with the terrible burden of guilt that he sees in human faces, in our diffidence and violence, in our servile distance from the Father. . . . The ministry of Jesus to the sick is closely tied in the New Testament to his ministry of forgiving sins. This is explained by the cultural thought patterns of his time, which associated sickness with moral guilt in ways we would consider strange.[65]

There still exists in modern times a residual effect of such thinking; it is demonstrated when religious bodies sit in judgment and attach the label *sickness* to much that they assess as immoral.

The Jewish emphasis on judgment as a value is characterized by Lawrence Kohlberg's states of moral judgment. Furthermore, his approach is in step with aspects of Christian thought:

Rejecting both psychoanalytic and social conditioning explanations of morality, he [Kohlberg] affirms notions of conscience, freedom and responsibility wholly consistent with Christian traditions. He charts moral development at three levels: preconventional, conventional and postconventional morality:

Level I—Moral value resides in external, quasi-physical happenings, in bad acts, or in quasi-physical needs rather than in persons and standards.

A Religious Foundation of Human Relations

Level II — *Moral value resides in performing good or right roles, in maintaining the conventional order and the expectancies of others.*

Level III — *Moral value resides in conformity by the self to shared or shareable standards, rights, or duties.*[66]

In Kohlberg's writings the key concepts which govern the values of both Christianity and Judaism are set forth in the affirmation of human conscience, freedom, and responsibility. It is unfortunate that human history has been fraught with great chasms of unmet needs within both of these traditionally oriented religious settings.

The Humanist Manifesto of 1933 prophetically projects human problems aggravated by the "acids of modernity": "Science and economic change have disrupted the old beliefs. Religions the world over are under the necessity of coming to terms with new conditions created by a vastly increased knowledge and experience. In every field of human activity, the vital movement is now in the direction of a candid and explicit humanism."[67]

George F. Thomas put Christian ethics in proper perspective: "While Christian faith and love are an adequate *basis* for all morality, they do not by themselves provide the whole *content* of morality. This does not imply that Christian ethics is imperfect. Christian ethics . . . was not intended to be a new code of laws specifying what men should do or should not do in every kind of situation. . . . To hear Jesus' words and to follow him is to have one's house built upon a rock. But Christians have the *responsibility of building* upon this foundation the best and fullest lives they can."[68] There is ample documentation in the New Testament to support the assumption that in order to love other people and to serve the Lord, we must first love ourselves in proper perspective. Earl C. Dahlstrom put it this way:

To know one's own worth or value, to be able to accept one's own liabilities, and to appreciate one's own uniqueness is to be prepared to serve. Among the major problems in our rela-

Toward Religious Identity

tions with others is the need for self-objectification that enables us to see both the best and the worst in ourselves as a preparation for not only seeing but understanding and accepting the best and the worst in others.[69]

To those who are still without answers or who are grappling with poor answers as they suffer the agonies of the damned in such circumstances as abortion, racism, sexism, homosexuality, drug abuse, and poverty, the words of Albert Schweitzer ring all too true: "How strong would Christian truth now stand in the world today, if its relation to the truth of history were in every respect what it should be! Instead of allowing this truth its rights, piety treated it, whenever it caused her embarrassment, in various ways, conscious or unconscious, but always by either evading, or twisting, or suppressing it."[70] The question of whether there is justification today for such an indictment of religious inadequacies in solving contemporary problems can be answered more confidently when specific problems are explored precisely within the Judaeo-Christian frame of reference.

A FINAL CAUTION

There are many difficulties in trying to use the Bible as a point of reference. It is not a single book; it is a large collection of eclectic writings. Its name is derived from the Greek word *biblia*, which means "books." The Bible consists of at least sixty-six books written by many authors over a period of approximately one thousand years. Furthermore, there are several different Bibles, including the Hebrew, the Greek Orthodox, the Catholic, and various Protestant versions.[71]

Despite their differences, three broad principles and five basic beliefs characterize Christian religions. The principles: there is a spiritual ground of all reality, there is a moral order in the world, and the good life is an aspect of religion. The beliefs: God is Creator and Father, Christ is Lord and Savior, the Church is the Body of Christ and the community of be-

33

A Religious Foundation of Human Relations

lievers, the Bible has unique religious value, and Christianity is relevant to personal and social ethics.[72] There are more than 260 Christian denominations, and they have more than 900,000,000 members.

It is also important to acknowledge that the Old Testament is a collection of history, codes of law, orations, and poetry and the New Testament is a handbook for practitioners of Christianity. The problems of nations chronicled in the Old Testament are dramatized in writings known as the Wisdom Literature: Proverbs, Ecclesiastes, Job, Ecclesiasticus, and Wisdom of Solomon; problems of Christian faith are discussed in the New Testament.

Most theologians have renounced metaphysical interpretations of the Bible in favor of historical interpretations. Therefore, errors of interpretation are not so much metaphysical as they are historical. Most theologians seem content to be guided by their own concepts of history. I would quickly add that although I am not a theologian, I, too, am guilty of this practice as I select the biblical quotations that I believe form a religious foundation for human relations.

The King James Version of the Bible illustrates language differences between earlier and contemporary societies. But more than language has changed; laws and mores have changed, too. Thus any effort to relate Scripture to present-day conditions will be somewhat iconoclastic. Being cognizant of the different emphases and traditions within the Bible, I also realize that the chapters which follow merely uncover the tip of a massive theological-human relations iceberg. Most of it remains submerged.

2
BROTHERHOOD

HENRI BERGSON points out Christianity's importance to the concept of brotherhood:

Humanity had to wait till Christianity for the idea of universal brotherhood, with its implication of equality of rights and the sanctity of the person, to become operative. Some may say that it has been rather a slow process; indeed eighteen centuries elapsed before the rights of man were proclaimed by the Puritans of America, soon followed by the men of the French Revolution. It began, nevertheless, with the teachings of the Gospels, and was destined to go on indefinitely; it is one thing for an idea to be merely propounded by sages worthy of admiration, it is very different when the idea is broadcast to the ends of earth in a message overflowing with love, invoking love in return.[1]

Brotherhood is an ideal state of human relations which has not yet been achieved. Through the ages, however, many theorists and philosophers have provided definitions. Those whose definitions are the most relevant are the men and women who have contributed significantly to brotherhood as it relates to contemporary society.

FOUR THEORISTS

Mohandas K. Gandhi provides an excellent example of such a contribution. He lived by the word of God and taught that word by personal example. He also sought truth and believed that "he who seeks the truth alone easily follows the Golden Rule."[2] Furthermore, Gandhi believed that all people are brothers and sisters, all are sons and daughters under one creator: "The distinction between heterogeneous and homogeneous [families] is discovered to be merely imaginary. We are all one family."[3] Although Gandhi spent his life serving his own people, he genuinely desired to aid all people. One concept in his *Satyagraha* movement was the eternal law of suffering. He disciplined himself to express it and accomplished much through his dedicated efforts.

Gandhi was called *Bhai*, meaning "brother," by the masses. It was a fitting name for a man who truly believed brotherhood to be the way of God. "To see the universal and all pervading Spirit of Truth face to face," he said, "one must be able to love the meanest of creation as oneself."[4] Reflecting this philosophy, Gandhi's concept of ahimsa not only held that all life is valuable but also promoted the unity of all life.

In America, Martin Luther King, Jr., was perhaps the most eloquent and renowned black practitioner of brotherhood in the Christian sense.[5] King's definition of brotherhood corresponds in basic meaning to that of the Bible. His central premise was that the whole of humankind are children of God and as such are, in essence, one in Christ. This premise, when extended, dictates that we should love our enemies because they are also our brothers and sisters. Such love includes an extension of charity, understanding, and forgiveness to our enemies. Even though oppressed by others, King advised his followers that they should wear down their oppressors with

Brotherhood

love and patience and appeal to their hearts and conscience. If this course of action is sustained, King believed, eventually unity will be the result. From this perspective, all of God's children are interdependent; in order to attain world peace and harmony, we must unite in such an expression of brotherhood.

Another black American, Whitney M. Young, Jr., discussed black-oriented brotherhood in his book *Beyond Racism*.[6] Brotherhood growing out of the black experience in America developed over the years out of necessity. Since blacks have not been able to assimilate into a predominantly white society by changing their names or modifying their accents as other groups have done, they have developed a pride in their own ethnic identity and have formed their own brotherhood. In his book, Young criticized churches which frequently have not supported by example the biblical message of love and brotherhood. For Young, the church represented a hypocritical and immoral institution that makes little attempt to put into practice what it preaches and professes. Defining racism as the major crisis in America, he offered his solution to the problem: the development of brotherhood between all citizens and, specifically, participation in an open society. Only through an open society, he concluded, will all men and women have an opportunity to develop their potential and fulfill their destinies.

In a somewhat different way, Rudolf Dreikurs refers to brotherhood as people working together to meet their common needs.[7] He believes human beings are social beings who need relationships with significant other persons if they are to achieve a feeling of self-fulfillment. This feeling of self-fulfillment and brotherhood can best be achieved through social interest by individual initiative, by valuing social equality, and by cooperative involvement. Unfortunately, the practice of brotherhood is not as simple as it appears by definition. Our society has many forces that counteract it, namely, competition, prejudice, social-class divisions, and institutional racism. Dreikurs feels that it is the responsibility of every person to develop within himself those social responses that will promote brotherhood.

A Religious Foundation of Human Relations

We find the following statement in Acts 17:26: "[God] hath made of one blood all nations of men." Gandhi's philosophy embodied this biblical truth. In keeping with it, he endeavored to hasten the day of universal brotherhood by devoting his life to the service and betterment of mankind. He had within him a humility and meekness that rarely has been matched. In *My Gandhi*, John H. Holmes says Gandhi's belief in God was so great that he lived in God and sought to know and do His will always. In this relationship he, Gandhi, was nothing and God was everything and he allowed nothing to interfere with that belief. Writes Holmes: "What he found or seemed to find, he conveyed to his disciples and ultimately to the great masses of his fellow countrymen, so that all became one company in God. Hence, the inner peace which prevailed in the midst of the most stupendous revolution in history."[8]

Gandhi stated that because all people are children under God, the good of each individual resides in the good of all. His lifelong effort to elevate the untouchables from their lives of degradation and shame is an example of the practical application of this philosophy. He saw the untouchables as creatures of God; not evil people with filthy living habits and ill manners, but victims of an evil social system. Believing that circumstances and their own limited experiences precluded their knowing better, Gandhi felt directed by God to alleviate the untouchables' suffering. Commenting on them in 1921, he said: "Two paths are open before India today, either to introduce the Western principle that 'might is right' or to uphold the Eastern principle that truth alone conquers, that truth knows no mishap, that the strong and weak have alike a right to 'secure justice.'"[9] Gandhi's philosophy and its relevance today were echoed by Adlai Stevenson: "The world is now too dangerous for anything but the truth, too small for anything but brotherhood."[10] For Gandhi, the uplifting of the untouchables represented a spiritual uplifting of the downtrodden peoples of all nations. He struggled valiantly for equal rights and dignity for his afflicted brothers in South Africa and for their emancipation from British rule. He wanted his people to

Brotherhood

have equal treatment so that they might bind up the wounds of long injustice. His thoughts reflected a phrase from Revelation 22:2: "and the leaves of the tree were for the healing of the nations."

King saw racism not necessarily as an evil inherent in a social system but, rather, as a tragic mistake passed on from one generation to the next. King was, however, painfully aware that in order for Americans to live together as one family, they must reason together. So committed was he to making this principle operative that he sacrificed his own life in pursuit of the ideal of brotherhood. "His sacrifice was for all men—Jew and Gentile, black and white," C. Eric Lincoln wrote of him. "Together, men could overcome the hatred and the perfidy which alienate them from God and from each other."[11]

Young agreed that the cited phrase from Revelation could serve as an ideal foundation for ending racism in America. However, the great necessity now lies in making nonwhite Americans and white Americans believe it is true. Too many religious leaders have preached the doctrine of brotherhood, but neither they nor their congregations have put it into practice. Young asked these questions: How many truly racially integrated churches are there in America? If we are all of one blood, then why should there continue to be overt differences in the church one attends and the treatment one receives from various members?

If it were only possible to eliminate the prejudices we all have, we could nurture the belief in every person that we are in fact all part of one nation—not a white nation, a black nation, a red nation, a yellow nation, or a Jewish nation, but, rather, one nation under God, with true meaning for the words *with liberty, justice, and equality for all.* In such a climate, racism would no longer exist and we could construct a new world rather than tear an outmoded one apart.

Dreikurs lends weight to this concept in his remarks on social equality. He says it is the fundamental requirement of social living. It is a concept that implies that everyone, regardless of race, sex, color, or creed, is to be viewed as a social equal.

A Religious Foundation of Human Relations

When converted into behavior, this belief leads to human equality.[12]

Other biblical thoughts relevant to brotherhood are found in Matthew 5:39, 43–44: "But I say unto you, that ye resist not evil; but whoever shall smite thee on thy right cheek, turn to him the other also. . . . Ye have heard that it hath been said, thou shalt love thy neighbor and hate thine enemy. But I say unto you, love your enemies, bless them that curse you, do good to them that hate you, and pray for them which despitefully use you and persecute you."

In keeping with these principles, Gandhi construed love to be an integral part of his nonviolent idealism, *Satyagraha*, or soul force. Reflecting its theological precursor, Gandhi's belief prescribes that good, truth, and love must in the final analysis be victorious because God is these principles. To Gandhi, all life was sacred and violence was completely incompatible with love. His aim was to practice and teach non-violence, which meant also to simplify life until violence became unnecessary. He believed that the essence of nonviolence is to combat weapons with the shield of the spirit. In this regard, Holmes remarked that Gandhi was repeating Paul's injunction when he exhorted his disciples to rely on "the sword of the spirit." His "arsenal of the spirit" included obedience, forbearance, long-suffering, good will, and courage: "If I hit my adversary, that of course is violence; but to be truly non-violent, I must love him and pray for him even when he hits me."[13]

Gandhi's never ending pursuit of brotherhood continued until his death. He prayed and fasted, and for his commitment he was clubbed and beaten, suffered insults, humiliation, illness, prison, was defamed, and endured extreme sacrifices without becoming embittered. Holmes observed of him: "He was never angry nor did he seek revenge. He knew that to forgive and love one's enemies was in the end to win the edge of their hate and overcome their hostility."[14]

In South Africa a mob set itself against Gandhi. Believing cowardice to be as distasteful as violence, he faced the crowd

Brotherhood

in broad daylight. He was attacked instantly, and the wife of the local police superintendant attempted to shield him and fend off the mob with her umbrella. He refused to prosecute his attackers and later was said to regard the incident as a useful test of his power to accept evil without retaliation. His action was in keeping with the message of Romans 12:14: "Bless them which persecute you: bless and curse not." Gandhi cautioned his followers that the true spirit of people is different from their deeds: "Hate the sin and not the sinner."[15]

Although he felt that it is proper to resist and attack a social system, Gandhi believed it improper to attack personally the people who run it. Passive resistance, he believed, is ultimately the most potent weapon; for only through love and brotherhood and the sacrifices of passive resistance can the inevitable tide of public opinion overwhelm racist opponents. Concurring with this philosophy, King made it mandatory that his followers put away their physical weapons and pick up the spiritual weapons of nonviolence: the breastplate of righteousness and the armor of truth.

To King, the biblical love-thy-neighbor dictum applied to all mankind. His was a profound belief that such love involved assuming a responsibility for mankind. To the question "Am I my brother's keeper?" King's answer was an unequivocal "Yes!" He dramatized the wrongs of his adversaries but always endeavored to make a face-saving alternative available to them. Inherent in all of King's major pronouncements was the Christian idea of brotherhood. He often equated this with creative good will: "overflowing love which seeks nothing in return" or "the love of God operating in the human heart."[16]

Although he was essentially an advocate of nonviolence, Young was quick to point out that in some cases violence will erupt no matter what one advocates. A case in point were the riots that broke out in many major cities after the assassination of King. The state of oppression and denied opportunities that blacks have endured for years has resulted in the past (and likely will in the future) in explosions of rage and hurt that ended in violence.

Possessing a deep awareness of the power of the individual human response, Dreikurs advocates that changes in society should take place through individuals intent on achieving the betterment of mankind. His philosophy would tend to be directed toward changes in attitude and behavior in each individual that would result in the realization of social equality. He cautions that this is an individual and not a group process or group responsibility. Personally adhering to the concept of nonviolence, he contends that we can achieve brotherhood by realizing the true meaning of democracy and living within the guidelines of the U.S. Constitution. The result is well worth the effort, according to Psalm 133: 1: "Behold, how good and pleasant it is when brothers dwell in unity."

Richard Shaull suggests several ways in which the Christian community can offer a structure for human liberation:

To do this, we will not only have to overcome the "privatization" of Christian existence so dominant in many circles, but also discover how to contribute effectively to the formation of personal and group self-identity over against the system, the development of increasing critical awareness, and the creation of a style of life that breaks the power of the old order over us, challenges its values, and makes it possible for us to play a new game by a new set of rules. If that is to happen, then it is our task to be especially sensitive to those individuals and groups who are open to and prepared for such an adventure.[17]

PASSIVE RESISTANCE

After his death, Gandhi's desolate followers and mourners were reported to have said of him: "We loved him because he first loved us."[18] Gandhi was able to see and understand how human relationships can be corrupted when one people rule another. He was instrumental in transforming Indian nationalism (freedom from the British) from a small movement led by the Western-educated elite into a mass movement supported

Brotherhood

by uneducated millions. His behavior provided his countrymen with a sense of dignity, self-respect, and purpose. Through his sacrifices, they learned to assist themselves in the search for unity, both national unity and unity with God. In hundreds of large and small ways, he taught his people that they were worthy of freedom. It was not enough, however, for them to attain freedom from British rule; they also needed intergroup changes. "The relations of rich man to poor man within India must change," he said. "The rich man must think of himself as his brother's keeper and must use his wealth as a trust for the benefit of the poor."[19]

Gandhi built and lived in two model villages in order to be near his people—people of all castes. He insisted upon identifying his life with that of downtrodden people; this gave practical testimony that he was trying to free himself of prejudice, and thus by example he taught acceptance. He felt that in order to help the Indian people in a significant way, a deep union between Indian leaders and the masses was necessary.

Gandhi recognized India as a pluralistic society in which all people of all creeds could live together in brotherhood. He believed that religion was a private matter and that attempting to create a religious state was patently unacceptable. He said each person should determine his own approach to God. He was deeply concerned about the hostility and lack of brotherhood between people of the Hindu and Moslem faiths. To protest it, he fasted twenty-one days; the result was a reconciliation between the two faiths. Despite all his efforts, partition became the rule after the British freed India. Jinnah, leader of the Moslem League, wanted a separate state of Pakistan and refused to accept any other option.

By way of contrast, Gandhi's beliefs revolved primarily around one subject: God. Understanding him is impossible unless this is kept in mind; he was intensely spiritual. In Holmes's words, "God represented to Gandhi not so much a presence as a pattern of life. It was this pattern which brought order alike to the outer and inner world of reality and therewith the sense of peace, which Gandhi recognized as truth."[20]

A Religious Foundation of Human Relations

Gandhi believed that Truth conceived as God is the Absolute. This is in keeping with the message of John 7:18: "He who seeks the glory of him who sent him is true and in him there is no falsehood."

In Gandhi's life, religion and politics bowed to the unrelenting search for truth. "To me," he said, "truth is God and there is no way to find truth except the way of God." He refused formal political power, believing that in possessing the formal power to direct others he would be depriving the people of their own right and opportunity to conduct their personal experiments with truth. In John 14:6 and 16:13, Jesus called himself the Truth, not for what he was but for what he did. All he did originated in the Divine Truth and made the latter a reality in this world. Christians are said to be worshippers of Truth, and it becomes their very nature if they accept or receive Christ in brotherhood: "Accordingly all progression in the apprehension of Truth depends on one's willingness to accept the indwelling Truth as the regulatory principle of both knowledge and action."[21]

Matthew 22:16 states: "And they sent out unto him their disciples with the Herodians, saying Master, we know that thou art true and teachest the way of God in truth, neither carest for any man, for thou regardest not the person of man." This has been interpreted as "The way of truth is the way of God." As I have said, Gandhi and King lived in God and in service to God. Their works of public service, their search for national identity, equality, and brotherhood are evidence of divine direction. Their quest for truth was insatiable. With their philosophy that morality is the basis of all things and that truth is the substance of all morality, both Gandhi and King believed that one man standing with truth on his side could wield immense moral power.

Gandhi's decisions were introspective, spiritual decisions, made, he would say, by God: "God has never allowed any of my own plans to stand. He has disposed of them in his own way."[22] It is said of Gandhi that he challenged the world, even as Jesus challenged Rome, to a duel between the sword and the spirit, in word and deed and drama. To his side he called truth, love, and peace. And since these were God as Mahatma knew God, the victory was his.

Gandhi derived and formulated his religious beliefs from many sources. Among them were the Bhagavad-Gita (Gandhi's favorite book and the scriptures of the Hindu religion) and the Christian Bible. He deplored much of the Old Testament but was inspired by the New, especially the Sermon on the Mount and Jesus' teachings of the Scriptures. Said Gandhi: "'But I say unto you that ye resist not evil: but whosoever shall smite thee on thy right cheek, turn to him the other also.' And 'if any man take away thy coat let him have thy cloak too,' delighted me beyond measure."[23] In Gandhi's search for brotherhood, the New Testament revealed to him the concept of renunciation; to him, it was the highest form of religion.

The two concepts of renunciation—truth, which Gandhi understood to be the embodiment of God, and loving-kindness, as expressed in ahimsa—were the basis for his passive-resistance *Satyagraha* movement. As has been noted, *Satyagraha* was more than just passive nonviolence; it was a way of life for Gandhi and his followers, a life of self-sacrifice leading to the inner-soul purity known as brahmacharya. This way of life demanded discipline of the highest order, so, in a spirit of true brotherhood, Gandhi divested himself of his property and other material goods and lived in poverty with his fellow men and followers. Triumphing over the flesh had a deep spiritual significance for him.

In 1906, at the age of 37, Gandhi began a life of sexual abstinence. Fasting was another form of self-denial; a stringent diet of fruit and nuts served to satisfy his body's needs and helped to eradicate any source of sensual pleasure afforded by eating. Of prayer he said: "I have not the slightest doubt that prayer is God's unfailing means to cleanse the heart of passions. But it must be combined with humility."[24] Correlative passages in Matthew 6:25, 33–34 state: "Therefore I say unto you, take no thought for your life, what ye shall eat, or what ye shall drink; nor yet for your body, what ye shall put on. Is not thy life more than meat, and the body more than raiment? . . . But seek ye first the Kingdom of God, and his righteousness

A Religious Foundation of Human Relations

and all these things shall be added unto you. Take therefore no thought for the morrow: for the morrow shall take thought for the things of itself. Sufficient unto the day is the evil thereof." The source of Gandhi's greatest strength was the absence of valuable possessions. Since he had none to lose, his enemies could not divest him of personal property.

The *Satyagraha* movement was characterized by disciplined nonviolence. Its followers could be identified by an inner power called "Spirit, the presence of God in the soul of men, the divine mystery of love in action . . . to still the fear and heal the hate of men."[25] Gandhi taught that *Satyagraha* should not apply moral coercion to its opponents but should aim at voluntary surrender to the elevated precepts of the philosophy. Its aim was to confront, not convert. Gandhi's philosophy was one of "endless becoming," a doctrine of permanent spiritual evolution. He felt that in their efforts to achieve true brotherhood his followers should always remain open to noble persuasion and be able to adapt to the here-and-now, to the demands of constantly changing human relations.

Clearly, Gandhi's way to brotherhood was the way of love: "Since it [love] is inspired by Jesus and his spirit, it is gentle, kind, patient, pardoning, self-effacing and sacrificial."[26] Many times and in a variety of ways Gandhi and his life have been compared to Jesus and His: "Both went to the people and led them in great movements of deliverance, from superstition within and oppression without. In both burned the pure and radiant flame of sacrificial love. They lived in Spirit and in Truth, and showed the way of life."[27] And both were martyred victims of religious fanaticism.

Romans 12:15 exhorts: "Rejoice with them that do rejoice, and weep with them that weep." Gandhi's empathy with the people of India helped him to show those who wanted freedom from British rule that they could do something for themselves and their cause. In a practical vein, he introduced the spinning wheel in Indian homes. This was designed to strike a mortal blow at Britain's fabric industry and at the same time enable

Brotherhood

the poor to earn a few rupees. To set an example, Gandhi devoted a part of every day to spinning.

In a decision devoid of brotherhood, the British ruled that only they could manufacture and sell salt; then they imposed an outrageous tax on it. Salt was indispensable in the lives of the Indians. In protest, Gandhi and some of his followers marched to the sea, brought out a pail of salt water, and from it produced salt. This was to symbolize the Indians' emancipation from British rule and encourage them to make their own salt.

Romans 12:17-18 cautions: "Recompense to no man evil for evil. Provide things honest in the sight of all men. If it be possible, as much as lieth in you, live peaceably with all men." Gandhi used these concepts as the foundation of *Satyagraha* first in South Africa, where he led the oppressed Indian people to strike in protest. The strike took the Indians from their jobs, paralyzing the country. Time and time again they marched; many of them were beaten and imprisoned. All of this was undertaken to call to the attention of the higher-class Indians in South Africa the plight of the peasants. Concurrently, Gandhi trained his followers to go out of their way to grant favors to their enemies, even to aid them when necessary.

The final portion of Gandhi's life was filled with dedicated service to others. Longing for humanitarian work of a permanent nature, he founded the Servants of India, a society dedicated to social work, including unionization of urban workers, famine relief, and general alleviation of the plight of the poor. In 1933 he made a twelve-thousand-mile pilgrimage of foot to dramatize the travail of the untouchables. He sought to rehabilitate villages, aid backward tribes, and deliver women from their role of servitude. Of his oppressors he said: "It has always been a mystery to me how men can feel themselves honoured by the humiliation of their fellow beings."[28]

In his efforts to achieve universal brotherhood, Gandhi remained uncorrupted. He even denied himself the pleasure of triumphing over his enemies by endeavoring to make every settlement a face-saving compromise. We find the precedent for this in Romans 12:19: "Dearly beloved, avenge not yourselves, but rather give place unto wrath; for it is written, Vengeance is mine; I will repay sayeth the Lord."

As the end of his life drew near, Gandhi became convinced, as did Jesus, that he would die by violence. When his time came, Gandhi died without anger and without fear. He died for what he had done and for what he had been. He taught and demonstrated that the meek and humble can emerge victorious in the end because God is on their side. In 1921, Holmes gave this sketch of him in a sermon:

Such is the Mahatma Gandhi. In this great spirit he lives among his people. As he moves from city to city, crowds of thirty and even fifty thousand people assemble to hear his words. As he pauses for the night in a village, or in the open countryside, great throngs come to him as to a holy shrine. He would seem to be what the Indians regard him—the perfect and universal man. In his personal character, he is simple and undefiled. In his political endeavors, he is as stern a realist as Lenin . . . at the same time he is an idealist, living ever in the spirit.

When I think of Gandhi, I think of Jesus. He lives his life; he speaks his word; he suffers, strives, and will some day nobly die, for his kingdom upon earth.

Do you recall how it is told of Jesus, that one day as he was journeying he heard his disciples quarreling. And he said, "What were you reasoning on the way?" And they said they had disputed who was the greatest among them. And Jesus said, "If any man would be first among you, let him be the servant of all."[29]

What, then, is brotherhood? What does the word mean? When I consulted dictionaries, I learned that brotherhood is defined as a bond between men; a feeling; an association with a common aim; or, perhaps, a religious order. These definitions are shallow. When I examined brotherhood in the context of Christian philosophy, I found its noblest meaning.

Brotherhood

Christian brotherhood is, unquestionably, a love of our neighbor. It follows, then, that such a love must involve an external benevolence toward other persons that includes assistance, encouragement, and an unqualified extension of general good will. And sometimes these things must be provided even when to do so causes personal inconvenience. In essence, from the Christian perspective, if we live our lives in the spirit of brotherhood as God intended and demonstrated, we must provide for other persons in need, even if to do so jeopardizes our own life and limb. Gandhi would have argued that anything less is sacrilegious.

NONVIOLENCE

The history of brotherhood in America has been dismal indeed, for citizens born outside the dominant group have suffered immeasurably. The treatment of black Americans is a typical example. One wonders what God was thinking about when that Royal Dutch Navy ship dropped anchor in Jamestown Harbor in 1619 and brought black indentured servants to America. There are those who would contend that since then things have changed for black Americans and all wrongs have been righted. Have they really? Black Americans only very recently have been accorded many of the legal rights denied them. But have they been accepted into contemporary brotherhood as defined in the Christian precept? Definitely not. Several dramatic examples could be cited to support this assessment, but conditions are improving.

When I think about American history, many individuals come to mind, but none of their deeds compares with what Martin Luther King, Jr., accomplished in twelve short years. More than any other American, he exemplifies to me the spirit of brotherhood in the Christian sense. He saw what many did not; he practiced brotherhood as many would not. His career began in a white-dominated America that lived in an illusory world full of democratic principles but predominantly undemocratic practices. Martin Luther King, Jr., had a dream, a dream of brotherhood that necessitated the awakening of white America. He wanted the same freedom and equality for all of God's people, black and white, Jew and Gentile, rich and poor. His strategy for achieving his dream was essentially a commitment to Christian brotherhood, a strategy of nonviolence.

Believing that King has been ignored by most theologians, Herbert W. Richardson suggests that he was *the* theologian of our times:

The most important proponent of a theology of reconciliation was Martin Luther King, who developed this theological principle into a new method for effecting social change. In his theology, therefore, faith affirms reconciliation in opposition to the relativism that denies its possibility. In intellectual discussion, faith hopes for agreement and not only dialogue. In war, faith expects and works for peace. In economic struggle, it calls for the common good. In the working together of churches, it anticipates ecumenical reunion. . . . One thinks immediately of King's support of the United Nations, of his development of the Southern Christian Leadership Conference, and of his concern for peace and ecumenism. These are the institutions where God is working in the world today. But only the eyes of faith can see it.[30]

King brought into clear focus the players in his version of an American tragedy: suffering, nonviolent protesters; their oppressive, racist adversaries; the onlooking general populace, black and nonblack. His entire approach was woven into a fabric of Christian brotherhood that, he hoped, would awaken the conscience of white America and ultimately lead to full freedom for blacks.

The turning point of the civil-rights campaigns was achieved when the oppressed minority willingly suffered and turned the other cheek. Such conduct demonstrated the integrity, honesty, courage, and Christian righteousness of the oppressed. Their adversaries were shown to the world as cruel, unjust, and completely lacking in any appreciation and prac-

Brotherhood

tice of sincere Christian brotherhood as it should apply to all of mankind, not just a favored few.

From the beginning, King sought situations that would crystallize public opinion, involve it, and direct it to such an extent that a thoughtful American could not help but recognize the hypocrisy of racial segregation and discrimination in America, land of the free. In communicating his dream, King sought unyielding commitment from his followers: "If tokenism were our goal this administration has adroitly moved us toward its accomplishment. But tokenism can now be seen not only as a useless goal, but as a genuine menace. It is a palliative which relieves emotional distress, but leaves the disease and its ravages unaffected."[31]

He stripped the mask of pseudoequality from the face of a hypocritical America. In view of his philosophy, personal commitment, and example, King's rise to a role of leadership and greatness was inevitable. From the Montgomery boycott, the sit-ins, the freedom rides, Birmingham, Selma, St. Augustine, Chicago, Memphis, and other struggles, Martin Luther King, Jr., and his followers, in the face of denial and in some instances failure, waged a war on racism. His critics say that King won a few battles but lost his war. In the end, the critics say, blacks still are not free. I do not agree. King did not lose; his war goes on.

One would think that Martin Luther King, Jr., a theologian, certainly would have had the support of the religious community in his quest for brotherhood and equality for all people; by and large, such support did not materialize. For example, while King sat in jail in Birmingham on Easter Sunday 1963, groups of blacks attempted to integrate worship services. The record of their efforts for dynamic brotherhood is dismal: only two of six white churches welcomed them.

Throughout King's campaigns, the religious community appeared fraught with indecision and ambiguity. Few religious leaders seemed to realize the lateness of the civil-rights hour; many urged restraint, patience, and moderation. Eight white ministers of Birmingham issued "An Appeal for Law and

A Religious Foundation of Human Relations

Order and Common Sense," suggesting that racial problems be solved through the courts and that the action of the demonstrators was unwise and untimely. The statement concluded: "We further strongly urge our own Negro community to withdraw support from demonstrations." The message was not addressed to King, nor did it accord to him or to his movement the dignity of recognition by name; instead, it referred highhandedly to "some of our Negro citizens, directed and led in part by outsiders." Although he was incarcerated at the time, King provided a thoughtful reply. In content, it was both polite and reflective of brotherhood:

You deplore the demonstrations taking place in Birmingham. But your statement, I am sorry to say, fails to express a similar concern for the conditions that brought about the demonstrations. . . . Oppressed people cannot remain oppressed forever. The yearning for freedom eventually manifests itself, and that is what has happened to the American Negro. Something within has reminded him of his birthright of freedom, and something without has reminded him that it can be gained. . . . The Negro has many pent-up resentments and latent frustrations, and he must release them. So let him march; let him make prayer pilgrimages to city hall; let him go on freedom rides—and try to understand why he does so. . . . I hope the church as a whole will meet the challenge of this decisive hour. But even if the church does not come to the aid of justice, I have no despair about the future. I have no fear about the outcome of our struggle in Birmingham, even if our motives are at present misunderstood. We will reach our goal of freedom in Birmingham and all over the nation, because the goal of America is freedom.[32]

Throughout his campaigns, King was closely attuned to the humanistic aspects of the Bible. Like Gandhi's, in so many ways King's way of life bore a striking similarity to the life of Christ. In short, King lived his Christianity. His teaching invariably reflected the way as exemplified by Jesus. King, Gandhi, and Jesus demonstrated vividly that we can choose

Brotherhood

to free ourselves from group pressures. In some instances, this choice will result in ostracism or death. But we do not have to remain silent partners with people engaging in inhumane behavior.

It is appropriate to note that Martin Luther King, Jr., focused on much more than the plight of blacks in a white-dominated America. Indeed, the range of his involvement in brotherhood expanded beyond any single problem area. He said any affront to human dignity must be countered. Thus his fight was directed at many evil forces, poverty, racism, and war among them; in the end, he sought world peace. Despite many setbacks and cruel adversity, he did not lose faith in his fellow man or abandon hope for the eventual union of all Americans into a truly United States. In *Where Do We Go From Here: Chaos or Community?* he noted that the aims of civil-rights movements had transcended integration and moved to pluralism.[33] This meant the races could come together, but not to inculcate only white values.

One can well imagine the resistance encountered by King in his crusade for Christian brotherhood. Certainly, rabid racists and ignorant and misguided whites were formidable foes. But not all of his critics were white. One of the sharpest attacks of King's nonviolent strategy was made by Malcolm X: "Just as the slavemaster of that day used Tom, the house Negro, to keep the field Negros in check, the same old slavemaster today has Negroes who are nothing but modern Uncle Toms, twentieth-century Uncle Toms, to keep you and me in check, to keep us under control, keep us passive and peaceful and non-violent."[34]

Nor did all theologians agree with King's appraisal of the potency of nonviolence. George Celestin offers the following rebuttal to nonviolence:

For Christians who are horrified at the thought of revolution, perhaps the greatest fear is of the violence that history demonstrates is inevitably involved. Power and particularly its violent use generates traumas of conscience for many Christians. As

A Religious Foundation of Human Relations

they see it, the way of Christ is the way of peace and nonviolence. Witness the interest of Père Régamery and of the late Martin Luther King, Jr., in the life and teachings of Mahatma Gandhi. . . . Karl Rahner, in an excellent analysis of the Christian understanding and use of power, points out that the struggle for power is inevitable. It is a struggle, moreover, from which the Christian cannot absent himself. To do so would constitute a false spiritualism, an escape from the real material world. Rahner considers blanket renunciation of any kind of physical force not merely impracticable but also immoral because it is in effect an abdication of responsibility under God.[35]

The issue of revolution remains ambiguous. Harvey G. Cox observed of American Christians: "We are living in an age of revolution without a theology of revolution. The development of such a theology should be the first item on the theological agenda today."[36]

It is ironic indeed that many blacks failed to recognize King's contribution to their freedom. Before his ascendance to leadership, there was little unity and almost no sense of national purpose or direction among the black masses in their struggle for freedom. Most black Americans recognized their plight, but few knew what to do about it. Why? Primarily because of the inherent sense of inferiority among blacks that had developed and crystallized since slavery.

Through a confrontation with white citizens, blacks developed an awareness of self and ethnic pride. Each confrontation tore a piece off the myth of white supremacy. Black people learned that no matter how much violent force whites could muster, they were not invincible and could be dealt with. As blacks marched, suffered, and met their opponents head on, the new sense of black unity grew. This was the dawn of black power.

The Malcolm X's, Stokely Carmichaels, and H. Rap Browns belatedly realized that were it not for the development of a black identity and a sense of brotherhood among black people as encouraged by King, they probably would not have been

Brotherhood

heeded by blacks at all. The sense of inferiority still would have been embedded, and all the fiery rhetoric of the violence-oriented revolutionists would have fallen on socially deaf ears.

Was Martin Luther King, Jr., successful? As stated earlier, even a cursory examination of his impact and achievements would dictate an unqualified yes. Using the concepts of Christianity and brotherhood as defined in the Bible, King pointed a way to freedom and justice. As a result, a social revolution is still taking place in America. The day of blacks' automatically being relegated to second-class citizenship and accepting it is over. Many discriminatory practices common only a few years ago have become past history. Although much has been achieved, much remains to be achieved, especially when we consider the plight of the previously silent minorities, such as the Spanish and Mexican Americans, American Indians, and Asian Americans.

TOWARD AN OPEN SOCIETY

In *Beyond Racism,* Whitney Young, Jr., indirectly referred to brotherhood when he wrote of black Americans' adopting, in the 1970's, a strategy different from that to which they had subscribed previously:

Previous periods saw blacks accommodate themselves to an openly brutal society, followed by a period of organization building, and finally a period of confrontation and demonstrations. Now we are on the threshold of a new period. Black people have the pride, the dignity, the skills, and a measure of power necessary to negotiate from a position of strength.[37]

This new period is one of black brotherhood, an association of persons with a common aim. Young did not, however, advocate that brotherhood is the answer to racism in America. On the contrary, he believed that building what he called an open society was the ultimate answer.

The theory of brotherhood has existed from biblical days

to the present, yet its true meaning seldom has been put into practice. Many of the Old Testament books are history; in them are the crowded and dramatic stories of people who lived thousands of years ago. Even then people were chided for their failure to obey the teachings and to follow the examples of brotherhood set forth in Scripture. In comparing the positive and negative aspects of brotherhood as recorded in the Bible, it is evident that acts of brotherhood were given lip service. And they are today. It is easy to speak of brotherhood, but far more difficult to practice it.

Young said America has relentlessly persecuted black people for three hundred and fifty years and in the process has created a second America, separated geographically and psychologically. Contending that black explorers were here before the *Mayflower* arrived, Young noted that this nation belongs to blacks as well as everyone else. Throughout his book, he encourages the building of an open society, his vision of which is one that can be shared by people of every ethnic group.[38] In an open society, people do not try to displace one another but instead try to live together as one nation, under God, with liberty and justice for all.

Commenting further, Young said: "The black man today is fully aware of his inferior status. He knows that it is man-made, not God-given."[39] This is true even though black Americans' blood, sweat, and tears have been a driving force in our economy—an economy that places them on the bottom rung of the ladder of success. Daily there are increasing expressions from blacks that they are no longer satisfied with crumbs; they want their fair share of the meal of survival. We can either work together in harmony and brotherhood, which brings dignity to all persons, or we can die together in the pain of hate and violence.

Outwardly, many "liberal" whites in this country pretend to oppose racial segregation, yet they will sell their homes if a black moves into the neighborhood or transfer their children into a private school if their public school is scheduled for desegregation. But not all whites have behaved this way. Many others have championed the cause of brotherhood in general and racial integration in particular.

In biblical history, the Israelites, not wishing to assimilate into the local populace, conquered the Land of Canaan and dispossessed its citizens. What has deterred the blacks from doing the same thing in America? Most black Americans exhibit no desire to conquer white Americans; they are simply striving to attain full equality and brotherhood in a society that, in principle, promises these things to them. "Black people today are placing more and more emphasis on the need for unity and on the desirability of creating a strong, stable black community capable of dealing with the white holders of power on a basis of equality," Young observed. "To some extent this emphasis on black brotherhood is a retreat from the constant confrontation with a hostile society."[40]

According to Young, the church, neglecting its responsibility to act against prejudice, has become the most hypocritical and immoral institution in America. In these times of moral conflict, many churches have become complacent and even condone or tolerate racism: "Some churches so completely mirror their members' bigotry," wrote Young, "that their creed might be 'I am my black brother's keeper; I keep him in his place.'"[41] Many congregations that willingly donate money to African missions still do not permit black people to pray in their Stateside churches. This caused Young to write: "Eleven o'clock on Sunday morning is still the most segregated hour in America. The church has failed to bring its purported message of love and brotherhood to its own members."[42]

It is sad that pseudo-Christians who ostensibly support brotherhood have been notorious for turning their backs on the poor and dispossessed. A few church schools have become havens for parents who remove their children from public schools just to keep them in an all-white atmosphere. Other church leaders know that if the church is to survive and contribute to the ideal of brotherhood, it will have to become more responsive to the urban and racial crisis. This is a profound moral crisis which the church cannot and should not ignore.

A Religious Foundation of Human Relations

It is debatable whether American Christian churches betray or transmit the Christian tradition and the church traditions which make up their foundation. William A. Clebsch makes this point lucidly:

Writings by Will Herberg, Gibson Winter, Reinhold Niebuhr, Martin Marty, Theodore Wedel, Peter Berger, and Harvey Cox, to name a few, have scored a variety of American churches for their cultural accommodations and their religious neologisms that, according to these writers, betray the faith once delivered to the saints.

At the same time other students were showing how the same churches have brought forth and transmitted important and long-neglected aspects of the Christian tradition and, indeed, of individual church traditions. These writers, largely of historical orientation, include Sidney E. Mead, Sydney Ahlstrom, Daniel Day Williams, H. Richard Niebuhr, and John Tracy Ellis.[43]

A campaign against racism, Young suggested, should not be limited to old clichés about brotherhood; these appeals have been falling on deaf ears for years. Instead, such a campaign must show that measures taken to benefit black people will benefit all Americans. The Old Testament would lead some religious groups to believe that they are God's chosen people. If America or the world is to survive, Young observed, we must all consider ourselves God's chosen people and live together, not only with platitudes, but with action.

To skeptics, Young wrote: "Some people believe that attitudes cannot be changed. I disagree: I have seen people do an about-face overnight when their own self-interest was at stake."[44] An example of this occurred when Jackie Robinson joined the Brooklyn Dodgers. Many players said they would never play with Jackie on the team, but when he started hitting balls and stealing bases, they began to realize that it was better to share the World Series money than go back to segregated non–World Series days. A second example is that of a young southern white lad who stuck like glue to a veteran

Brotherhood

black sergeant in Vietnam. His option was to become either a segregated dead white soldier or an integrated live white soldier. Prejudices of a lifetime can dissolve in seconds when one's own survival or self-interest is at stake.

Whitney Young suggested actions that everyone can take to help build an open society. This list is by no means complete, but it does offer guidelines to make a significant beginning:

Communicate. Listen to the emotions behind the words black people are expressing. Listen to how people are expressing themselves. Listening to the words alone is not enough.

Learn. What has the black man contributed to his country? In the past, most media portrayed blacks as happy slaves, domestic servants, or lazy janitors. Lately, our media are showing that blacks have contributed much more to our history than earlier books and histories told.

Help black people get jobs. Ask questions when there are no black employees in the department store, supermarket, or restaurant you patronize.

Boycott. When there is an awareness of racial discrimination, write the offending party a letter and tell him that you do not intend to purchase his products until the discriminatory situation is rectified. Tell your friends about it, too.

Buy Black. Black businesses need and want to serve the entire community, not just black persons. They need to secure and retain some of everyone's business if they are to make their maximum contribution to the gross national product.

Volunteer. Tutor low-achieving black children, supervise recreational activities, teach homemaking skills, or do whatever else your knowledge and experience qualify you to do.

Educate other white people. Don't ignore bigoted remarks by whites or minorities. Bigotry begets bigotry.

Bring open housing to your neighborhood. Put pressure on landlords not to discriminate. Pass along information on housing vacancies to the local Urban League.

Desegregate your job, your school, your club, your pro-

fessional organization. Make it possible for blacks to become an integral part of community activities.

Use your power. Use prestige, influence, or power to open jobs for blacks, and get involved in social action. If all else fails, read Saul Alinsky's book, *Rules for Radicals,* and consider some of these examples for bringing about change.

Although these guidelines focus on black-white relationships, they are relevant for interaction with all groups, especially disadvantaged Chicanos, American Indians, Puerto Ricans, and Asian Americans. Nor should we neglect women, aged, and physically and mentally disadvantaged persons.

INDIVIDUAL INITIATIVE

According to Rudolf Dreikurs, our society is in a constant state of turmoil, with much unrest and chaos. At the time his book was being written, high school and college students throughout the nation were marching, demonstrating, picketing, and rebelling. Their causes varied, but their emotions were basically the same: anger, indignation, and discontent. Those in our society who are still being denied dignity and excluded from human brotherhood are not unlike the rebelling youths.

There have been advanced many theories to explain some of the reasons for the lack of brotherhood in America. Dreikurs has suggested that one significant cause is anomie, the feeling of rootlessness, or being cut off, or not belonging with other members of society.[45] Other authorities suggest that the primary cause involved in the entire range of society's problems is the rapid and overwhelming social upheaval of our era; technology has advanced faster than society's capability to promote brotherhood. The effects of rapid change on the whole fabric of the societal system are graphically illustrated in Alvin Toffler's book *Future Shock.*[46]

Another expert, Alfred Adler, contends that man must develop social interests if he is to calm current social turmoil.

Brotherhood

The fundamental prerequisite for societal living is the concept of equality; without it there can be no stability or social harmony. Through all of time, whenever one group establishes itself as superior, it creates instability in other groups; sooner or later it is overturned, and another dominant group replaces it. A biblical parallel is found in Mark 3:25: "And if a house be divided against itself, that house cannot stand." Social interest and social equality can bring about the unity that will result in true brotherhood for all of mankind.

Adler concluded that we can determine our own destiny and initiate our own fate.[47] This view is congruent with existential philosophies which state that: man is aware of his being and has the capacity to choose his own behavior; man assumes responsibility for his own behavior, and life is what he makes it; man displays the courage to exist when he makes his own decisions, asserts himself, and accepts the consequences.[48] A biblical correlate is apparent in Leviticus 19:18: "Thou shalt love thy neighbor as thyself." This Old Testament teaching supports individual responsibility and explicitly pronounces that man is his brother's keeper.

If we acknowledge the validity of individual determinism, then each person is constrained by the conditions of his existence and influenced by his life experiences. Sometimes the latter provide us with an opportunity to recognize the deeper, spiritual meanings of life. Because we make our own experience, which we may then use as we see fit, we can determine its meaning and decide what stimuli we will respond to.

Dreikurs states that the moving force behind all of our actions is an inner plan according to which we act and which is scarcely known to us. The plan includes our attitude toward others and toward life; it is essentially what we think of ourselves. We can respect others only if we respect ourselves, and trust life only if we trust ourselves. Our self-concept shapes our interests, strivings, feelings, and capacity to participate in brotherhood. The importance of self-concept in realizing brotherhood should motivate us to examine ourselves closely. In other words, it is essential for us to understand our reactions

A Religious Foundation of Human Relations

to various environmental stimuli and the impact of our reactions and behavior on other people.

As we develop self-insight, there will come to most of us the realization that we are prejudiced, for ourselves and against others. We must deal with these prejudices if we are to implement and perfect the state of brotherhood. We are told in I John 4:7: "Beloved, let us love one another: for love is God." Logical argument and rationale alone are not enough to overcome prejudices, but prejudices can be overcome if we are aware of them and are willing to reconsider the facts upon which they are predicated.

Dreikurs says we are all products of the society in which we live: "The time has come for us to realize that we, even though being influenced by our environment, also can influence our environment."[49] A similar concept is found in Matthew 28:19: "Go ye therefore, and teach all nations." In the human situation there is constant interaction between the individual and his institutions. We must realize that each of us has the right and responsibility to shape our social institutions. It is through social participation and communion with others that brotherhood can be achieved, and it is through nonviolent, interpersonal human relationships that a peaceful, harmonious, and rewarding society can be realized. Finally, it is each person's privilege and responsibility to work toward this goal, or, as in Philippians 2:12, "work out your own salvation with fear and trembling."

The community is the basic societal unit from which we must work to encourage brotherhood. We are all part of our communities (at least physically); we have rights, privileges, and duties because of this membership. Others may try to deny us the right to our place in the community, Dreikurs cautions, but we must have the courage and conviction to stand up for our rights. This will help offset efforts to deprive others of their rightful heritage.

Currently, the cultural atmosphere in most communities is characterized by turmoil. Inflation, unemployment, and distrust of political figures grow daily. Society is being torn apart. Individuals focus on their own rights and disregard the rights of others in an attempt to survive, physically and emotionally. Minorities in communities are divided into various segments; each with a common enemy: the Establishment. But the Establishment varies, depending upon each individual's definition. For some blacks, it is white racists; for some women, it is unfair social and employment practices; for some labor leaders, it is an exploitive management; for some children, it is their parents. Instead of consolidating their struggle against injustice, domination, and deprivation of rights, each group fights its own battle. Such division is the Establishment's most potent weapon.

There is a polarization between those who call for law and order, hoping to suppress rebellion with power, and those who support the underprivileged and openly or tacitly support their rebellion. How long will it be before most people realize that there will be no law and order until we have peace and brotherhood in our communities? So long as authorities feel that they can establish order through oppression, violence and destruction will be the counter forces. Dreikurs concluded: "The strife for an egalitarian society expresses man's desire for social harmony. Democracy requires the recognition of human equality. Our present dilemma arises from the fact that while we all have legally become equals, we do not know how to deal with each other as equals."[50]

People everywhere are striving for their political freedom; they are striving for participation in the decision-making processes that they feel now lie in the hands of too powerful bureaucrats, many of whom have proved themselves unfit to wield the power that has been vested in them. Richard McKeon has commented on the danger that emerges when citizens lose faith in their social systems:

We are in danger of forgetting what equality has come to mean in the centuries of discussion of its meaning. And we are in danger of losing the equalities which we have achieved during the centuries of struggle for equality. We have forgotten

A Religious Foundation of Human Relations

the meaning of equality to such an extent that reputable scientists devote ingenuity and scientific erudition to demonstrate that men are unequal. We have lost the moral motivation toward equality by supporting that equality is at best an effective though descriptive catchphrase or by excusing inaction because the times or circumstances are not right to put equality into effect.[51]

A disproportionate number of ethnic-minority members can attest to the fact that judicial equality is impotent without economic and social equality. In our society we have judicial equality in the law, but this legislated equality does not have its counterpart in the experiences of the everyday world in which ethnic minorities live. Law-enforcement officials accord the power elite, social elite, and others in the community treatment that is vastly different from that accorded persons who are poor, uneducated, or nonwhite.

The rich and powerful have a special niche in our society. It is apparent that wealth and power are unevenly distributed among the haves and the have-nots. We tend to measure a man by what he has in his bank account. Some theorists suggest that in order to foster the principle of brotherhood, the economic goods in society must be more evenly distributed. This, the theorists continue, can be done within the democratic political structure through an equitable graduated-tax program. Congressional reaction to this suggestion indicates it is not a popular option to most persons in power. In the meantime, we appear to be circumscribed by our ineffectual competitive remedies and errors.

The danger in allowing competition to provide the sole basis for personal superiority is becoming increasingly recognized, even though competition is cited as a necessary requirement for social mobility. It is characteristic of our society that individuals endeavor to elevate themselves, moving up the economic ladder out of habit, conditioning, and fear that if they cannot keep up with their neighbors they will be labeled a failure. The brotherly love that remains a symbol of great religious devotion has not become an ingredient in the formula for economic success.

Brotherhood

Growth and brotherhood will be achieved when everyone works toward a common goal, moving on a similar plateau, growing through the desire to contribute and expand, without stopping the progress of others. It is of interest to note that highly competitive persons tend to stand competition only if they win; if they do not win, they either withdraw, become aggressive, or manifest other behavior aimed at defeating their competitors. We frequently hear about the work addict who works himself to death to achieve success. Conversely, the goal of brotherhood is to establish a cooperative atmosphere. A cooperative person is more concerned about the plight of other people and how he can contribute to mankind rather than improve his own position at the expense of other persons.

Ideally, then, what does democracy represent? To Dreikurs, it represents government by the people, who exercise their rule through their representatives. In addition, democracy is deeply concerned with fundamental human rights, among which is the recognition of equality: social, political, economic, and personal. Dreikurs believes that democracy can succeed in building a community of brotherhood based upon mutual respect, cooperation, trust, and consideration for all. Recognizing that humans do not live as isolated islands but, rather, are social beings dependent upon others in their environment, Dreikurs emphasizes the necessity of developing social interests, especially interest in other people. For him, we can achieve brotherhood only if we realize social equality, for social equality is the cornerstone of brotherhood. John Donne has expressed these ideas a bit more poetically:

No man is an Iland, intire of it selfe; every man is a peece of the Continent, a part of the maine; if a Clod bee washed away by the Sea, Europe is the lesse, as well as if a Promontorie were, as well as if a Mannor thy friends or of thine own were. Any man's death diminishes me, because I am involved in Mankinde; And therefore never send to know for whom the bell tolls; It tolls for thee.[52]

3
LOVE

LOVE is one of the most complex and powerful of human emotions. "Love and religion," said Havelock Ellis, "are the two most volcanic emotions to which the human organism is liable, and it is not surprising that, when there is a disturbance in one of these spheres, the vibration should readily extend to the other."[1] Few persons would dispute the interaction Ellis suggests occurs between love and religion.

Displaying their awareness of the complexity of love, the Greeks employed three separate words to define it: *eros, philia,* and *agape*. In liberal translation, *eros* reflects the seeking love, *philia* the sharing love, and *agape* the giving or sacrificial love. For purposes of our discussion, *eros* means the philosophical (for the word *philosophy* means "the love of and seeking of wisdom"); *philia* means the psychological (for this word focuses on the interrelationships, or self-sharing, of human beings); and *agape* means the giving or overflowing love that is found in the Christian religion and in those of its followers who attempt to manifest Christian ideals.

PHILOSOPHICAL PERSPECTIVES

In *Symposium*, Plato discussed the various facets of love in the lives of the people of his day.[2] He began by praising the greatness and beauty of a particular god, the God of Love, saying this god had always been good to mankind and was a constant source of human happiness. Plato expressed disappointment that men and women had not written poems or songs of praise to the God of Love: "What a strange thing it is . . . that, whereas other gods have poems and hymns made in their honor, the great glorious god, Love, has no encomiast among all the poets who are many. . . . So entirely has this great deity been neglected."[3]

In his considerations of the human expression of love, Plato maintained that love should transcend the ordinary level of human emotion. For him, the ideal human relationship of love was expressed in the devotion between a lover and his beloved:

If there were only some way of contriving that a state or an army should be made up of lovers and their loves, they would be the very best governors of their own city, abstaining from all dishonor, and emulating one another in honor; and when fighting at each other's side, although a mere handful, they would overcome the world. For what lover would not choose rather to be seen by all mankind than by his beloved, either when abandoning his post or throwing away his arms? He would be ready to die a thousand deaths than endure this. Or who would desert his beloved or fail him in the hour of danger? The veriest coward would become an inspired hero, equal to the bravest, at such a time; Love would inspire him. The courage which, as Homer says, the god breathes into the souls of some heroes. Love of his own nature infuses into the lover.[4]

Plato described love as, first, the desire to attain something good beyond one's self or circumstances. Next, it is attraction between the sexes; in this type of love, the participants seek immortality by reproducing themselves. Plato stated: "All men will necessarily desire immortality together with good: wherefore love is of immortality."[5] He submitted that all humans seek this end by one means or another. Thus there are those who give birth to other human beings to represent them here on earth long after they are gone, and there are those who seek immortality through paintings, poems, plays, and music.

Discussing yet another manifestation of love, Plato described the friendship which develops between two people of the same sex. This relationship occurs when two people come together and educate each other to their individual virtues. A strong bond is effected in this unique human relationship, and Plato assessed that those in this bond are closer to immortality and to love than those who seek to satisfy their longing for the eternal in the procreation of children. Indeed, for Plato the constant association of two people in the relationship of seeking truth and sharing beauty represented the noblest form of love. Defending the merits of such an association, he said:

Above all, when he finds a fair and noble and well-nurtured soul, he embraces the two [wisdom and virtue] in one person, and to such a one he is full of speech about virtue and the nature and pursuits of a good man; and he tries to educate him; and at the touch of the beautiful which is ever present in his memory, even when absent, he brings forth that which he had conceived long before, and in company with him tends that which he brings forth; and they are married by a far nearer tie and have a closer friendship than those who beget marital children, for the children who are their offspring are fairer and more immortal.[6]

Plato concluded his eulogy of love by indicating that he would pay homage to the God of Love as fully as he could and would urge others to do so, since love is the way to immortality. To repeat, clearly explicit in Plato's philosophy is the principle that all persons seek immortality. In the male-female relationship, couples seek it through the procreation of children, in

Love

the hope that their offspring will continue to reproduce and thus keep their name and lineage alive. Other persons strive for immortality through the arts. For example, they may be moved by the beauty of nature and wish to re-create it on canvas, which is a method of recording expressions and responses of themselves. Such works of art may come to be admired and revered by others, thereby affording a certain immortality to the artist. Plato, however, considered art an imitative exercise and defined the seeking of truth as the highest form of love. Therefore, it was in the friendship between two people who seek wisdom that Plato found love's highest expression. Friendship, in his view, stands beyond comparison with a painting or a newborn child, for it has no physical properties. Such a relationship has been created in the minds and through the wills of the individuals involved. Since it is closer to the immortal (which is nonphysical) than the other two types, Plato believed that two people seeking wisdom will have a better chance of achieving the eternal status for which all people strive.

For the Greeks generally and for Plato specifically, it is well to remember that the final emphasis was not placed on wisdom but, rather, on the love of seeking wisdom. As a matter of fact, in Plato's day, those who sought knowledge for its honor or public display were denigrated by Greek men of wisdom. It was the love of wisdom, or the search of knowledge for its own sake, that the Greeks considered to be the highest virtue. The umbilical cord between the Greek belief in immortality and our own Christian tradition of yearning to transcend human existence remains unsevered.

As Plato sought to elevate the relationship between the lover and the beloved to the highest expression of love, so, too, did his student, Aristotle. Characterizing friendship as the highest level of human relationship, Aristotle said of man: "He cannot live in complaisance with others, except it be a friend."[7] In *Nicomachean Ethics*, Aristotle describes his theory of love in friendship; when he writes of friendship, he is implying love, particularly the merits of self-love. His starting point for love begins with self-love, then moves to self-love in friendship, and finally resides in three basic facets of friendship, each of which revolves around a specific type of love.

In Aristotle's time, it was generally accepted that we should love our best friend, and our best friend is someone who wishes for our well-being.[8] This is an expression of the self-love a person should feel in his own behalf, and the same should be true of our feelings toward anyone defined as our friend. Only if a man has strong feelings for himself and is in fact a self-lover, said Aristotle, can he have these feelings for another. Self-love therefore becomes the basis for the ability to establish a friendship with another person. Commenting on lack of self-love, Aristotle admonished that a bad man's disposition is not friendly even toward himself because there is nothing lovable about him.[9] It follows, then, for Aristotle, that in order to be able to love, one must himself be lovable.

Aristotle disputed the derogatory connotations that are usually associated with the term *self-love*. He submitted that those who gratify their appetites and emotions in irrational indulgence do not qualify for his higher meaning of the term. He also asserted that if a person directed his attention above all else to acting justly toward himself in the terms of self-control and virtue, he would develop to the point of having self-love and of expressing the kind of love that true friendship requires. Thus, Aristotle concluded, a person who has the capacity for being a good friend should be a self-lover because he will enhance not only himself but also his fellow man by performing noble actions.

After establishing that it is not necessarily bad to love ourselves, Aristotle went on to say that self-love, in fact, is a prerequisite to participation in the various types of friendship. He supported his thesis by observing that the friendly relations which we have with our neighbors and which serve to define the various kinds of friendship seem to be derived from our personal needs.[10] To qualify as one with the capacity for love that friendship requires, Aristotle described five behaviors and sentiments that a man should exhibit toward a friend: he wishes for and does what is good for, or what appears to him to be good for, his friend's sake; he wishes for the existence and life of his friend for his friend's sake; he spends his time in his friend's company; his desires are the same as his friend's; he shares sorrow and joy with his friend.[11]

Aristotle cited three causes for the love that expresses itself in the affection of friendship: what is good, what is pleasant, what is useful. It was true in Aristotle's time and is true now that we do not feel affection or love for everything, but only for the lovable. Neither do we wish good things for inanimate objects that cannot return our affection or love. According to Aristotle, when the motive of love in friendship is based on pleasure or usefulness, the partners do not feel love for each other as persons; rather, they enter into an arrangement for what each can gain from the other. A relationship formed merely because of the pleasure or usefulness persons derive from it is not love. Another term should be given to this type of interaction.

For Aristotle, friendship based on contributing to the self-realization of the good in another person was the perfect form of friendship: "It exists between good men who are alike in excellence and virtue."[12] In this type of friendship, feelings of affection (self-love) exist in their highest and best form. To attain such a relationship requires that each partner convey to the other that he is worthy of affection by engendering confidence and trust. Since this requires a great deal of time and patience, Aristotle suggested it is impossible to express true affection or love toward many; this relationship must be reserved for a very few.

In ancient Greece (as is the case now), most people, perhaps because of personal ambition, wanted to receive love rather than give it. Receiving love was regarded as being honored, and to most Greeks this was highly desirable. But Aristotle's love as defined by friendship placed its emphasis on giving rather than receiving: "Since, then, friendship consists in giving rather than in receiving affection, and since we praise those who love their friends, the giving of affection seems to constitute the proper virtue of friends, so that people who give affection to one another according to each other's merit are lasting friends and their friendship is a lasting friendship."[13]

When characterizing the love between a man and woman, Aristotle was somewhat more charitable than Plato. He believed the affection between a husband and wife was inherent in the laws of nature inasmuch as man is by nature a social creature and prefers not to live alone. He felt also that men and women live together not entirely because of their social nature but also because of the desire for procreation and to secure the needs of life that the male-female balance provides. Aristotle remarked of the male-female relationship: "This kind of friendship brings both usefulness and pleasantness with it, and if the partners are good, it may even be based on virtue and excellence."[14]

Passages in the Bible agree with the philosophy that friendship, which is based on goodness, is in fact based on love:

Thou shalt love the Lord thy God with all thy heart, and with all thy soul, and with all thy strength, and with all thy mind; and thy neighbor as thyself. — Luke 10:27

I love them that love me; and those that seek me early shall find me. — Proverbs 8:17

Thou shalt love thy neighbor as thyself. — Leviticus 19:18

A friend loves at all times. — Proverbs 17:17

Owe no man anything but to love one another: for he that loveth another hath fulfilled the law. — Romans 13:8

Aristotle's theories of love have very close parallels in modern psychology and apparently have influenced theories that involve self-actualization. Most of these contemporary theories point out that we must know and love ourselves before we can truly know and love others. Witness further correspondence between ancient and modern thought: Aristotle said it

Love

is impossible to have a perfect friendship with a large number of people; today we hear the same thesis in human-relations workshops. Communicating at a real core level in contemporary society, most authorities agree, occurs with only a very few people, if any, in an entire lifetime.

The following frequently quoted passages of I Corinthians 13:1–8 synthesize the essence of Aristotle's position:

Though I speak with the tongues of men and of angels, and have not charity, I have become as sounding brass or a tinkling cymbal. And if I have the gift of prophecy, and understand all mysteries, and all knowledge; and if I have all faith so that I could remove mountains, yet do not have charity, I am nothing. And if I bestow all my goods to feed the poor, and if I deliver my body to be burned, yet do not have charity, it profits me nothing. Charity is patient, and is kind; charity does not envy, is not pretentious, is not puffed up, is not ambitious, is not self seeking, is not provoked, thinks no evil, does not rejoice over wickedness, but rejoices with the truth; bears with all things, believes all things, hopes all things, endures all things.

In the writings of Plato and Aristotle, love is variously defined as a passion for immortality, as self-regard, and as the expression of two people in perfect friendship. In the Bible's list of things that endure, including faith, hope, and love, the greatest of them is love. There are similarities between Plato's and the Bible's ideas of love. Although Plato's *Symposium* was written four hundred years before Paul's letters to the Corinthians, both give immense praise to love. Plato cited the example of an army of lovers and beloveds which would be the greatest of its kind in the world. The New Testament, through Paul in Corinthians, indicates a regard for a similar principle with the statement that greater love hath no man than to lay down his life for his fellow man. However, Paul did not condone homosexuality. In answer to Plato's complaint that love had not received the kind of praise it deserved from poets and songsters, certainly Paul in his passage on the excellence of love provides an eloquent description and praise of love.

Plato repeatedly expressed the idea of love as the passion for immortality and contended that all people are drawn to it in order to be closer to the God of Love. By contrast, Paul would take exception to the idea of such a god and would insist that there is only one true God and he *is* love, not simply a god of love. Clearly, there is a basic difference of perspective regarding love in the monotheism of Paul and the polytheism of the Greeks. However, both would contend equally for the reality and desirability of immortality and love as the path that leads to it. The Greek position concerning love resides more in *eros*, or in seeking truth with another to gain love, whereas the biblical perspective emphasizes *agape*, or love of God. Anders Nygren saw the two types of love as being dichotomies:

There cannot be any real synthesis between two forces so completely contrary to one another as Eros and Agape—the Eros which, beginning with a sense of poverty and emptiness, seeks God in order to find in Him satisfaction for its own wants, and the Agape which, being rich through God's grace pours itself out in love. The measure in which such a synthesis appears to have been successful is from the point of view of the Agape motif the measure of its failure, for it has meant the betrayal of Agape. Whenever a synthesis seems to have been reached and the two motifs are united, it becomes the task of a succeeding generation to untie the knot and thereby bring about a deeper understanding of the nature of the Christian love-motif.[15]

Karl Barth took issue with Nygren's dichotomy and elected to mix *eros* and *agape*.[16] In still another interpretation, Jacques Maritain[17] and Bernhard Häring[18] defined Christian love as being friendship with God and man. And certainly there are other interpretations that we will not discuss in this book.

Despite dissimilarities, many of our values and much that conditions our human relationships today derive from the foundations and influences we find in early philosophy and the Christian theology which followed.

PSYCHOLOGICAL PERSPECTIVES

Erich Fromm and Sigmund Freud are not only psychoanalysts but also men of philosophical profundity; their theories of love bridge the gap between philosophy and psychology. The influence of ancient philosophers is evident in modern psychological works related to love. An example that bears this out is Fromm's view that "any theory of love must begin with a theory of man, of human existence."[19] This parallels the early Greek philosophical thought which has already been presented. Also closely akin to Greek ideal is Fromm's prime concern, which focuses on the creation of a sane society based on human needs and the establishment of harmonious relationships among men and women and nations in a chaotic age. However, both Freud and Fromm depart somewhat from the ancient Greek writers in defining what constitutes man's basic nature and his true priorities.

I would also point out that there are differences between Freud and Fromm. We may better understand their concepts of love by exploring those differences regarding the basic nature of man. A strict Freudian at first, Fromm gradually modified his position because of Freud's early emphasis on the unconscious and lack of focus on social and economic factors. In contrast to the Freudian theory of the biological foundations of the human character, Fromm believes man is a product of his culture. The principal problem for Fromm, apart from a consideration of love, is the specific way an individual adjusts to his world. Fromm especially concerns himself with the dilemma of Western man, whose individuality leaves him isolated, insignificant, and doubtful about the meaning of life. Fromm's concern was reflected in a 1956 statement: "The danger of the past was that men became slaves. The danger of the future is that men may become robots. True enough, robots do not rebel. But given man's nature, robots cannot live and remain sane."[20]

Commenting on the basic nature of man and animals,

A Religious Foundation of Human Relations

Fromm maintains that the equivalent of love in animals is instinct. When man the animal became man the human, he transcended his animal nature but did not leave it. From this transcendence there is no return but, rather, a continual growing away from bestial instincts. It begins at birth when we leave the protective cover of the womb.

At birth, man the human is equipped with awarenesses: of himself, of others, of his past experiences, of the possibility of future experiences, of the inevitability of death. Our awareness of death is a significant key to our sense of separateness, which makes urgent our need to love. The insight that we will experience death alone and, probably, not in a manner or time of our choosing accelerates our urgency to find love. It soon becomes apparent to all of us that we will die before or after experiencing love. Both possibilities accentuate the need to experience love. Circumscribed by the bounds of their own being, most humans exist as entities apart, completely separate, from others. If we did not reach out to others from this state of isolation, Fromm says, we surely would become insane. Thus insanity is the inability to unite with another person: the insane person retreats within himself or herself and blocks out all others. In this view, the greatest tragedy is not to be loved.

At whatever emotional level of existence we participate, Fromm noted, being isolated produces anxiety in us. We feel as helpless as the proverbial leaf which is at the mercy of every wind that blows. Gradually, we are confronted with the knowledge that only if we can reach out, unite with another person, and participate in love can this bond of solitude be broken. Man has forever attempted to solve the problem of his sense of separateness, whether he lives in a cave, a hogan, a monastery, a castle, or an apartment. It is, in fact, from this sense of separateness and the mystery of existence that much of philosophy and theology have derived. Psychology attempts to augment these philosophical and theological foundations in examining love's place in the human relationship.

Establishing the bond between psychology and religion, Fromm traced the transcendence of man from animal to

Love

Genesis and expulsion from the Garden of Eden. Unable to return to the protection of his innocent natural world, man the animal was confronted with the necessity of developing into civilized man. Fromm conjectured that upon their departure from Paradise, Adam and Eve were ashamed not so much of their nakedness as of their separateness and inability to love. This separateness is illustrated when Adam chooses not to defend Eve for eating the forbidden fruit but, rather, places the blame on her.

Knowledge, which the fruit represented, is a key concept in philosophy, psychology, and theology, although in each discipline it is represented differently. In the jargon of philosophy, we move in the direction of knowing truth; in the jargon of psychology, we move in the direction of knowing the self in relationship to another person; in the jargon of theology, we move in the direction of knowing God, who often represents but an aggregate of all the mysteries that we do not understand.

Fromm suggests unity as a solution to our anxiety. Some persons explore the possibilities of this unity through orgiastic states which may be drug- or sexually-induced. So long as this behavior is socially acceptable, there is no attendant guilt, but if it is not socially acceptable, intense guilt surrounds it. For example, although the orgiastic state of drunkenness often is employed in an attempt to participate in the love relationship, this manner of expression has a long tradition of Christian disapproval. In Samuel, Nabal becomes drunk and slips into a stupor and is dead within ten days. In Deuteronomy, the Israelites are told to stone a son if he is rebellious, a spendthrift, or a drunkard. The stigma attached to drunkenness is apparent in the laws and mores of our culture.

The roots of conformity reach deep into Old Testament traditions. Modern conformity, an attempt to be related to others intimately, has strong ties with the biblical traditions of the Hebrews. The ancient Hebrews believed they were the chosen people of God and that marriage should be among the chosen. Some Hebrews even believed that they should enslave the Gentiles and destroy the nonbelievers. Fromm cautioned

A Religious Foundation of Human Relations

against exerting conformity at the expense of others in the name of love.

We can gain insight into Freud's views of love by examining Fromm's comments about them. After the First World War, Fromm wrote, Freud developed a new theory concerning love, a complete departure from previous theories: *eros* is present in every cell of living substance and has as its aim the uniting and integrating of all cells. Thus Freud discovered nonsexual love. He called it the love instinct, the form of love identified with life and growth. He submitted that the life instinct fights with the death instinct and the outcome determines the course of human existence. Clearly, this view was contrary to his earlier theory of man as an isolated system driven by just two instincts, survival and pleasure. Man at the mercy of only these two instincts had but one reason to enter into a relationship with another person: to gratify his need for sensual pleasure.

In Freud's new theory of love, man was no longer thought of as totally isolated and egotistical but as related to others and impelled by life instincts to require union with others. More fundamental than sexuality and pleasure, Freud's new theory proclaimed the importance of life, love, and growth. Commenting on his new theory in *Why War?* Freud wrote: "Anything that encourages the growth of emotional ties between men must operate against war. These ties may be of two kinds. . . . They may be relations resembling those toward a loved object, though without having a sexual aim. There is no need for psychoanalysis to be ashamed to speak of love in this connection for religion itself uses the same words: 'Thou shalt love thy neighbor as thyself.'"[21] The second kind of emotional tie is identification: whatever leads men and women to share important interests and produce this community of feeling.

The change in Freud's position to one more in keeping with biblical tradition of what constitutes love is apparent in the following passage:

Nothing short of a radical change of viewpoint had occurred. Freud, the enemy of religion, which he had called an illusion preventing man from reaching maturity and independence, now quotes one of the most fundamental commandments to be found in all great humanistic religions as support for his psychological assumption. He emphasized that there is "no need for psychoanalysis to be ashamed to speak of love in this connection" but, indeed, he needs this assertion to overcome the embarrassment he must have felt in making this drastic change with regard to the concept of brotherly love.[22]

Fromm agrees with Freud's later view. He believes that the most fundamental of all loves is brotherly love; the caring, respecting, responding, and furthering of the self-realization of another. Here we can plainly see the imprint of Aristotle's concept of love in friendship. Fromm believes that in brotherly love we become at one with all other humans because it makes the human core-of-being common to all persons regardless of race, intelligence, or culture. By Fromm's measure, in order for us to become aware of this common bond, we must penetrate facades and reach other people's core-of-being. We must not focus on the facade, for when we do, we concentrate on differences. Psychology as a discipline displays a keen awareness of the alienating factors which result from emphasizing the differences in human beings.

As was discussed earlier, brotherly love is characterized by the Greek concept *philia*, which connotes a love between equals. Fromm submits that ideal brotherly love is between equals, but, being human, we are not always equal and at various times stand in need of varying degrees of help. Thus from time to time the love relationship requires more than a half-way effort by one of the participants. In agreement with concepts of love expressed in several biblical passages, Fromm's brotherly love begins not with loving a brother but with loving a stranger, a poor person, a helpless person, and those who hold ideas different from ours. To love our brothers and sisters—our own flesh and blood—cannot be construed to be a great achievement. Even lower animals seem to display this kind of love or nurture. Brotherly love can unfold only when we love someone who does not serve some useful or pleasurable purpose in our own lives.

A Religious Foundation of Human Relations

In Psalms it is written that the man who remembers the weak and the poor will be happy, will be delivered on the day of trouble, will have his life preserved, will be safe from his enemies, and will be protected from illness. Similarly, in Exodus, God admonishes the Hebrews to protect the widows and orphans or he will slay them and make their wives and children widows and orphans.

In addition to brotherly love, Fromm has written of motherly love:

Motherly love . . . is unconditional affirmation of the child's life and his needs. But one important addition to this definition must be made here. Affirmation of the child's life has two aspects: one is the care and responsibility absolutely necessary for the preservation of the child's life and his growth; the other aspect goes further than mere preservation. It is this latter attitude which instills in the child a love for living, which gives him the feeling: "it is good to be a little boy or girl, it is good to be on this earth!" These two aspects of motherly love are expressed very succinctly also in the biblical story of creation. God creates the world and man. This corresponds to the simple care and affirmation of existence. But God goes beyond this minimum requirement. On each day after nature—and man—is created God says, "it is good." Motherly love, in this second step, makes the child feel it is good to have been born; it instills in the child the love for life, and not merely the wish to remain alive. The same idea is shown to be expressed in another biblical symbolism. The promised land [land is always a mother symbol] is described as "flowing with milk and honey." Milk is the symbol of the first aspect of love, that of care and affirmation. Honey symbolizes the sweetness of life, and the love for it and the happiness in being alive. Most mothers are capable of giving "milk," but only a minority of giving "honey" too. In order to be able to give honey, a mother must not only be a "good mother," but a happy person—and this aim is not achieved by many. The effect on the child can hardly be exaggerated. Mother's love for life is as infectious as her anxiety is. Both attitudes have a deep effect on the child's whole personality; one can distinguish indeed, among children — and adults — those who got only "milk" and those who got "milk and honey."[23]

Fromm concluded that both brotherly love and motherly love have a universality: if I love my brothers and sisters, then I love all brothers and sisters; if I love my child, then I love all children. In contrast, erotic love does not have this universality but is rather an exclusive love. Erotic love, Fromm noted, is the most deceptive of all loves. It is confused with the spontaneous experience of falling in love and the subsequent tearing down of social barriers between two people. This type of love results in a very short-term closeness: the couple becomes intimately known to each other with no more barriers to overcome and no more sudden closeness to experience. In this instance, love becomes equated with short-term physical contact. Consequently, the erstwhile lovers look for new partners and new thrills.

The exclusiveness of erotic love can cause two people to attempt to become one and deliberately exclude the rest of the world. By doing this, the couple becomes separate from other persons and, to a degree, separate from each other. A healthy love relationship does not eliminate the rest of mankind but, rather, includes it. Although difficult, it is not impossible that erotic love can be healthy love; this can be achieved by involving other persons. I would add that this does not imply sexual intercourse as a requisite for erotic love. Healthy love does entail accepting the premise that we are all interrelated and are all part of the whole of humankind. If this is true, then it follows that it makes no difference whom we love; it becomes merely a matter of the will to love. Perhaps this lends weight to the statement that beauty is in the eyes of the beholder.

In his theory of love, Fromm stated that we are all identical in that all men are part of Adam and all women are part of Eve but nevertheless we are all separate entities. Each of us exists as a common person, yet a unique individual. By this very uniqueness we attract some people and repel others.

A Religious Foundation of Human Relations

The complexity of the love relationship is illustrated in the marriage of Jacob, Leah, and Rachel. Jacob fell in love with Laban's younger daughter, Rachel, and agreed to work seven years for her. After the seven years passed, he went to his marriage bed only to discover the next morning that it was Leah, Rachel's older and ugly sister, who was his bride. He complained to Laban, who convinced him to complete a marriage week with Leah, marry Rachel, and work another seven years. Even though he loved Rachel more than Leah, it was the latter who bore him four sons during the seven years. At this time in the Hebrew culture, a man was allowed more than one wife and was required to provide each a separate and individual family life. Jacob loved Rachel in a deep emotional way and at the same time loved Leah in a dutiful way.

Erich Fromm observed that men and women must love in order to overcome their anxiety at being a separate entity. The love can be brotherly love between equals, or motherly love for the helpless, or erotic love, a unique and willful experience between two individuals. Each type of love is sanctioned by various passages in the Bible. I say it again: in psychology, the umbilical cord between religiously seated tradition and modern experience remains unsevered. C. L. Becker defined this tie as the values of our existence that need no justification:

Whatever success men have had since the Stone Age in lifting themselves above the level of brute existence has been the result of the slowly developing capacity of reason to distinguish fact from illusion and to prefer the values that exalt the humane and rational qualities of the human personality to the values that deny and degrade them.... They are values which, since the time of Buddha and Confucius, Solomon and Zoroaster, Plato and Aristotle, Socrates and Jesus, men commonly employed to measure the advance or the decline of civilization, the values they have celebrated in the saints and sages whom they have agreed to canonize. They are the values that readily lend themselves to rational justification, yet need no justification.[24]

Love

THEOLOGICAL PERSPECTIVES

Anders Nygren's *Agape and Eros* is a classical theological study of love. Nygren characterized *agape* as being spontaneous and unmotivated, indifferent to human merit or worthiness, creative, and opening the way to fellowship with God.[25] To this definition, Paul Tillich added that Christian *agape* "accepts the other person in spite of resistance": it suffers and forgives.[26] In yet another vein, Paul Ramsey stated that Christian love has the special task of creating community where none exists.[27] Fulton J. Sheen popularized all of the preceding concepts.[28] In this section, we will focus our attention on Nygren and Sheen.

Generally, Nygren's ideas convey the same concepts found in the Bible but in terms more easily understood and related to those in contemporary society. He wrote that love has many shades and many depths; it is a mirror which reveals the soul and the character of the one giving love. In the many kinds of love which we have the capacity to express, each is subject to the true inner feelings of the giver. Generally speaking, the more closely a person relates to the giver of love, the deeper the love will be. Love will be returned only when true love is given. Commenting on the expression of love, Nygren states that *eros* is not unlike Platonic love, which seeks to be more than merely sensual.

An examination of Nygren's writings has convinced many persons that he held within his own heart the art of true love. In Matthew 13:3-8, Christ says: "Behold a sower went forth to sow; and when he sowed, some seeds fell by the wayside and were devoured by the birds, some fell where there were stones and could not grow, and others fell into good ground and brought forth fruit." Sheen's writings reveal that the roots of his own theological thinking were seated in this passage, that we will receive the yield of love from the heart of another in return.

In a further refinement of his concept of love, Nygren stated that Christian love is directly opposed to all rational computation and calculation. He further cautions that Christian love is not a part-time affair. True love requires commitment in order to grow and endure. Sheen drew from this point and stated that life is love and love is life: "Love is the fulfillment of dreams and making anyone who touches our life happy because of the encounter."[29] He continues by saying that grief and pain build love, for love can grow better in a contrite environment. We must continually grow in love or stagnate into oblivion, with no love and no growth. Furthermore, he admonishes that if humans do not grow in spirit and love, this is in direct opposition to God's law of order in the universe. Love is necessary to build faith, for love is the foundation of spiritual growth.

God loved the world very much, so much in fact that he was willing to give his son to die for the sins of the world. This was done so that the world could grow in wisdom and pursue eternal progression. Commenting on the power of such love, Nygren says love was meant to be a sign, a symbol of the divine. Symbolically, love is like the sunlight that bathes the trees, which in turn sink into the ground to rise again as bigger, stronger, and more beautiful trees. Some of the trees that die and sink into the ground will grow again, and some will be used centuries later as fuel to warm the body as love warms the spirit.[30] Nygren gave his theological support to the plan and structure of the universe by asserting that although one never knows how love will be returned, it can only be returned as good. This mystery of the unity of the workings of the universe is characterized in New Testament theology when Christ, while being crucified, asked, in perfect love, that his heavenly father forgive his tormentors because they did not know what they were doing.

God does not love that which is already in itself worthy of love, but on the contrary, that which in itself has no worth acquires worth just by becoming the object of God's love. . . . Agape loves, and imparts value by loving. The man who is loved by God has no value in himself; what gives him value is precisely the fact that God loves him.[31]

Love

According to Nygren, love requires three components: the lover, the beloved, and the mysterious bond (God) which unites these two. Self-love is excluded from Nygren's interpretation of *agape*. Identifying the Christian or giving type of love, he said love means being considerate of others. For him, it will never be the carnal aggressiveness which seeks to devour the prey and be glutted; rather, it means listening to others, putting oneself in their frame of mind. In essence, to love means to become identified with a soul in crisis.

Commenting on love in society, Nygren and Sheen pointed out that there are many expressions of love. For instance, there are people who say they love the poor but do not help them; there are people who say nothing, but their deeds express love for the poor. It is apparent that many persons neither say they love the poor nor do they exhibit any love for the poor. Sheen asked: "How many of those who say they care have ever given of their time, money or energy?" No one can say he loves the poor until he has put the love he professes into practice. Therefore, Sheen, as does the Bible, encourages us to translate the spirit of God's love into works of love.

A parallel theological concept is expressed in a biblical parable. A very rich man asked Christ how he could guarantee his getting into heaven. Christ told him to give all that he had to the poor and to follow Him. The man went away sad because he did not love the poor enough to follow Christ or even enough to try to make the suggested compromise relative to his material goods. The Bible also provides much information about the results that can be expected to accrue from either love or the lack of it. As was noted earlier, I Corinthians 13:1–4 states that if one has all the attributes of a holy person but does not have love, one has nothing: "Though I speak with the tongues of men and of angels, and have not charity [love], I am become as sounding brass or a tinkling cymbal."

When Jesus makes the righteous and sinners change places, it might at first sight appear as if this were a matter of simple transvaluation, or inversion of values. . . . Actually, something of far deeper import than any "transvaluation" is involved here—namely, the principle that any thought of valuation whatsoever *is out of place in connection with fellowship with God.*[32]

For Nygren and Sheen, the love of other persons is inseparable from the love of God. If we truly love God, we will be served and loved. Conversely, if we truly love another person, God will be served. Like Aristotle and Fromm, Nygren and Sheen caution that love is separate from usefulness. A relationship with another person would not qualify for their concept of love if it were maintained for the purpose of enhancing personal well-being. They say emphatically that love does not cherish another person because of the pleasure the other person gives; love is not controlled by the value of objects.

When fellowship with God is conceived of as a legal relationship, Divine love must in the last resort be dependent on the worth of its object. But in Christ there is revealed a Divine love which breaks all bounds, refusing to be controlled by the value of its objects, and being determined only by its own intrinsic nature.[33]

Warning against human ambition, Nygren and Sheen say the only really progressive thing in all of the universe is love. Because of man's ambition, love, which God made to bloom and blossom through all time, is that which is most often nipped in the bud. There seems to be paradox. If love is what the heart wants above all else, why does it not grow in love instead of rejecting love in favor of lesser material values? Sheen submits that love is not given, not understood, and not wanted because it entails responsibility and this inconveniences people. Most people want love on their own terms, at their own times of convenience, and in a way that corresponds with what they expect it to be by their measure. However, when love is meted out to them in their own measure, they are bitter because it does not correspond with a higher type of love they dream of but are actually unwilling to participate in.[34]

Contending for the universality of love, Nygren and Sheen say love should be practiced as a condition for living. This is in keeping with the biblical tradition that one should love for

Love

the sake of an abundant life and in order that salvation may be achieved. For both Sheen and the biblical writings reflect, all things begin with love. Love is eternal and is the only enduring quality of mankind. Both in contemporary theological thought and the traditions from which it springs, it is promised that love will return many times that which is given. If you love very little, it will be returned to you in the same small measure; if you love abundantly, so will you receive love.

Addressing the question of how to love Christ says in Matthew 16:24: "If any man will come after me, let him deny himself, and take up his cross and follow me." Here is where divine love enters the human dimension. Without such love, little is given or accomplished. Depriving oneself for the sake of love does not mean that one should not care for oneself. Just as charity in its literal sense begins at home, so, too, does love. If we do not love ourselves in humility, we can never love anyone else in tenderness.[35] Here we see a correlation not only between contemporary theology and theological traditions, but also between contemporary theology and psychological principles.

Leviticus 19:18 advises: "Thou shalt love thy neighbor as thyself." If we love and have enough understanding of ourselves, we will be able to love our neighbors. In fact, we will be able to relate to and love all with whom we come in contact. This is truly the Christian or *agape* type of love; it is the love which is pure giving and which overflows its infinite abundance in every direction.

If God's love were restricted to the righteous it would be evoked by its object and not spontaneous; but just by the fact that it seeks sinners, who do not deserve it and can lay no claim to it, it manifests most clearly its spontaneous and unmotivated nature.[36]

Commenting on the power of love, Sheen asserted that if people truly have love in their hearts, they will never know the agony of hate and the misery which attends it. In a parallel commentary, John 4:10 states: "If thou knewest the gift of God, and who it is that saith to thee, give me to drink; thou

A Religious Foundation of Human Relations

wouldest have asked of him, and he would have given thee living water." What is being suggested here is that if the person had known who was asking for a drink, he could have asked and received the gift of love and would never have had to ask for love again. Love unquestionably is a gift, one that requires making oneself vulnerable by opening the self to receive. In our present-day society, as in the days of antiquity, this is very difficult to do. Love is both difficult to receive and difficult to give because of the fear of rejection and self-doubts that cloud our vision.

Regarding a means for people to express love, we can advance the concept that one way we can love one another is to owe one another nothing except love; when this is accomplished, God's law of love is fulfilled. The Bible states this in many instances. Resorting again to allegory, Sheen likened love unto a tree: love is the tree, and the branches twist away from the tree to touch all those who love; love returns through the trunk of the tree into the roots, which make up the reserve fountain of love. There should be no limits on love; it must be allowed to grow and flourish. Peter once tried to place a limit on love by asking Christ how many times a person should forgive another. Christ replied that if you truly love your fellow man, you will forgive him seventy times seven.

Using the sun to symbolize love, Sheen suggested that love is like the sun with regard to all whom we love. The closer we feel to people and the more we love them, the warmer they will be in their feelings toward us. The closer they are to the source of your love, the warmer you will be. According to Sheen, there are various degrees of love. We can be loved by few and hated by many, loved by many and hated by few, or anything in between. If we are loved by few, we need to review our tree and our sun to determine whether we are giving love in sufficient quantity to ensure that it will be returned to us. If we are being loved in sufficient quantity to justify our existence, our peace of mind is assured.

Although it is the most important human emotion, love often is both the most overused and most underused or unused emotion in the human body. Nygren says we spend too much

Love

time pursuing things we desire and think we love but which really do not contribute to our growth in spirit and our ability to love. We say we love certain persons, but are we ready to love them as they are instead of as we want them to become? One of the requirements of Christian love is that it be unconditional.

What we find wrong with our world today and what we found wrong with our world yesterday is likely to be what will be wrong with our world tomorrow: we simply do not have real concern for our fellow human beings. If love is to become the predominant force in our world, we must be willing to care and to care first if necessary. This is the message found in the Bible, especially the New Testament.

How much should we love? Why should we love? Who should we love? What are the rewards for loving and what are the rewards for not loving? And who is to give us our reward for loving? According to Nygren and Sheen, we are our own rewarders. In the biblical tradition, we will reap what we sow. If a man fails to give of himself and ends up not caring for or loving people, then he may rest assured that there will be no love for him in the lives of other people. There is so little time in life, and to live without loving is, Nygren and Sheen concluded, to go through life in an unnatural frame of mind. This demoralizes the soul and creates a person who is not fit to live among people who have time to live, love, and develop that potential in themselves and others to the fullest degree. In the words of C. S. Lewis:

If you want to make sure of keeping your heart intact, you must give it to no one. Avoid all entanglements, lock it up safe in the coffin of selfishness. But in that coffin—safe, dark, motionless, airless—it will change. It will not be broken; it will become unbreakable, and irredeemable.[37]

HOMOSEXUALITY

Homosexuality has been addressed by sociologists, psychologists, philosophers, politicians, and theologians alike. The

A Religious Foundation of Human Relations

1960's brought a wave of sex-revolution rhetoric and a new public frankness that was seized upon by the news media, which reported that homosexuality was interpreted in three basic ways: as a problem, as a way of life, and as a personal right. To extremists on either end of the spectrum, homosexuality is seen as either a reenactment of the fall of Rome or a long-overdue liberation of the personal right to express sexual preference. Various cultures have differed in the degree of their acceptance, or rejection, of homosexuality, exacting penalties that range from burning at the stake in medieval Europe to relatively mild mockery among Navaho Indians. American society stands near the middle of the continuum and is gradually moving toward increasing tolerance, or even acceptance, of most forms of homosexual activity.

Religion has played a significant role in the evolution of public response to homosexuality, which Oscar Wilde described less than a century ago as "the love that dares not speak its name."[38] Many persons who cite religious bases for their condemnation of homosexuality make biblical reference to Sodom and Gomorrah, Leviticus, and Paul's letters to the Romans and the Corinthians as proof of God's displeasure with this practice:

But modern Scripture scholars insist Sodom and Gomorrah has nothing to do with homosexuality. The legendary destruction of the cities was brought about by the wickedness, and perhaps inhospitality, of the people. In the 16 references in Scripture to the Genesis 19 account, there is not one support that the fire and brimstone which hailed from heaven came as the result of homosexual love.... Those persons who quickly quote Leviticus and that book's condemnation of men lying with men had best read the entire law and be amused at the variety of violations we all merrily incur daily. Those who pick and choose what they wish to quote should read Leviticus 11:9-12 the next time they sit down to lobster or New England clam chowder.[39]

The Old Testament clearly states that the homosexual act is to be punished; the New Testament is less specific. Per-

Love

haps the difference is found in the historical fact that during the early days of Christianity in the Roman world, homosexuality was widely practiced.

Although there are historically substantiated accounts of death by stoning for the homosexual offense, Brian McNaught offers an explanation that lies outside the strict Judaeo-Christian tradition: Jewish condemnation of homosexuality and sodomy did not appear until after the Babylonian captivity. Until that time, there was no law against homosexuality. The Jews were few in number, however, and were threatened constantly by larger tribes and races, so they began protecting themselves by insisting that the purpose of all sexual activity be procreation.[40]

The taboo of men having sexual intercourse with men, some scholars aver, was instituted because this practice wasted the seed of procreation and thus diminished the only means of increasing the numerical strength of the Jewish people. No law is cited against women having sexual intercourse with women, which may, of course, simply indicate the unimportance of women in ancient Jewish culture. It also has been suggested that the condemnation of sodomy may have been a rejected people's response to a practice used by their Babylonian captors as a visible sign of supremacy. Homosexual prostitution, another target of Jewish condemnation, was very closely identified with the idolatry of Ashtoreth and Baal. In the Jewish mind, the terms are often interchangeable: "Condemnation of one was condemnation of the other — much like the late Senator McCarthy's association of homosexuality and treason."[41]

Despite the fact that most scholars agree that Christ's message of love never mentions homosexuality, his followers, principally Paul, transmitted condemnatory messages. The first formal church legislation against the homosexual emerged in A.D. 300 from the Council of Elvira, during which pederasts were denied last rites. When Christianity was declared the state religion by Constantine in the early fourth century, worldwide suffering began for the homosexual: "In 342 A.D. a decree imposed the death penalty for sodomy. In 390, Emperor Valentian initiated death by burning, in the tradition of Sodom and Gomorrah. In 538, Justinian codified the Roman law and subsequently prescribed torture, mutilation, and castration for homosexuals."[42]

From a theological perspective, the effect of Justinian's policies has great impact on the whole of the Christian world. In Novella 77, he blames homosexuality for famines, earthquakes, and pestilences. Consequently, sodomites were put to death lest the entire city and its inhabitants perish. Justinian's Novella 141 describes homosexuality as the state of those who have gone to decay through abominable and impious conduct which is, most deservedly, abhorred by God. From Jewish roots, all of Christianity became imbued with revulsion for homosexuality: "Thus what was originally an exclusively Jewish attitude towards homosexuality and phallic symbolism had gained ascendancy over the whole Christian world. A true Christian believer was marked out from then on by his unconditional condemnation of everything homosexual. Correspondingly, homosexual acts were regarded as unshakeable proof of heterodoxy."[43]

During the Dark Ages, the Church punished homosexuals with excommunication, denial of last rites, mutilation, torture, castration, and death by burning, with burial of the victim transacted in unsanctified earth. Heresy and homosexuality became almost inseparable in the eyes of the Church. During the Middle Ages, heretics were accused of unnatural vice routinely, and so closely were sodomy and heresy associated that the same name was applied to both. Sodomy was described as a sin so horrible that it must not even be mentioned in the presence of Christians. The influence of the Church had broad ramifications, the extent of which is apparent in English criminal law, where theological terminology, such as *unspeakable* and *horrible*, remained unamended until the nineteenth century.

During the Spanish Inquisition, great delight was taken in burning homosexuals alive. Homosexuality was treated as the ultimate crime against morality and was referred to as

Love

abominable or unspeakable. When Protestants broke from the Roman Catholic church, they carried with them their predecessors' sexual code of condemnation. The legacy of homosexual annihilation was further perpetuated by Henry VIII in England and the Calvinists in Amsterdam. In England, it was not until 1861 that the death penalty for sodomy was removed; in Scotland, it remained in practice until 1889. In Nazi Germany, homosexuals were condemned and shot without trial; other thousands were removed from society for extermination in Hitler's concentration-camp ovens. All of this took place under the guise of the Judaeo-Christian ethic. It is important to note that there was no homosexual taboo in China, Japan, India, the Arab countries, or pre-Columbian America.

At this writing, homosexual activity is still construed as an offense punishable by law in every state in the Union. In some states, the punishment is lengthy incarceration in penal institutions; in others, an alternative is treatment in state hospitals, where homosexuals are given shock treatment and vomit-inducing drugs to motivate a sexual response considered more acceptable. Medical experts disagree on the causes of homosexuality. Some experts define it as a congenital anomaly directly related to physical causes of glandular secretions. Other experts—the majority—define it in psychogenic terms. Whatever the cause, it is obvious that imprisonment is an undesirable therapy. According to Benjamin Karpman, this type of therapy is "as futile as hoping to rehabilitate a chronic alcoholic by giving him occupational therapy in a brewery."[44]

Commenting on homosexuality, John W. Dixon, Jr., wrote: "The fear of the feminine and the terrible fear of homosexuality that infects so many American men is most publicly evident in acts of public and private violence that are supposed to demonstrate manliness."[45] Dixon described homosexuality as a negative response that indicates fear of the opposite sex rather than a positive response or love for one's own sex. In rather simplistic terms, Dixon concluded: "It would take a professional skill that I cannot claim to tell to what degree homosexuality in general and any particular case of it is fear of the genitals of the other sex or an idolatry of the genitals of one's own sex."[46]

A somewhat more temperate view was expressed by Robert Springer in *New Catholic World*:

Specifically I ask how can the Catholic community in New York City go on public record as opposing civil rights for homosexuals in the form of "Intro 475," the bill currently before the city council? Can we as Christians oppose equal access to jobs and housing for homosexuals and lesbians? How can I eat the Body of the Lord and drink his Blood on Holy Thursday and be party to legislation that denies opportunity to food in the belly and to a roof over the head of my Christian brother and sister standing beside me?[47]

Springer recommends the doctrine of forgiveness and reconciliation of celibate with married, male with female, oppressor with oppressed, and heterosexual with homosexual, for he reminds us that in Christ Jesus there is no male and female, nor is there slave or master. An editorial commentary on a National Council of Churches Governing Board meeting in the spring of 1975 defends the view that the equal-rights amendment and the civil rights of homosexuals are valid causes:

They [homosexuals] have been made to appear as threats to that mythical "stable society" that now serves as a memory reservoir of what once was and is now gone. A public frustrated to the point of employing force to retain something that it has lost—and probably never really had—is a public ripe for hearing a word from either a dictator or a source of freedom. We have the word of freedom, but our communication in the past has too often sounded like a further threat to Middle America's way of life with its advocacy of those causes that appear to be undermining "their" stable society.... Consider the homosexual civil rights resolution: We must protect the civil rights of persons regardless of their "affectional or sexual preference."[48]

Methodists, who make up the nation's second-largest Protestant denomination, are sharply divided on the central issue or ordaining self-acknowledged homosexuals. The evangelical wing, represented by the unofficial publication *Good News*, "deplores sex perverts teaching to us," while the Council of Youth Ministry wants the church's general conference to declare that "sexual orientation shall not be a bar to the ordained ministry."

In evaluating the rights of homosexuals to receive ordination, arguments will have to begin at the point of whether homosexuality is a natural pattern of sexual adjustment for some persons or an aberration—an inadequate pattern occasioned by differing emotional circumstances in the growth of the individual. If it is natural (for physiological or psychological reasons), then the case could be made that discrimination against the homosexual seeking ordination is as immoral or illegal as discrimination for reasons of gender or race. But if the presupposition is that homosexuality is an inadequate pattern of life that has developed for any number of reasons, discrimination could not be charged.[49]

Three basic schools of thought have emerged from the Methodist examination of the homosexual issue. Some Methodists view homosexuality as normal, others see it as a sinful pattern of life, and a third group looks upon it as an inadequate pattern of sexual adjustment. Because of the complexity of human sexuality, it seems that nothing said at judicatory gatherings is likely to change the majority position that marriage between people of the same sex is not recognized by the Church.

Most commentators quote Paul to disparage homosexuality: "The women exchanged natural relations for the unnatural, and the men likewise gave up natural relations with women and were consumed with passion for one another."[50] Perhaps, as Robert H. Mayo concluded, the boredom of our modern culture causes some people to "become weary of clean, wholesome, entertainment. We turn to nudity, pornography and homosexuality."[51] Presbyterian authority Richard Lovelace sees current concern for the acceptance of homosexuals as a repetitive historical pattern: "To anyone with a knowledge of Church History this is a familiar pattern. Again and again the church has seen the appearance of antinomian movements permitting complete sexual license and pitting 'the witness of the spirit' against the teaching of scripture."[52]

There have been a few cracks in the religious wall restraining homosexuals. In 1972 the Northern California Conference of the United Church of Christ ordained the first avowed homosexual to the ministry. In 1976 an avowed lesbian was appointed deacon in an Episcopal Church. But such cases are rare. Most Catholics, Protestants, and Jews seem unwilling to accept known homosexuals in religious leadership roles.

Subsuming homosexuality under the broader mantle of interpersonal human relations in general, Paul Blanshard writes:

The honest answer to all these agonizing doubts and questions seems to be that Christianity no longer has an answer. The pulpit has relied for so long on scriptural generalizations about purity and sin that it is not capable now of supplying a moral framework for sex for the younger generation. If marriage and love are to be saved, and I think they are both worth saving, the salvation must come not from organized religion but from plain people not motivated by any religious dogma and from secular prophets and scholars who make use of all the learning that the social and physical sciences have to offer.[53]

The contradictory conclusions drawn from Jewish and Christian perspectives offer hope that research on the physiology and psychology of sex, on personality development, and on both homosexual and heterosexual life-styles will continue. Perhaps when society is at last ready to consider profoundly the question of social controls of sexual behavior, it can do so with greater knowledge and understanding instead of passion and prejudice, which in the past have divided religious organizations and the people they are charged to serve.

4
MARRIAGE

MARRIAGE is a delicate and mutual human relationship entered into by two people with the legal sanction of the state and, in most cases, the moral sanction of the church. It has been said that marriage is the most cherished of all human institutions. As such, it is affected by many diverse factors. The popular notion that marriages are made in heaven grew out of Tobit 6:17: "For she is appointed unto thee from the beginning." Experience suggests that successful marriages are not preordained. To achieve a successful marriage, mutual supportiveness and an open, straightforward relationship seem to be the predominant prescription of writers commenting on the subject.

Most Christians would endorse Emil Brunner's definition of marriage:

It is in community of two persons of different sexes, a community which is complete, based upon the natural foundation of sex love, but only fulfilled in the recognition of the fact that by divine appointment they belong to each other; through whose created distinctiveness the creator maintains the human race, and through which the sex nature of man, which is dis-

A Religious Foundation of Human Relations

posed for community, can and should realize its personal character.[1]

In an attempt to establish a philosophy of marriage, we will discuss the views of several present-day theorists. The discussion will, I hope, show that much of contemporary thought has theological antecedents in the Bible.

ADJUSTING TO MARRIAGE

James A. Peterson says the initial adjustments in marriage are the ones most likely to be lasting.[2] Many newly wed couples find it necessary to seek advice from a marriage counselor or friends in the early stages of their marriage. For most couples, marriage presents a new situation in which they find new and unfamiliar roles thrust upon them. At this point, it is evident that observing their parents was, at best, inadequate preparation for marriage. Indeed, it is usually after the ceremony that each learns that our society does an inadequate job of preparing children for marriage. Consequently, each partner begins an on-the-job training to be a husband or a wife. In this crucial period of defining their roles, if the couple cannot successfully adjust to role expectations that are new to them during the early years of marriage, they may never be able to do so. The longer role conflicts remain unadjusted, the more likely the situation will result in separation or divorce.[3]

The highest incidence of separation and divorce occurs during the second year of marriage. Gradually, as individuals become accustomed to married life and each other, the romanticism of courtship must be transformed into a more lasting kind of affection. Many would contend that the human nature is not conducive to such an adjustment. "Marriage is primarily a matter of mutual destiny," Herman Alexander Von Keyserling wrote: "[It] sets up an indissoluble state of tension, and its very existence depends upon the preservation of this state. Man and woman, both as individuals and as types, are funda-

Marriage

mentally different, incompatible and essentially solitary. In marriage they form an indissoluble unit of life, based upon fixed distance."[4]

Those who believe that marriage can work commonly agree that it is only successful when romantic illusions fade and a lasting companionship grows in their place. This type of love manifests stability; it grows out of maturity and results in greater capacity to cope with frustrations. The strength of this type of relationship is rooted in the mutual agreement of realistic marital goals. It is important to note that these are best built upon the solid foundation of past experiences that have been shared and found jointly rewarding.

Early problems concerning sexual adjustment in marriage are made more difficult by the fantasies and mythologies that are conjured up regarding the honeymoon and engagement experiences. Partly as a result of fantasies and mythologies, the most difficult adjustment in marriage tends to be the sexual one. Despite an abundance of authoritative how-to-do-it manuals, most couples belatedly discover that there are no universal sexual standards that apply equally to everyone.

Otto Piper suggests that because sex in marriage allows two people to express their personal love, it serves to draw individuals out of their isolation and put them in touch with each other.[5] Some individuals seek sexual intercourse with their spouses during or shortly after quarreling. Analyzing this behavior, Ruel L. Howe concluded that some persons need love most when they are most unlovable.[6]

Reinhold Niebuhr outlined three ways in which sexuality is likely to seduce us: it gratifies hunger and thus is self-love; it facilitates an escape from an uneasy sense of guilt; it provides an escape from the responsibilities of freedom by entrance into subconscious or unconscious forms of existence.[7] However, it is wise to consider Brunner's declaration that sex per se is not evil or impure:

The evil in the life of sex is the isolated function, *which manifests its* hostility to the Divine order *by reducing the awful process of procreation and sexual union to a mere trifle, and by refusing to accept responsibility for "the other two."*[8]

Consequently, from this perspective, sexuality must be rejected as an end in itself, as a mere physical indulgence—a passion without fidelity. In Brunner's words: "So long as love does not become fidelity, sex union simply means . . . that one 'makes use' of the other."[9]

It is also important to note that early inappropriateness of response in marriage by either husband or wife should not be considered as an irreversible tragedy. While it is true that anxiety over sexual success or failure can result in frigidity in women and impotence in men, this is not necessarily the result. When such negative results do occur, some writers call this development a "low order of sexual adjustment."[10] Headaches, psychosomatic complaints, irritability, and sharpness of tongue are examples of a low order of sexual adjustment. "Sex lies at the root of life," said Havelock Ellis, "and we can never learn to reverence life until we know how to understand sex."[11] The attainment of a pleasing sexual life is the most intimate form of tenderness and loving, but as a rule it comes only to those couples who have found happiness in other areas of their lives.

The temper of many things a married couple does indicates the appreciation and degree of their physical responsiveness. In both husband and wife, sexual adjustment influences glandular and emotional responses. But there are other reasons for glandular and emotional disturbances, including conflicts over money, differences over religious training, and neglect and discourtesies. One reason sexual adjustment is so crucial is the fact that failure in any one of the other areas tends to be reflected in the sexual relationship.[12] However, a couple that has achieved a satisfactory, cooperative framework in non-sexual areas will find a minimum of difficulty in relating sexually; and "sexual pleasure, wisely used, and not abused, may prove the stimulus and liberator of our finest and most exalted activities."[13]

Marriage

A sophisticated view of attaining sexual completeness in marriage is the conservation of sufficient psychic and physical energy in order that there may be a reserve for expenditure in coitus. This, of course, is an oversimplification of a much more broadly based matter. *If* men and women realize the differences in their sexual rhythms and arousal patterns, *if* they are happy in their other marital relationships, *if* they are creative in their lovemaking, *if* they are capable of coping with fears of pregnancy and insecurities, *if* they are in good health and are not perpetually fatigued, *if* their home is orderly and their privacy assured, they may look forward to a happy future of sexual interaction within their marriage bonds.[14]

Problem solving, or the adjustment of conflicts, is one of the most hazardous aspects in a marriage. Adding to this jeopardy is the fact that problem solving in marriage varies greatly from couple to couple. If the basic approach used to solve problems is either exploitative or coercive, no amount of verbal veneer can overcome the psychic scars created by such maneuvering. Running away from problems by leaving the scene or by indulging in alcohol or drugs are common but counterproductive approaches. Another problem-solving technique is to retreat into anger. To be sure, anger has its place—particularly when there is much hostility that needs to be ventilated before rapport can be established—but productive anger is different from the outbursts of anger that are used exploitively to force a spouse to yield because of fear. Aristotle observed: "Anybody can become angry—that is easy; but to be angry with the right person, and to the right degree, and at the right time, and for the right purpose, and in the right way—that is not within everybody's power and is not easy."[15]

Many methods of problem solving in marriage are evasions of open and honest discussions and are means of getting one's own way rather than developing a mutually satisfying method of resolving differences. In most instances, the use of a specific problem as the battleground for dominance precludes interpersonal growth. To ensure long-range interpersonal relation-

A Religious Foundation of Human Relations

ships that will be mutually satisfactory, the dominant-submissive relationship has to be resolved.

Emotional interdependence is a necessary achievement for a married couple. This includes the expectation and reception of sympathetic understanding, emotional support, and encouragement. Furthermore, it is sharing laughter, grief, and puzzlement. Peterson lists four types of relationships that a couple may have in marriage: independent-independent, in which individuals keep their feelings and emotions to themselves; dependent-independent, in which there is a giver and a receiver of feelings and emotions; dependent-dependent, in which both marriage partners want to receive support; and emotionally independent individuals. Emotionally independent people can readily and easily admit their need for support as well as their need to give support to others. When individuals can both give and receive support, Peterson says, they are prepared to grow, to interlock their life with another, and to become emotionally interdependent with another individual.[16] It is apparent that in this type of relationship, marriage is most likely to succeed.

Money is another variable. The amount of money a couple has is not of paramount importance as long as their basic necessities are provided. What is important are the motives which direct the use of that money. Living wisely with money is a skill that most of us lack before marriage. The wise use of money involves the capacity to view it rationally, to live with it intelligently, and not to use it as a psychological tool or escape from other problems. It also involves carefully choosing goals of life that are truly representative of our innermost purposes. Once these goals are defined, their achievement rests upon painstaking planning. In it, a couple must consider three basic areas of spending: life goals, yearly plan, and monthly budget.[17]

In a successful marriage, a family budgets its time with as much care as it budgets its money, so that a maximum number of hours will be available for family activities. The expertise with which money and time are handled can strengthen or weaken individual growth, family growth, and overall marital solidarity and security. The couple that intelligently plans the expenditure of time and money is likely to be a happily married couple.

Now for a look at planning for children. Peterson cautioned that although there is no right time to have a child, there are some pragmatic considerations that facilitate a wise decision. When the arrival of a child is imminent, the couple should have enough financial resources so that the baby will not cause an economic burden; they should have matured in their love through successful early adjustments so that a warm, emotional place will exist for the baby; they should have made progress toward sexual adjustment so that the entire period of pregnancy is not a period of uncertainty concerning their future life together; and they should decide upon the proper spacing of subsequent children to safeguard the health of the mother and child.[18]

After the birth of a baby, it is essential that the mother give loving attention to both the baby and the father. Many marital difficulties begin with pregnancy or the first child because the husband is not prepared to share his wife's physical and emotional affection. The wife should make every effort to include her husband in the care of the child so that he will not feel isolated or abandoned. Peterson cautions that the enlargement of the circle of love should not stretch its bonds in one direction so far that the circle is broken. Most husbands who are partners in conception are prepared to do more in the important period which follows: that of childhood.[19]

Robert O. Blood, Jr., observed that all marriages encounter conflicts at one time or another.[20] Even if one partner always gives in, conflict is there but the dominant partner may be impervious to it. The longer a conflict remains, the greater the tension becomes. Because tensions within a marriage are inevitable, working at resolving them should be a never ending process. John Dewey observed that

conflict is the gadfly of thought. It stirs us to observation and memory. It instigates to invention. It shocks us out of sheeplike passivity, and sets us at noting and contriving. Conflict is a sine qua non of reflection and ingenuity. In a creative marriage, conflict will be used as an opportunity for the growth of both partners.[21]

In addition to those I have mentioned, there are other sources of marital conflicts. For example, immaturity in either partner can precipitate problems or prevent a successful solution of problems. Because an immature person is unable to trust wholly, he tends to be secretive, and secrecy can destroy the sense of mutuality found in honest, trusting marriages. La Rochefoucauld remarked in *Maxims* that "sincerity is an open heart. Few people show it; usually what we see is an imitation put on to snare the confidence of others."[22] A mature person, on the other hand, can admit his mistakes because he has a foundation of security; with a sense of security, he is more flexible in making proposals and accepting counterproposals to resolve conflicts. If only one partner is willing to make concessions, this is usually sufficient to set a climate for resolving most marital conflicts.[23]

When conflicts arise and anger is one of the resulting emotions, the nonangry partner should realize that anger is an indication of how strongly the other person is feeling about the situation. In the words of La Rochefoucauld: "It seems that nature that so wisely ordered our bodies for our happiness, gave us pride too, to spare us the mortification of knowing our shortcomings."[24] In a marriage, feelings are emotional barometers that should be carefully read in order to predict and prepare for coming storms. Silent suffering is rarely productive, particularly in a relationship as intimate as marriage. If grievances are held in, tension will build up and eventually explode outward against the partner or inwardly against the self.

Marriage counselors advise couples to view their problems with the understanding that they often symbolize deeper needs than those that have surfaced. With this caution in mind, the parties can then work out more lasting and creative adjustments. If one partner is supersensitive and cannot bear

Marriage

for her spouse to be angry with her, this may short-circuit the openness needed to allow submerged issues to surface. Those persons contemplating marriage should not only know that consideration, awareness, patience, tenderness, and understanding are all needed to make a successful marriage, but also that slow, careful effort is required to achieve and maintain it.

In some marriages, alcohol creates conflict, especially if the drinking releases all inhibitions against aggressive remarks and behavior. In such cases, drinking increases the likelihood that discussions will disintegrate into quarrels. If couples are aware of this potential, they can avoid controversial topics when drinking occurs. Similarly, if marriage partners become aware that the only time they quarrel is when they are tired, they should avoid controversial topics when fatigued. Blood, like Peterson, views money as a primary cause of conflict in many marriages. How much they have, how it is spent, and who manages it may all have a serious impact on a marriage relationship. Having enough money is only one side of the coin; spending it is the other. Some husbands perceive the wife's spending as a threat to their need to dominate. No exercise of dominance, man over woman or woman over man, is conducive to the development of a healthy marriage.[25]

Many wives are independent and dislike asking their husbands for money. Female role fulfillment rarely resides in being a submissive wife but, rather, in being an appreciated human being. If every dollar the wife spends seems to her husband a surrender of power, serious problems can result.[26] They may become engaged in a battle of wills that only tangentially touches on money. Conversely, the trusting marriage partner proclaims: "I will give you what you want before you have to take it, because I trust you." Trust is putting aside aggression and having confidence that the other marriage partner will not inflict hurt but will enrich. This is especially important in money matters.

Perhaps the most difficult of all problems to cope with in marriage is infidelity. Because sex is a very intimate aspect of marriage, extramarital intercourse is its most profound betrayal. A shaky marriage will be destroyed by it, but a good marriage can survive it. Blood commented that people who have any kind of marital inadequacy are disposed to extramarital involvement. Primarily two types of people fall into this classification: the nonreligious and the emotionally immature.[27] Another authority, Alfred Kinsey, estimated that half of all married men and one-fourth of all married women commit adultery sometime during their married life.[28] How a husband or wife handles this breach of trust will, in large measure, determine whether their marriage survives.

The marriage relationship needs to be free and open for love to flourish and grow. Kahlil Gibran wrote:

Love one another, but make not a bond of love; let it rather be a moving sea between the shores of your souls. Fill each other's cup but drink not from one cup. Give one another of your bread but eat not from the same loaf. Sing and dance together and be joyous, but let each one of you be alone, even as the strings of a lute are alone though they quiver with the same music.[29]

Unless married love is constantly growing and expanding, the capacity for psychological fulfillment and even sexual enjoyment will atrophy. A married couple should early come to the realization that marriage is sometimes painful, difficult, and in need of the constant exercise of self-control. To be sure, marriage partners should be aware that the joys of a marriage are purchased at a high price, but it is a price that enriches and does not impoverish the spenders. Therefore, each partner should be prepared to sooth the other's suffering, remembering that "a pearl is a temple built by pain around a grain of sand."[30]

The role expectations brought to a marriage are likely to be formulated on the basis of sex. The propriety of these male-female roles is determined to a great extent by society. For instance, our society tends to be more comfortable when the man cuts the grass and the woman makes the beds. No two people, however, come into marriage with the same expectations. And male-female role expectations are changing to a more egalitarian view. Within this framework, if the trash needs carrying out, the important thing should be that it is carried out, not who does it.

Carl Rogers commented that individuals whose behavior continually falls short of what they believe it ideally to be are likely to be plagued by self-hate and feelings of inferiority.[31] A man may believe he should be the breadwinner and yet, because of illness, discrimination, or unemployment, be unable to fill this role. If his wife has a job and is the breadwinner, he will be forced into a role reversal, and this experience can be demoralizing to him and detrimental to his marriage. In some marriages, couples compete for the same role; they disagree on which one will make certain decisions. In an egalitarian or balanced marriage, there is little competition in decision making. I would hasten to add that there are few egalitarian marriages.

In most subcultures it is socially accepted that two of the primary female roles in marriage are wife and mother; likewise, the corresponding male roles are husband and father. The father role and mother role are concerned mainly with providing love and discipline to their children. To do this effectively, some parents delegate discipline as the father's responsibility and love the mother's. In a balanced marriage, however, mothers and fathers share the responsibility for providing love and discipline. There is no valid reason to attribute feminine behavior to a woman in her wife and mother roles and masculine behavior to a man in his husband and father roles. What seems to be more important in terms of effective parenthood is that there be teamwork in caring for and rearing children. Besides, a wife will find marriage less burdensome if her husband shares the housework and shows an interest in her as an individual apart from her wife and mother roles.

A man's occupation role has a significant effect on his marriage, and it may be either positive or negative. Even if the wife is employed, it is the husband's occupation that most often is considered the main source of family income. When this condition obtains, the husband's occupation provides not only income but also social status. If he is classified as a professional employee, the husband is likely to be respected in the community, even if he holds a low-paying professional job. For instance, a clergyman will have considerably more social standing (as well as considerably less income) than a skilled tradesman. It is sad that in many instances people hurry to improve their social status at the expense of love. This is a factor that often receives too little consideration in evaluating the marital relationship.

An important responsibility for both partners in marriage is the role of listener. If one partner is troubled, the other needs to understand, and this requires listening. Along with listening, empathy and care should be extended; these can go a long way in easing a partner's troubles. Goethe once said: "Whatever you cannot understand, you cannot possess."[32] Summarizing one of his surveys, Blood concluded that wives who communicate their troubles to their husbands are more satisfied in their marriages than wives who do not and that both sexes are more satisfied with marriages in which the channels of communication are open. It is important to remember that communication is not always verbal. Gibran wisely stated: "The reality of the other person is not in what he reveals to you, but in what he cannot reveal to you. Therefore, if you would understand him, listen not to what he says but rather to what he does not say."[33]

Love which grows into lasting marriage needs both attachment and release. Attachment is in the form of closeness, companionship, and caring for each other; release is in the form of trusting, respecting, and being interdependent but free of each other in some instances. If one partner cannot let go and wants to control the other, love will be strangled. If the husband and wife have respect for each other as separate beings, love becomes a releasing force.

When love is young, married couples make new discoveries about each other, themselves, and their relationship. As they age, often new discoveries cease. It is at this point that partners begin to take each other for granted; the average marriage begins a downhill descent. The longer such matter-of-factness persists, the greater the decline. Marriage is never perfect, never fulfilled, and never incapable of more growth. Unfortunately, in many marriages couples become weary of trying to discover each other, and as they grow older, they lose their enthusiasm and energy. In other instances, the marriage is old before it gets started.

Not all marriages turn sour, but most become colder. Studies have indicated that as couples age, disenchantment with marriage increases. In reviewing research findings, Blood concluded that old married couples evaluate their marriages less favorably than do younger ones.[34] As marriage progresses, disengagement tends to be the rule rather than the exception. Couples begin to pay less attention to each other; they frequently become bored with each other. If we examined marriages that have succeeded, it is clear that married love need never stop growing, but the married couple must work to see that it does not.

With rare insight, Paul Claudel commented: "Love is not two people looking at each other, but two people looking together in the same direction." This is especially true of a creative marriage.

OPEN MARRIAGE

George and Nena O'Neill's book entitled *Open Marriage* is highly critical of the closed-marriage concept, which they label a cultural ideal subtly inculcated by training from childhood. They charge that the clauses of a closed-marriage contract dictate that husband and wife must always appear together as a couple, must share the same friends and forsake those persons their marriage partner cannot tolerate, must always share vacations and most hobbies, must always be available for each other's whims and loneliness, must both put their funds into a conjugal financial pot, and must never feel attraction toward anyone else of the opposite sex.[35]

For these reasons, the O'Neills assert that the traditional closed marriage is a form of bondage for both husband and wife. Specifically, they cite the negative aspects of closed marriage to be possession or ownership of the mate, denial of self, maintenance of the couple front, and rigid role behavior. The O'Neills further claim that although one originally marries for love, warmth, and companionship, the clauses of the closed contract gradually stifle one's freedom and individuality, making both partners slaves of the marriage. To counter this form of slavery, they suggest open marriage: the couple share their love with others and experiment with various patterns of love and lovemaking.

In their counsel to the young on sex, the churches' appeal to Biblical texts and simple punitive prohibition has been less overt and more discreet than in earlier eras. Sociological and, above all, psychological arguments count for much more. . . . The gist of the socio-psychological advice is that sex is too dangerous for the young. It may call down community censure or set up dire psychic reverberations. The significant point in this counsel—whether purely religious or prudentially socio-psychological—is that it does not cultivate maturity. Consequently, the counsel is caught by its own logic: Getting married does not necessarily extract from sex all the danger threatening the immature. The one decisive gain in marriage would be the freedom from community censure.[36]

Marriage is a covenant, the very fabric of which consists not in forced cohabitation and counterfeit performance of duties, but in unfeigned love and peace.[37] This type of marriage is neither open nor closed. Love and marriage cannot exist or grow unless there is reciprocity; and where love cannot be, there can be nothing in wedlock but the empty husk of an external matrimony. Both open and closed marriages without

Marriage

love are as undelightful and unpleasing to God as any other kind of hypocrisy. Solomon advised men that they should live joyfully with the wife whom they love. How, then, if we find it impossible to love, can we obey this exhortation in an open or a closed marriage?

DIVORCE

In the seventh chapter of I Corinthians, Paul, speaking of marriage and divorce, says plainly that God has called us to peace and not to bondage. God commanded in his law more than once through his prophet Malachi that he who hates, let him divorce. Malachi also cautions against the misuse of the legal privilege of divorce. In Matthew 5:32, Jesus sanctions divorce only for adultery, but in Matthew 19:3-8 he makes no exception. Jesus' two different attitudes on divorce have become the basis for different church positions on it; the less strict churches regard it as a fundamental human and spiritual need. Concerning biblical passages pertaining to divorce, Hans Martensen wrote:

The important question now arises whether there may be also other cases, besides those expressly named in Scripture; in other words, whether these sayings of our Lord and his apostles are to be regarded as literally laws, as ecclesiastical appointments delivered as such to the church, or whether, on the contrary, we have found in them a principle to be applied by the church in such cases as should occur? The latter is our view of the passages quoted, and according to our conviction the only evangelical one.[38]

This view permits divorce for reasons other than those specifically mentioned in Scripture—if divorce will protect the religious and ethical standards of the family. Perhaps nothing separates the various religious denominations more than their norms pertaining to sex, marriage, and divorce.

A Religious Foundation of Human Relations

To grind in the mill of an undelighted and servile copulation, must be the only forced work of a Christian marriage, ofttimes with such a yokefellow from whom both love and peace, both nature and religion mourns to be separated. Man ought even for love's sake and peace to move divorce upon the good and liberal conditions to the divorced. And it is a lesser breach of wedlock to part with wise and quiet consent, promptly, then still to toil and profane that mastery of joy and union with a polluting sadness and perpetual distemper: for it is not the outward continuing of marriage that keeps whole the covenant, but whatsoever does most according to peace and love, whether in marriage or in divorce, he it is that breaks marriage least; it being so written, "Love is the fulfilling of every commandment."[39]

Some marriages—more than 25 per cent in America—simply do not work, no matter how hard those involved try to preserve them. When a marriage fails, it takes courage to face the enormous changes that are bound to occur. Divorce is one trauma that can shatter a person's identity; a part of a married person's identity lies in his or her role as husband or wife. Each marriage partner is accustomed to viewing himself or herself as half of a couple. Thus contemplating the change back to independence can be frightening indeed.

The remarriage of persons who have been divorced also is a marital problem. Having got unmarried, most divorcees are soon ready to marry again. The loneliness of life without a mate can be even more difficult once the comforts and emotional security of marriage have been experienced, however fleetingly. Many divorced people prefer having a spouse to being single and are, quite simply, unhappy when living alone.[40]

In contrast to colonial times, when widowhood accounted for nearly all remarriages, in the last few generations a new element has been injected into the American marital pattern, namely, the gradually swelling tide of remarrying divorcees. About two-thirds of women and three-fourths of men choose

Marriage

to remarry sometime during the postdivorce period. This means divorcees are more vulnerable to marriage than single or widowed people. Furthermore, divorcees have a tendency to remarry quickly after a divorce has been granted. The modal periods of remarrying are the second and third years; half of those who remarry do so within five years. Interestingly, divorced persons are inclined to select mates who also have been divorced.

Most persons are not merely interested in achieving a state of marriage, they are very eager to be successfully married. Therefore, in most instances, divorce is an unintentional and unpremeditated outcome. The predictions of marital adjustment among remarried people are contradictory. Some researchers have demonstrated rather conclusively that the chances for remarriages ending in divorce are greater than for first marriages; others report that most persons in their samples had second marriages which were satisfactory. Remarriage itself acts as a highly selective force.[41]

In the final analysis, it seems that a divorce by either party weakens the strength of the marriage bond and a second divorce experience lessens greatly the chance of survival for a third marriage. It has been suggested that twice-divorced persons, sometimes referred to as the neurotics, have only about a 20 per cent chance for a lasting marriage. Certain factors seem to be highly correlated with success in remarriage, including social class, adaptability, and resiliency. In general, middle-class persons are more successful in marriage than those of the lower class. The will to succeed is especially important in the second marriage. Persons possessing such a drive and those who have the maturity and adaptability are most inclined to be successful the second time around.

Several factors explain the higher failure rate in marriage after divorce, including these: since divorced persons tend to marry other divorced persons, these marriages may have traits that make it difficult for them to succeed; there is less hesitation to resort to divorce a second time (generally, moral com-

A Religious Foundation of Human Relations

punctions against divorce are overcome at the time of the first divorce); most divorces are means of escaping, rather than working through and resolving, interpersonal problems; marriage after divorce may be the result of so-called rebound or of other conditions unfavorable to making a wise choice.[42]

There are cumulative problems to confront remarried couples. Specifically, previous marriages and divorces result in an assortment of in-law and personal-friend problems. This is the case even when the remarried honestly believe that "all that is past." Researchers who have studied divorce point out that in many instances the second marriage has too many people in it: it does not consist solely of the married couple, but also includes their children, former spouses, and in-laws.[43] In short, divorced persons who remarry are living not only with the second spouse, but to some degree with the residual remains of the first marriage. This may either help or hinder the second marriage, but there is little doubt that the specter cast by antecedent mates poses a problem for most remarried people. To brush aside all thoughts of a former marriage and to tell oneself that the past does not matter is to invite failure. A previous marriage is a fact of life to be lived with and, it is hoped, one from which some vestige of profitable experience has been derived.

If a married mate has financial responsibilities for children of a previous marriage, another kind of marital adjustment is necessary. Financial pressure may be extremely severe if the husband or wife must pay alimony or child support. Few persons earn sufficient money to support two families adequately. Thus frequently it becomes necessary for the other spouse to work in order to help defray family expenses. This kind of financial pressure can and often does impair or destroy second marriages.

Accepting children of a spouse's previous marriage is a factor in marital adjustment. Some people find it very difficult to accept situations that arise when their spouse has visitation rights with children of a former marriage. To know that the spouse is seeing his or her former mate when visiting the

Marriage

children may arouse feelings of jealousy, uneasiness, and outright hostility.

ADDITIONAL BIBLICAL INSIGHT

Viewing marriage from a biblical perspective reveals that many roots and modifications of contemporary thought are seated in theological convictions. Peterson says a couple must be able mutually to resolve the problem of marriage, but most writings in the Bible are emphatic that the husband should be the dominant partner. Ephesians 5:23 states: "For a husband is the head of the wife, even as Christ is the head of the church." Ephesians 5:24 cautions: "Therefore as the church is subject unto Christ, so let the wives be to their own husbands in everything." I Corinthians 7:3 does, however, recognize that the wife is not subservient to her husband in the same manner as a servant: "Let the husband render unto the wife due benevolence." This recognition is reflected in Peterson's idea that understanding, emotional support, and encouragement are basic requirements of a successful marriage.

Passages in the Bible frequently reiterate the husband's and wife's responsibilities to each other. For example, Ephesians 5:33 says: "Nevertheless let everyone of you in particular so love his wife even as himself; and the wife see that she reverence her husband." In Peter the Bible warns that a husband should be careful of his wife and be thoughtful of her needs and treat her as the weaker sex; if she is not treated well, his prayers will not be answered. Peterson stresses the importance of sexual adjustment in a successful marriage relationship. I Corinthians 7:4 points out the importance of the physical relationship: "The wife hath not power of her own body, but the husband; and likewise also the husband hath not power of his own body, but the wife."

Blood remarks that infidelity may be the single most difficult problem to cope with in marriage. The Bible also contains extensive commentary on this subject. I Corinthians states that people who live immoral lives and are adulterers

A Religious Foundation of Human Relations

will not share God's kingdom. Several biblical passages emphasize that sexual sin is never right; marriages are not made for that, but for God, and he wants to fill our bodies. In the words of I Corinthians 6:18: "Flee fornication. Every sin that a man doeth is without the body; but he that committeth fornication sins against his own body." Matthew specifically states that man shall not commit adultery. Supporting this, other Scripture tells the married to honor their marriage and to be pure because God will punish those who are immoral or commit adultery. Leviticus 20:10 expands this dictum: "And the man that commits adultery with another man's wife, even he that commits adultery with his neighbor's wife, the adulterer and the adulteress shall surely be put to death." Later, this injunction was lifted (Ecclesiasticus 23:26) and adultery was deemed punishable by public disgrace.

Conservative Christians stand in conflict with Blood's belief that it is possible to preserve a marriage in spite of infidelity. Conservatives quote several biblical passages that treat adultery as a grievous sin. However, Blood is in accord with conservative Christians when he says there should be reciprocation in marriage. For example, I Corinthians admonishes the husband to give his wife all that is her right as a married woman. Colossians 3:18–19 further reflects this idea: "Wives, submit yourselves unto your own husbands, as it is fit in the Lord. Husbands, love your wives, and be not bitter against them."

On the subject of divorce, I Corinthians 7:10–11 admonishes that the Lord says a wife must not leave her husband, but if she is separated from him, she must remain single or else go back to him. And the husband must not divorce his wife. Paul dealt with a subject Jesus did not discuss: marriages between Christians and non-Christians. Paul counsels that if a Christian man has a wife who is not a Christian but she wants to stay with him, he must not leave or divorce her. And if a Christian woman has a husband who is not a Christian but she wants to stay with him, he must not leave or divorce her. The reasoning is clear: the spouse who is not

Marriage

a Christian may become one with the help of his or her Christian partner. Otherwise, if the family separates, the children might never come to know the Lord, whereas a united family may, in God's plan, result in the children's salvation. However, I Corinthians 7:15 advises, "if the unbelieving depart, let him depart." This passage could be interpreted to mean that divorce is acceptable if the marriage is no longer blessed by God.

Paul's opinion (I Corinthians 7:16), which he said was not the Lord's command, was that mixed marriages should be maintained but that in the case of disagreement, separation should be initiated by the Christian partner. Thus evolved the rationale for the Roman Catholic regulation known as the Pauline privilege, which under certain conditions permits the marriage of a Catholic to a person divorced before baptism.

The concept of open marriage finds little acceptance within the context of the Bible. Critics of open marriage caution that sexual attractiveness may extend beyond the mate. However, open-marriage proponents note that this relationship does not necessarily imply that any physical interaction will occur. Matthew 5:28 takes a very narrow view in this matter: "But I say unto you, that whosoever looketh on a woman to lust after her has committed adultery with her in his heart." Even the most liberally translated interpretation of this passage cannot escape the clarity of its intent. The open marriage, as seen by the O'Neills, would unstructure marriage roles more than the most liberal biblical interpretation would allow.

Despite the differing views of theorists and sources that I have cited, marriage remains the holiest of human relationships, and it is also one of the most enduring institutions in our civilization. Thus how people relate to each other in marriage is as crucial as what they relate to each other.

5
EDUCATION

FOR past generations, one of the major roles of schools has been to instill in the young society's traditional goals, values, and practices. It should come as no surprise, then, to learn that in this endeavor societal goals have shaped the educational means. Quite naturally, the inculcation of traditional goals has rested on traditional methods of education. Yet, because of our rapidly changing environment, it is clear that traditional goals, as well as obsolescent teaching methods, cannot adequately prepare future generations for a world which, in the words of the Greek philosopher Heraclitus, will be entirely in a state of flux. To become an integral member of society in the future, the individual will be required to learn how to make decisions rapidly while functioning as an integrated human being.

J. Christiaan Becker says today's students are confused:

There are types of confusion. Ours is no longer a nihilistic confusion of a Sartre-type, personal despair in the face of death: ours is a confusion of too much rather than too little. There are many possibilities — too many. Indeed, we rejoice in a new sense of freedom — freedom from all the heteronomies which

Education

bound us in the past and to the past and which still chain our fathers in our opinion—and we are determined to establish ourselves as men of sober integrity—men with a sense of autonomy—men who truly belong to a mankind come of age. All this is possible—but our too many possibilities of explicating reality turn in on us, and they erode commitment. Possibility may be our new idol and a life of noncommitment our new "possibility." For Hegel the real was the rational, for us the real is the relative. The possibility-syndrome produces our identity-crisis, so that it becomes increasingly rare to meet students with a mature sense of vocation and commitment.[1]

The watchword of education in future years must be not *tradition* but *liberation*. Perhaps this point can be made through an analysis of the works of four theorists who have changed traditional modes of education in this century: John Dewey, Abraham H. Maslow, James S. Coleman, and Warren G. Bennis. Concurrently, I will compare the work of these men to Scripture in order to show how, in their attempt to liberate the minds and spirits of twentieth-century students, these theorists have followed or strayed from our Judaeo-Christian heritage.

PROGRESSIVE EDUCATION

In his greatest work, *The Republic*, Plato spoke of the "true education of the inner being"[2] and cautioned that knowledge which is acquired under compulsion obtains no hold on the mind.[3] Education must be at once both a profound and a freeing experience or else it is nothing. Nearly twenty-five hundred years later, John Dewey, another philosopher, took up Plato's prescription and expanded it to construct a pedagogical system relevant to the needs of young minds in a vastly complex industrial environment.

Dewey was far ahead of his time in the task of trying to instill in children the mental and moral commitments needed in an enlarged and intricate world. As the father of progressive education, he revolutionized learning methods in this country and other parts of the world. Although he lived to see and to deplore some of the excesses of his theories as perpetrated by misguided disciples, he never changed his mind regarding the need to focus on diverse, child-centered curricula. As Dewey put it: "The teacher who does not permit and encourage diversity of operation in dealing with questions is imposing intellectual blinders upon pupils—restricting their vision to the one path the teacher's mind happens to approve."[4]

Although education claims Dewey as its own, he was also a profound thinker in the fields of psychology and philosophy, having taught the latter subject at Minnesota, Michigan, Chicago, and Columbia universities. At the University of Chicago, he became director of the School of Education and gained national fame. Dewey's philosophy of education reflected the Industrial Revolution and the development of democracy, and from the combination of these two influences evolved his principle of learning by doing. Repelled by the classical approach to education, which he characterized as talking about things rather than showing how to do them, Dewey warned repeatedly against authoritarianism in the classroom, which he felt could only stifle the imagination of the child.[5]

Dewey rejected the idea that children could be studied apart from society. Rather, he viewed children as individuals who grow and think in a vast complex of interactions and relationships, not in a solitary interaction cut off from others. Armed with this premise, he posited faith in education as the soundest instrument of social, political, and moral change:

The child is to be not only a voter and a subject of law; he is also to be a member of a family, himself responsible, in all probability, in turn, for rearing and training of future children, and thus maintaining the continuity of society. He is to be a worker, engaged in some occupation which will be of use to society, and which will maintain his own independence and self-respect. He is to be a member of some particular neighborhood and community, and must contribute to the values of

Education

life, add to the decencies and graces of civilization wherever he is.[6]

Ancillary to Dewey's faith in education was his firm belief in democracy. He held it not only because democracy gave every citizen a vote, a voice, and an influence, but also because it assured opportunity to all. And he saw democracy as a necessary prerequisite to good education, industry, and even foreign relations: "A society of free individuals in which all, through their own work, contribute to the liberation and enrichment of the lives of others, is the only environment in which any individual can really grow normally to his full stature. An environment in which some are practically enslaved, degraded, limited, will always react to create conditions that prevent the full development even of those who fancy they enjoy complete freedom for unhindered growth."[7] We would not be far amiss in calling Dewey a staunch proponent of equal-opportunity employment in education.

Likewise, we might well hail John Dewey as the grandfather of human-relations methods, for democratic education forms the foundation of human-relations training. According to Dewey, voluntary association should replace autocracy in industrial relations, and conference and law should replace war in foreign affairs. In advocating such revolutionary approaches, Dewey was not a pessimist; he saw man as an organism in an environment, remaking the environment as well as being made by it. The starting point of Dewey's system of thought was always biological. He described his educational system as follows:

First, that the pupil have a genuine situation of experience— that there be a continuous activity in which he is interested for its own sake;
Secondly, that a genuine problem develop within this situation as a stimulus to thought;
Third, that he possess the information and make the observations needed to deal with it;
Fourth, that suggested solutions occur to him which he shall be responsible for developing in an orderly way;

Fifth, that he have opportunity and occasion to test his ideas by application to make their meaning clear and to discover for himself their validity.[8]

For Dewey, education should be aimed not only at understanding the world but also at changing and refashioning it. How closely he parallels later writers in the field of human relations! If we consider ourselves as falling short of our potentialities in the practice of human relations, here, at least, is one inspiring man who tried to move us ahead in the evolutionary process of becoming truly humane.

How does Dewey's philosophy compare to that of Scripture? Can there be found in the Bible any evidence that would substantiate, fortify, or disprove his beliefs? At the outset, we can find many biblical references to knowledge, teaching, and truth, including these:

Who is a wise man and endued with knowledge among you? Let him show out of a good conversation his works with meekness of wisdom. — James 3:13

Understand, ye brutish among the people: and ye fools, when will ye be wise? He that planted the ear, shall he not hear? He that formed the eye, shall he not see? He that teacheth man knowledge, shall he not know? — Psalms 94:8-10

Wise men lay up knowledge. — Proverbs 10:14

And thou shall teach them diligently unto thy children. — Deuteronomy 6:7

Go ye therefore and teach all nations. — Matthew 28:19

And ye shall know the truth and the truth shall make you free. — John 8:32

But speaking the truth in love, may grow up into him in all things. — Ephesians 4:15

Although John Dewey would have been quite reluctant to claim Judaeo-Christian foundations for his philosophy of

Education

education, he was very much concerned with those things of which Scripture speak about. Still, the main parallel which becomes apparent is not that between Dewey and certain Old Testament prophets, but that between Jesus and Dewey.

Jesus was a true revolutionary in his day; Dewey's theories also opened him to criticism from those who thought of him as a dangerous radical. Jesus was concerned with every individual, regardless of his or her origin or station in life; Dewey stressed the preciousness of each and every human being. Jesus helped people became more than they ever thought they could become; Dewey never tired of pointing out that all children have the capacity for intellectual growth. Jesus and Dewey fought authoritarianism, ignorance, prejudice, and bigotry.

Like Jesus, Dewey brought a new vision into the world. He looked at the life of modern people and at the archaic educational processes which enslaved them, and he revealed to all that they need no longer be burdened with inhumane values. Committed to the undying worth of all people, Dewey saw, and made countless others see, the undeveloped potential of the human organism and the limitless possibilities for growth — intellectual, moral, social, and political. Like Jesus, Dewey went beyond the surface of pessimism to declare that man was both worthy and capable of achieving a new ethic. Jesus stood for the spiritual perfection of man; Dewey fought for man's ability to grow intellectually and morally. Both men were completely caring individuals, and both effected an inestimable change in human affairs.

Dewey was not sympathetic to traditional religion. He believed that too often in the past religion had inhibited free inquiry, thus forcing religious philosophy into a mold that became dogmatic and obscure. Further, throughout his life he clung tenaciously to the view that metaphysics can in no way further man's goal of intellectually controlling nature.[9] To counteract this condition, Dewey advocated the understanding of truth and reality as an evolving by-product of cooperative human endeavor rather than an established closed doctrine of divine revelation.

A Religious Foundation of Human Relations

For Dewey, *religion* was one thing and *religious* was something quite different. The former he understood as a particular collection of tenets setting an organization apart because of its belief and procedures. The latter had a much broader meaning. "The religious," he said, "is 'morality touched by emotion' only when the ends of moral conviction arouse emotions that are not only intense but are actuated and supported by ends so inclusive that they unify the self."[10] An experience of this sort will have religious value in proportion to the effect it produces from the practical standpoint of adjustment to existing conditions; it is the modification of conditions to bring about the fruition of purposes and necessities. This adaptive process in human experience is given impetus by the combination of various factors, and Dewey believed it is not a religion but a religious element that brings it about.

He took sharp issue with the claim of religious persons who said they offered the only avenue through which religious values may be experienced. Furthermore, he opposed religions that contended they had a monopoly on ideals and the supernatural means by which ideals could be acquired. Dewey felt that such a view of religion impeded the realization of growth-producing religious values immanent in natural experiences. Contrary to common opinion, Dewey believed that religion could be, and should be, subject to scientific investigation. For him, even the personal elements of mystic experience required intellectual substantiation. The true existence of a mystical experience was not questioned by Dewey. He maintained that faith is an inadequate substitute for reason.

God, Dewey said, is a word that denotes "the unity of all ideal ends arousing us to desire and actions."[11] He criticized Christianity for leaving too much to grace. For Dewey, the ideal should not be identified with any particular Being, especially if the Being resides outside nature. Natural conditions, he suggested, agitate and promote expression, and ideals are not dependent for validity on any antecedent external Utopia. Thus the good life is attainable through human effort and desire expressed in art, knowledge, education, friendship, and love. As free agents with selective choices, we have the intelligence

Education

to evaluate conditions and predict consequences within ourselves and our environment. While Christians feel that there is something that transcends life, Dewey and his disciples found the same heartening inspiration in life itself.

Those who see Jesus as the Son of God might consider it in bad taste to compare him with Dewey. But no disrespect is intended in my likening of these two great teachers. Neither do I desire to disturb Dewey's rest by giving a distorted picture of him as a conventionally religious man when he was not. It can be cogently maintained that the greatest legacy of Jesus was the power of love, which he shared with others, and the life of love, in which he was an overpowering example to those who knew him. In his own way, John Dewey also lived a life of love, dedicated to all human beings and their betterment. As Adlai Stevenson remarked of Mrs. Eleanor Roosevelt, we might also say of John Dewey that he preferred to light a candle than to curse the darkness.

It is enlightening to compare the teaching methods of Jesus and John Dewey. Neither man merely lectured; both demonstrated. They employed an eclectic approach, and their students learned by doing. Jesus and his disciples were a cohesive group whose effectiveness lay in a coordinated effort within a communal life, a life which was to edify and inspire hundreds of millions through the ages. In his laboratory school at the University of Chicago, Dewey organized his students into a close and concerned group who worked in concert, with the result that the lives of millions of children and adults were changed.

Jesus' teaching is concrete, rather than abstract. It is filled with examples and images taken from nature and from everyday life. He uses rain clouds before a storm, the lilies of the field, or the soil of the earth to illustrate his meaning; likewise the grain and the weeds, a lost sheep or lost coin, the bridegroom and the bride, lambs and wolves, bread and stones, and many other figures. The gospels abound with his pictures of the countryside and its dangers, of little details of home life, and of the motives that fill men's hearts, their lusts, fears, joys,

A Religious Foundation of Human Relations

and sorrows. Unlike modern teachers for whom "the beginning of wisdom is the inspection of terms or the definition of words." Jesus tells a story, either taken from everyday life or based upon it, and he carries his listener to the very heart of his message.[12]

The teachings of both Jesus and Dewey were at once simple and revolutionary: simple because they sprang from the heart, revolutionary because they necessitated a completely new moral outlook. Jesus taught "love thy neighbor as thyself" in an age when "an eye for an eye and a tooth for a tooth" was the guiding principle of conduct. Likewise, Dewey's educational watchword was "let's do this together" when the authoritarian commandment "do as I say" dominated most of the classrooms.

The hardships and martyrdoms of the early Christians were certainly not unknown to Dewey and his followers. For nearly twenty years after the 1916 publication of his masterful exposition of the philosophy of progressive education, *Democracy and Education*, school personnel throughout the nation were told by many well-meaning but ignorant citizens that they had better not adopt Dewey's teachings for, as it was alleged with absolutely no proof, he and all his associates were disguised Bolsheviks. The opponents of progressive education missed no opportunity to lay the blame for every sin of modern man at the doorstep of progressive theories of learning. Nevertheless, Dewey and his followers persevered in expounding their new theories. And when given a fair hearing, they succeeded in winning converts. The final proof of the relevancy of Dewey's ideas is seen in the fact that no other educational principles have given rise to so many constructive innovations in curricula and teaching methods.

Since the days when Jesus of Nazareth walked the earth, his followers have attempted repeatedly to set down on paper their interpretations of what the Gospels imply for humane, compassionate living. We cannot but wonder even today at the enormous vitality of the Good Shepherd's messages, which

Education

have so far transcended the cultural barriers of the age in which they were inspired. Both Jesus and John Dewey were far ahead of their time simply because they taught the most fundamental and eternal lessons of the heart: love, brotherhood, knowledge.

To some writers, it seems apparent that in the twenty-first century we will make decisions in a consensual manner. In a world as complex as the one we inhabit, these writers argue, obedience no longer can mean following a leader blindly. If obedience is to mean anything in the years ahead, it must be defined in terms of responsible, cooperative relationships with peers and superiors. Both the religious message of Jesus and the educational philosophy of John Dewey demand of each of us that we engage in a humane and meaningful dialogue with others. The one thing neither man enjoins upon us is that we dispense with reason and accept ignorance in the form of dogma.

John Dewey was not the first man to disagree with organized, traditional religion. Jesus engaged in a struggle with those who had substituted human pronouncements for God's law. Today we find that in each denomination there are two churches: the official church of ecclesiastical, dogmatic leadership, and various subgroups of lower clergy and concerned laity. Many problems for organized religion and public education grow out of entrenched, centralized, dogmatic authority.[13]

Centralized, authoritarian decision making has proved costly to most other institutions as well as religion and education. As Andrew Greeley said:

The team of astronauts, the pro football champions, the missile launching experts, the computer programmers, the combat squad are all collegial, because if they are not, they are going to fail and they know it. The risks are too great, the costs too high, the potential payoff too important for there to be any room for prima donnas in these activities — neither the prima donna who wants to give all the orders nor the prima donna who wants to do passively what others tell him to do. Similarly, on that wandering pilgrimage of ours, since we cannot go it

A Religious Foundation of Human Relations

alone, we must go with others in the most intelligent and cooperative fashion possible.[14]

John Dewey's theories are not antithetical with the spirit of the New Testament for the very reason that he remained throughout his life a constant foe of dogma and obscurantism. Those persons who would force authoritarianism on students and rob them of their divine freedom have distorted the basic Judaeo-Christian teachings to which we are all heirs. Those persons who would deprive students of their liberty of thought make religion seem irrelevant. Yet in an age of extreme authoritarianism and academic rigidity, young people are continuing to search for the spiritual significance of life. Instead of denying God, many of them are rebelling against a society that has left him out. In spite of those persons who would demean both man and religion, the spiritual aspect of life is too fundamental to be denied a central role in helping us come to grips with present social realities. The spiritual content of Jesus' and Dewey's teachings are virtually identical, and as men they would have understood and appreciated each other in full measure. Each would have felt equally at home with John Ruskin's pronouncement in *Stones of Venice*:

Education does not mean teaching people what they do not know. It means teaching them to behave as they do not behave. It is not teaching the youth the shapes of letters and tricks of numbers, and leaving them to turn their arithmetic to roguery and their literature to lust. It means, on the contrary, training them into the perfect exercise and kingly continence of their bodies and souls. It is a painful, continual and difficult work to be done by kindness, by watching, by warning, by precept, and by praise, but above all—by example.[15]

BEYOND BASIC NEEDS

We seek answers to the meaning of life by means of acquiring wealth, power, pleasure, popularity and any number of other things. All of these things, so long as they are external, leave us at the mercy of circumstances and in the power of others. If the basis for the worth of a man's existence does not lie within him, then the significance of his life can be destroyed by forces beyond his control. . . . Far too often we strive to meet the problem by having *something significant instead of by* becoming or being *something significant.*[16]

All human beings, Abraham H. Maslow maintained, strive to satisfy five basic needs: physiological, safety, belongingness and love, esteem, and self-actualization.[17] The location of the student on the physiological self-actualization continuum determines how and to what extent he or she is motivated to satisfy the other needs. Physiological needs, Maslow said, are the first to be satisfied by every person and the need for self-actualization is the last to be fulfilled. According to this theory, the basic physiological needs to not contradict the need for self-actualization but, rather, complement it.

Maslow explained the relationship between needs by relating them to the growth of a child. A small child needs food and shelter as well as safety and love, but as she grows older her attention turns from these necessities to the needs of her inner being, such as self-esteem, and to the pondering of such things as fate, destiny, potential, and fulfillment of a life's mission. As the child grows into adulthood, Maslow maintained, the self-actualizing aspect of the personality develops. Just as the trees need sun, water, and food from the environment, so, too, do all people need adequate physiological comforts and safety in their environment. However, these various ingredients are just the beginnings for self-development. Once the basic needs have been satisfied, each person then seeks a greater amount of psychological and social growth. Thus when the basic needs are satisfied, the development of each individual is then primarily determined from within rather than from without.

Maslow believed that satisfied needs are not motivators, but he did recognize the problem of recurring need satisfaction.

Specifically, the satisfaction of a need for food is a motivator only when one is hungry, but in most societies people tend to plan ahead for need satisfaction. Because of this, a student's action may not be directly related to the classroom situation requiring immediate attention but, rather, be directed in some manner to satisfy a nonschool need.

What roots can we find in our Judaeo-Christian heritage that might confirm Maslow's theories? To answer this question, I will have to describe more fully each of the five human needs which make up part of Maslow's hierarchy of needs.

Physiological Needs. Maslow defined a physiological need as one that is felt by a human being who has nothing, who is lacking everything except life. Further, he maintained that in a normal, healthy person such a need would overshadow all other needs, including the need for safety. For example, a student who is lacking food, safety, love, and esteem would in all probability desire food most. This is to say, when all of a student's needs are unsatisfied, his actions are controlled by his physiological needs. All other needs are forgotten for that instant; they become nonexistent or are pushed back into a remote corner of the mind until the need for food is alleviated. According to Maslow, the whole organism can be characterized as hungry, for its entire consciousness is almost completely dominated by the desire to satisfy its hunger. All capacities are concentrated on the effort to satisfy the urge for food, even to the point of making the individual dangerous to others if this very basic need is thwarted. For this reason school breakfast and lunch programs for low income students are important.

Genesis 42 and 43 give an account of the famine in Egypt and Israel. Jacob sent ten of his sons from Israel to Egypt to buy corn, but he was fearful for the safety of his youngest son and did not allow him to go. When the ten returned and remarked that if more food was to be purchased they would have to take their youngest brother with them, Jacob said no. However, as food became more scarce, Jacob reconsidered and let his youngest son go: food had become the uppermost thought in his mind.

Education

Jesus also realized the need for food and often showed his awareness that it is a basic need. In Matthew 14, as he spoke to the multitudes, his disciples came and told him that many people were leaving because they had to go and find food. He then performed one of the greatest of his many miracles: he blessed the bread and fish and fed the people, thereby satisfying their basic need for food. Nor should we forget that the Lord's Prayer opens with the petition *Give us this day our daily bread.*

Many other passages in the New Testament speak of the importance of food. James 2:15–16 states: "If a brother or sister be naked and destitute of daily food and one of you say unto them, 'Depart in peace, be ye warmed and filled,' notwithstanding ye give them not those things which are needful to the body, what doth it profit?" In I Timothy 6:7–8 we find: "For we brought nothing into this world and it is certain we can carry nothing out, and having food and raiment let us therefore be content." The basic need for food is recognized in Matthew 6:31: "Therefore take no thought, saying what shall we eat, or what shall we drink or wherewithal shall we be clothed . . . for your Heavenly Father knoweth that you have need of all these things. . . . But seek ye first the Kingdom of God and his righteousness and all these things shall be added unto you."

It might be pointed out here that although Maslow considered food man's basic need, Scripture often speaks of it as if it were a gift which will be added to the individual who has faith and righteousness. Thus while the Bible does not deny that food is a basic need, it does seem to imply that an individual cannot be certain of need satisfaction unless he has attempted to satisfy his spiritual hunger. It is evident that the most important things for Jesus and his disciples were eschatological and that Maslow's major focus was on people in their earthly state.

Safety Needs. Maslow believed that once basic physiological needs have been filled, our actions then are controlled by the need for safety and we will marshal all our available resources to act as a safety-seeking mechanism. According to Maslow, everything would seem less important to the organism than safety and protection, and he further suggested that even the physiological need might take second place if it had recently been satisfied. Consequently, physically safe schools are important, too.

The Bible contains several passages, in both the Old and New Testaments, indicating that fear and its concomitant reaction, the seeking of safety, are very important needs to the individual. We find in Job 21:9: "Their houses are safe from fear." Other passages refer to houses prepared against the day of battle and seeking safety in the Lord. Fear is a common emotion and safety is something to strive for constantly. We are told often in the Old Testament that cities had walls for protection and men bore arms when going into battle to keep them safe. Safety was as important in biblical times as it is today, and Scripture often confirms Maslow's theories regarding the significance of this need.

Belongingness and Love Needs. After the first two needs, physiological and safety, are fulfilled, the student will feel, as he or she has never felt before, the absence of close personal relationships. Thus emotional hunger will take the place of physiological hunger in each person's consciousness, the hunger for affectionate relations with people. Human beings are social creatures who desire a place in their group or family, and they will seek, usually with great intensity, such a place. The paramount role once played by hunger, thirst, and fear in their consciousness is then replaced by pangs of loneliness and friendlessness.

The Bible spells out the human need for love and belongingness. Jesus says in the Gospel of Matthew: "Ye have heard it hath been said, 'Thou shalt love thy neighbor, and hate thine enemy,' But I say unto you, Love your enemies." Other scriptural passages echo the same theme: "Thou shalt love thy neighbor as thyself." "Owe no man anything but to love one another." "For he that loveth hath fulfilled the law . . . and if there be any other commandment, it is briefly comprehended

Education

in this saying, 'Thou shalt love thy neighbor as thyself.'" "Love worketh no ill to his neighbor; therefore love is the fulfilling of the law." To love our neighbor as ourselves implies that we will interact with our neighbors as a Thou.

There is really no need to ask or even discuss the question, "Who is the neighbor?" To accept God's act in Christ at the very core of one's existence means a radical identification with all men. No one is excluded. Every man necessarily becomes one's neighbor; his place in existence becomes ours, including the non-Christian. It is this radical identification with neighbor which prevents God's grace from becoming "cheap grace" and mistaking of worship for faith.[18]

There can be no doubt that certain passages in the Bible assign at least as important a place to love as did Maslow. In fact, the Bible contains more than five hundred specific references to the word. Further, both the Old and New Testaments tell us that it is not enough to receive love; one must return it in equal measure. It must also be remembered that belonging to a group is of paramount importance in the Bible. One of the great revelations of Jesus is that all men, women, and children belong to one another, that each and every individual is a loved and loving child of God.

Esteem Needs. Maslow believed that all people in our society have a need and a desire for a stable, firmly grounded, high evaluation of self, for self-respect, and for the esteem of others. Esteem needs, he concluded, can be divided into two sets: self's view of self and others' view of self. Those persons whose esteem needs consist of a need for a high evaluation of the self and for self-respect can be described as self-directed, self-looking individuals who want to be strong, competent, and full of self-confidence as they look out at the world.

The Bible tells us little about self-respect, at least in a direct manner, but it does often caution us that we must live with our conscience. We will not be respected by others, various Scripture passages imply, unless we have acted according to what is right, and this cannot be the case unless we have followed the commands of the Creator. As far as holding in esteem only high-status persons, Scripture is abundantly clear on this matter. Deuteronomy 1:17 tells us: "Ye shall not respect persons in judgment; but ye shall hear the small as well as the great." Likewise, Proverb 28:21 cautions: "To have respect of persons is not good, for for a piece of bread that man will transgress."

It would appear that Scripture and Maslow are not far apart regarding the necessity for self-respect, but Scripture does not seem to set a high value on being greatly esteemed by others, at least in a worldly sense. Perhaps the only type of esteem to which approval is clearly given in the Bible is that which comes from spiritual riches. Jesus declared that all people should be esteemed and respected by others because they are all sons and daughters of God and are all part of a universal brotherhood. Maslow pointed out that we like for others to admire our reputation, our status, our fame, our dominance. So far as Scripture is concerned, students should be taught not to put a high value on such earthly things because people are fallible and the vast majority of us do yearn for things that are not praiseworthy in a spiritual sense. In the words of Ecclesiastes 1:2: "Vanity of vanities, saith the Preacher, vanity of vanities; all is vanity."

Self-Actualization Need. Self-actualization as defined by Maslow refers to the individual's desire for self-fulfillment, that is to say, the tendency for a student to become in reality what he or she is potentially capable of becoming. Self-actualized persons, Maslow said, are far more self-sufficient and self-contained individuals than nonactualized persons, and the determinants which control their behavior are primarily inner determinants rather than social or environmental ones. Such persons stand out from their fellows in their self-direction and often are responsible for giving others new values in many different fields.

Scripture is not lacking in references to self-actualization and inner strength. Isaiah 30:15 speaks directly to the question: "For thus saith the Lord God, the Holy One of Israel; In

Education

returning and rest shall ye be saved; in quietness and in confidence shall be your strength." Psalms 27:1 contains a good summary: "The Lord is my light and my salvation; whom shall I fear? the Lord is the strength of my life; of whom shall I be afraid?"

Both Maslow and Scripture tell us that humans cannot survive without something to believe in. Drug addicts and alcoholics are vivid reminders of this truism. Maslow, however, indicated that an individual can achieve self-actualization by his or her own will, whereas the Bible tells us that we must believe in God before the inner self can achieve peaceful harmony. Nevertheless, the characteristics of Maslow's self-actualized individual and the Bible's God-directed person are, at base, not dissimilar. Both individuals, one self-actualized from within and the other with an inner self in communication with God, are at peace with themselves even though the world around them may be in constant turmoil.

EQUAL EDUCATIONAL OPPORTUNITY

Most people adopt the *laissez faire* economics interpretation of equal opportunity. According to this notion, every person ought to compete under equal legal and political rules for the goods of society. Obviously, those with the most talent will win, advocates of this thesis maintain. Albert Hofstader has posited another interpretation of equal opportunity.[19] For him, the ultimate concern is the development of each person's unique capabilities to the highest level. From this perspective, equal opportunity means equal opportunity for self-actualization. In order for this to occur, political, economic, educational, and social equality must be considered basic human rights.

The Civil Rights Act of 1964 directed the Commissioner of Education to undertake a survey to assess the lack of availability of equal educational opportunities for individuals by reason of race, color, religion, or national origin in public educational institutions.[20] James S. Coleman, a well-known

A Religious Foundation of Human Relations

social psychologist, was given the task of coordinating the survey and was instructed to complete it by 1966. He was the principal (though not the sole) author of *Equality of Educational Opportunity*, the official report on the status of American education. Even so, the 737-page volume, with 548 additional pages of statistical explanations, is best known as the Coleman Report.

Soon after its publication, the Coleman Report became a focal point of controversy; there was scarcely a prominent educator who did not take sides in the matter. Equal educational opportunities in the past, the report pointed out, were considered in terms of the quality of instructional staff, textbooks, class size, age, and condition of the physical plant. Coleman found that when one looks at equality of education in terms of school output, a whole new set of factors must be examined.[21] Godfrey Hodgson described two of the report's major findings:

Children were tested at the beginning of grades 1, 3, 6, 9, and 12. Achievement of the average American Indian, Mexican American, Puerto Rican, and Negro (in this descending order) was much lower than the average white or Oriental American, at all grade levels . . . the differences are large to begin with, and they are even larger at higher grades. Two points, then, are clear: (1) These minority children have a serious educational deficiency at the start of school which is obviously not a result of school, and (2) they have an even more serious deficiency at the end of school which is obviously in part a result of school.[22]

In contradiction to traditional belief, Coleman found in his research that of the existing educational influences, the child's family background was the most important. And the two most salient factors pertaining to family background were the educational history of the parents and their economic status. Therefore, according to Coleman, if a child comes from a home with poorly educated parents who also are in a low eco-

Education

nomic position, the chances of educational success for the child are low.

One of the most interesting questions to arise from the study of the influence of family background on school achievement was whether large numbers of low-income children in a school would have a negative effect on children from affluent, well-educated families. Coleman answered this question by saying that as long as at least sixty per cent of a student body came from the middle class, there would be no detrimental effect on school achievement. He amplified this view by asserting that middle-class norms prevail in middle-class schools. Conversely, in a predominantly lower-class school, there prevail standards that oftentimes are antischool.[23]

A further conclusion of the Coleman Report, that the second most influential factor in a child's educational motivation is his peer group, surprised many reputable educators. "I guess what I'm saying," Coleman wrote, "is that a child's learning is a function more of the characteristics of his classmates than of those of the teacher."[24] He drew this conclusion both from his earlier work with adolescents and from substantial survey material contained in the report. Because most parents are engaged in making daily ends meet, a juvenile subculture arises as children are compelled more and more to seek emotional security from their peers rather than from traditional nurturing agents, the parents.

Without doubt, for educators the most shocking conclusion of the Coleman Report was its denial that school conditions play the major role in influencing the education of the child. In no uncertain terms, the report stated that "when other things were equal factors, such as the amount of money spent per pupil, or the number of books in the library, or physical facilities such as gymnasiums or cafeterias or laboratories or even differences in curriculum, it seemed to make no appreciable difference in the children's level of achievement.[25]

Stephen C. Rose was one of several writers who disagreed with this finding:

A Religious Foundation of Human Relations

The schools are increasingly trapped in a structural milieu, aided and abetted by administrative myopia, that leads to what Paul Goodman has called "compulsory miseducation." Imaginative teachers are often the first to sense the limitations of a system which overcrowds classrooms, burdens frontline educators with back-room bureaucratic form filling, and refuses to demand enough money to do the job that needs doing.[26]

Given the enormously important conclusions of the report, what did Coleman suggest as prescriptions for educational change? Since the family is no longer the chief educational institution of the child, it is clear that the child must turn elsewhere for education. Few children can turn to a full-time job as a viable educational alternative because laws forbid them to work at what society considers too early an age, but few schools educate students. As Francisco Ferrer noted: "All the value of education rests in respect for the physical, intellectual, and moral will of the child. Just as in science no demonstration is possible save by facts, just so there is no real education, save that which is exempt from all dogmatism, which leaves to the child itself the direction of its effort, and confines itself to the seconding of that effort."[27]

Coleman argued that because family structure has broken down, the child no longer can turn to this traditional unit for education. Currently, children receive too much schooling and not enough education. In other words, children increasingly have nowhere to go to learn certain practical skills and habits, among which are learning about work; learning how to function in society; learning how to be a father, mother, husband, or wife; and learning responsibility for others.[28] Consequently, an alarmingly large number of today's youth are simply being deprived of a chance to realize their full potential as human beings. And to make matters worse, the traditional school too often hinders the child instead of helping him. Consequently, most students do not drop out; they are pushed out. Coleman summed up the dilemma which formal schooling poses for contemporary society:

Education

Schooling, meanwhile, continues to mean much the same thing it did before—the learning of intellectual skills. Thus although schooling remains a small portion of education, it occupies an increasingly larger portion of a young person's time. Consequently, if an appropriate reform of education is to be made, it must begin with this fact: Schooling is not all of education, and the other parts of education require just as much explicit planning and organization as does schooling.[29]

Not content simply to analyze the problem of schooling, Coleman also delineated the task before us. The young, he said, must be given training in those skills which the economic institutions of our society demand. If such skill development programs are to succeed, they must be carefully conceived and well executed. He gives us a broad clue to the implementation of such a venture:

In the free enterprise economy of the U.S. it could begin by providing the young with entitlements that could be redeemed by business and other enterprises that try to provide the appropriate learning experiences. The economic organizations of society would change radically to incorporate the young—to become institutions in which work is designed not only for productive effeciency, but for learning efficiency as well.[30]

It should be obvious to both lay and professional educators alike that the conclusions of the Coleman Report and the recommendations of its chief author overturned a number of accepted theories about school and its influence. But are the ideas of James S. Coleman as startling as they appear? Do they really mean a full break with all traditional concepts of education? Specifically, how do Coleman's views on education compare, for example, with those set forth in Scripture?

Education in the biblical tradition prepares a person to live his or her life as it relates to God and other people. It is said in Scripture that our sole purpose in life is to serve our Creator and thereby gain salvation. Writes J. D. Douglas: "Jewish education's whole function was to make the Jew holy, and separate from his neighbors and to transform the religion into the practical."[31] Education in the Old Testament was not economically centered but, rather, served two purposes: perpetuation of Jewish society and proper worship of Jehovah. "Actual details of schooling are few; it is strange that the very word 'school' occurs but once in Scripture, and then refers merely to a lecture room borrowed by Paul (Acts 19:9), and not to any Jewish or Christian school."[32] It also should be noted that in biblical times there was no school system as we use the term today.

The segregation and class distinction which Coleman found endemic to our modern educational system also was prevalent in Old Testament times. Daniel 1:3–4 notes that King Jehoiakim set up a three-year period of formal education for some of the youth of Israel: offspring of the royal family and of nobility, without blemish, handsome and intelligent and competent to serve in the king's place. Perhaps, as some writers have suggested, the Coleman Report has merely put before us an age-old problem in a new time, a new place, and in new terms.

Nor is Coleman's assertion that education is greater than schooling in any way opposed to the New Testament. We have no scriptural account that Jesus attended school, although he probably went to the synagogue for religious instruction, yet Jesus is the Christian model of the educated man, for he lived exactly what he taught and gave practical examples of his doctrines each day. The Sermon on the Mount is probably the greatest educational manual for practical living ever conceived for man.

Rosemary Haughton has outlined the difficulties of teaching Christian values in contemporary society:

. . . when daily living must go on in a world where Christian values are no longer taken for granted the old vehicles of teaching become inadequate and may tend to work against the purpose for which they were used. . . . Real knowledge does not come with words only. Words are necessary in this world, but

Education

are of value only when they crystallize knowledge gained by a mixture (varying widely in its proportions) of experience, in tuition, and thought about both these. Even doctrine expressed in clear, supple and meaningful terms remains barren without this.[33]

HUMAN RELATIONS IN HIGHER EDUCATION

Most Americans were shocked and angered only a few years ago as students on college campuses from one end of our nation to the other began what seemed, at least to many, the systematic destruction of their schools. This so-called university revolution was perhaps best symbolized by a young student hacking away at the Columbia University library with a pickax as his friends urged him on with violent obscenities rarely heard on any Ivy League campus. Violence reached a climax in the late 1960's as law enforcement officers inflicted physical beatings—and a few deaths—on picketing college students. Most tradition-minded Americans, bewildered as they were by what they considered to be a radical conspiracy, refused to believe that the demonstrating students might be reacting to an inadequate education. But those who did care to look beneath the surface of college life, behind the façade of athletic contests and Latin-enscribed diplomas, could see that something was seriously wrong with America's higher education system.

Nearly fifteen years ago, Roger Harrison and Richard Hopkins told us what was wrong:

With few exceptions, formal systems of higher education in the United States provide training in manipulation of symbols rather than things; reliance on thinking rather than feeling and intuition; and commitment to understanding rather than to action. These systems were designed originally for the training of scholars, researchers and professionals, for whom rationality, abstract knowledge, emotional detachment and verbal skills are primary values. These systems, however, are applied across the board to almost all students, regardless of their occupational goals.[34]

In short, too many of our colleges and universities have insisted on treating young human beings as robots.

Although most scholars have some idea of the problems that plague modern higher education, only a few of them have come forward with stimulating suggestions for change. Warren G. Bennis, president of the University of Cincinnati, is one of this small group. Stressing planned change as the key to institutional reform in the next few decades, Bennis, Kenneth D. Benne, and Robert Chin tell us that it is the most feasible alternative to nondemocratic methods. They define it as "methods that maximize freedom and limit as little as possible the potentialities of growth; methods that will realize man's dignity as well as bring into fruition desirable social goals."[35]

It is a truism that one of the major reasons for the dilemma in education today is that our schools influence students to move toward traditional goals which are all too often woefully inadequate for a new age. To counter this trend, Bennis and his colleagues developed a theory of what they called meta-goals which deal with what and how the individual learns in nontraditional manners. There is a bit of the following biblical flavor in meta-goals:

To know wisdom and instruction; to receive the instruction of wisdom, justice, judgment, and equity; to give subtilty to the simple, to the young man knowledge and discretion. A wise man will hear, and will increase learning; a man of understanding shall attain unto wise counsels. — Proverbs 1:2-5

Colleges and universities are traditionally research oriented, but the meta-goal system revolves around observation and questioning in nonresearch settings. Traditional education generally takes place in the classroom, but meta-goals expand the concept of the classroom to areas outside rooms designated as classrooms. In short, learning occurs wherever

Education

people are interacting. The traditional system of education seldom teaches the student how to initiate action in reaching solutions to human problems. However, as the importance of human relationships becomes clear to him, the student can develop behavior and attitudes that facilitate improved human relations.

According to Bennis, if problem solving is to be relevant for genuine human needs, it must deal with real-life situations. And it is important that students build on theory, which will remain useless if not applied; they must be able to take risks, think problems through to a humane solution, and move from the protective atmosphere of the university into the community. Real-life situations require that students respond to them as they exist, not as some theoretical model has told them to respond. This seems to fit yet another biblical passage: "And I gave my heart to seek and search out by wisdom concerning all things that are done under heaven" (Ecclesiastes 1:13). Harvey G. Cox engaged in such a search as he tried to communicate new ways of caring for the poor:

A tradition of concern for the poor could just as easily lead the churches today into the social-service rather than the political attitude toward poverty. The other operative theological and ethical tradition is the equalitarian vision of the blessed community in which everyone participates without distinction. Although this image recurs many times in the Bible, it is perhaps best seen in Jesus' parable of workers in the vineyard, each of whom receives the same pay although they have worked different lengths of time. . . . When the principle of radical equality before God and equal participation in the community is applied to the present society, and not just to the church or to the world to come, it has explosive consequences for secular polity.[36]

It is also important for students to learn that there is no single best set of societal norms. The normative values of our society are not necessarily the only ones that are worth while.

A Religious Foundation of Human Relations

Bennis has expressed often his belief that authority must not be used to force students into patterned responses or value judgments. Rather, authority must be supportive when students try to define their values. Nor should teachers punish them when they give a wrong answer. The reward system need not always be based on completing a task; for some students, merely attempting a task is as desirable as completing it. Nor should it be said that complete freedom is the right approach with students. The challenge to teachers is to find out how much freedom each individual can accept responsibility for, then allow him to assume it.

Bennis' meta-goal philosophy may revolutionize the relationship between student and teacher. Teachers must help students find their way to an inductive method rather than to the traditional deductive one. Teachers must show students that their own feelings, perceptions, and experiences need not, in fact cannot, be the same as those of their teachers. And finally, teachers must bring students to a realization that just as problems arise out of real-life situations, so, too, must viable solutions come only after they have considered the possible effects on other persons. Proverbs 12:18 seems appropriate for this process: "A man shall be commended according to his wisdom, but he that is of perverse heart shall be despised."

One may well ask: Why haven't more changes come about in higher education as a result of the upheavals in education we have witnessed during the past decade? Bennis blames bureaucracy for universities' slowness to change, defining bureaucracy as "a social invention which relies exclusively on the power of influence through rules, reason, and the law."[37] It was created to fill the need for more predictability, order, and precision. Now we are faced with the fact that bureaucracy has placed education in a subservient role and has attempted, with the influence of federal money and power, to control the minds of educators and students. As this condition grows, Romans 14:13 appears to be wise counsel: "Let us not, therefore, judge one another any more: but judge this rather,

Education

that no man put a stumbling block or an occasion to fall in his brother's way."

But changes are occurring. Within the past decade, educators and industrialists have begun to move away from their traditional roles and are pooling their knowledge to find new and more humane solutions to their organizational problems. Gradually, educators are beginning to realize that man is much more complex than was previously thought, not a simple robot; effective power is based on collaboration and reason, not coercion and fear; and democratic ideals are germane to problem solving.

The increasing emphasis on education in the modern world renders the old bureaucracy almost useless. The process of education has caused individuals to want more personal satisfaction, more opportunities for creativity, and more involvement in decision making. Bennis predicts that education, which is the most distinctive characteristic of our society, will become even more so in the future. He further predicts that members of most organizations will be permitted and even encouraged to use their imagination, fantasy, and creativity to an extent unheard of at present.[38]

Along with these developments will come the demand from all corners of our society that education teach people how to live with and tolerate ambiguity. It is in this endeavor that human-relations training will prove to be indispensable. It seems inevitable that more university educators will deal more with the relevant issues of society: racial equality, sexual equality, and social equality. In order to do this, behavioral scientists and educators in particular cannot be content with focusing on traditionally "safe" problems.

Only a few years ago, many approaches that have since proved effective in group situations—for example, sensitivity and encounter training—were rejected by shortsighted traditionalists. Yet the need for change has grown to such proportions that new roles have emerged for teachers: change agents and facilitators. Indeed, planned change challenges educators

A Religious Foundation of Human Relations

to find ways to use to the utmost and apply knowledge as an instrument or tool for humane changes. Bennis outlined three processes for educational innovation: development, diffusion, and adoption. The biblical relationship is clear:

Take fast hold of instruction, let her not go. Keep her, for she is thy life.—Proverbs 4:13

6
JUSTICE

IT MAY be that the greatest glory of Western civilization has been its long concern with justice, a concern which arose almost simultaneously with the desire of people to live together as a group. Civilized men and women learned very early that there could be no peace without at least some few stable tenets by which their actions could be evaluated and to which at least a sizable majority of a community could give its assent. We are the heirs of a long tradition of legal justice, including the Code of Hammurabi, the commandments of the Old Testament prophets, the edicts of Solon, the Roman Twelve Tables, the Code of Justinian, English common law, and the Magna Charta.

When English social reformer William Godwin said, "To a rational being there can be but one rule of conduct, justice,"[1] he was merely repeating what has been assumed through the ages: when justice ceases to be accepted by civilized people, so also do they reject reason itself. Whenever justice dies in a society, lawlessness takes hold. St. Augustine reminds us: "Justice being taken away, then, what are kingdoms but great robberies? For what are robberies themselves, but little kingdoms?"[2] Augustine's admonition was echoed nearly fifteen hundred years later by James Madison: "Justice is the end of government. It is the end of civil society. It ever has been and ever will be pursued until it is obtained, or until liberty be lost in the pursuit."[3]

Reinhold Niebuhr suggested that the question of social order cannot be answered until the question of justice is settled.[4] The significance of this position is that it acknowledges the importance of both order and justice. Within this framework, leaders are subject to the consent of their followers. "No oligarchy," Joseph C. Hough, Jr., wrote, "can finally make pretensions to ultimate power. . . . The distribution of power on the equalitarian model means that ideally human self-interest is balanced against human self-interest in the political structures of democracy in such a way as to allow change without recourse to complete disorder."[5]

Yet the question remains: What is justice? In an effort to answer it, we shall examine the writings of Plato, Henry David Thoreau, Martin Luther King, Jr., and William O. Douglas. In one way or another, all four men have championed the cause of justice.

PLATONIC JUSTICE

In describing the death of Socrates, his friend and teacher, Plato, talked about an unjust end for a just man: "Such was the end, Echecrates, of our friend, whom I may truly call the wisest, and justest, and best of all men whom I have ever known."[6] It was obvious to Plato that a state which would condemn the best of all men could not be a just state, for the man who had best exemplified justice in his life was not safe within its boundaries. What, then, is a just state and who is the just man?

These two questions were considered inseparable by Plato. And they form the basic themes of his greatest dialogue, *The*

Justice

Republic, a masterful example of the philosophical inquiry. Early in the dialogue, Thrasymachus maintains that injustice is more profitable for a man than justice,[7] and Socrates, ever eager to pursue truth, replies that an unjust state is forever torn asunder and no peace reigns within it. Likewise, the unjust man is always at war with himself and others.[8]

However, Socrates was not content to vindicate justice solely on the grounds that the practice of it is proper if the soul is to remain healthy: he proposed that a just man has a happier life than an unjust man. Thus the wise man will desire justice both for itself and for its consequences and in so doing set himself apart from the masses, who believe that if someone is just, it is only because justice will bring rewards and fame, not because it is desirable solely for its own sake. The ignorant, we are told, look upon justice as a means of compromise, between the best of all, which is to do injustice and not be punished, and the worst of all, which is to suffer injustice without the power of retaliation.

At this point in the dialogue, Socrates observes that it is in the state that we see the true nature of justice. His assumption was that whatever virtues or defects the soul may contain will be found in macrocosm in the structure of government.[9] Plato, through the mouth of his principal actor, Socrates, constructed the ideal state. He divided it into three classes: the guardians, the auxiliaries, and the masses. The guardians, those who will rule over the State and give it laws, will not be entrusted with government until they reach the age of fifty. Defining the guardians as the best men and women, Plato shared very little of the traditional Greek bias against the natural abilities of women.

The guardians will hold all things in common, including wives and husbands. They are expressly forbidden to possess gold and silver since, Plato said, "gold and silver we will tell them that they have from God; the diviner metal is within them, and they have therefore no need of the dross which is current among them, and ought not to pollute the divine by any such earthly admixture; for that commoner metal has been the source of many unholy deeds, but their own is undefiled."[10]

Plato called those who will guard the state from its enemies auxiliaries and specified that they, like guardians, should receive special training for their posts. Above all, these fine soldiers must be trained to recognize who is a friend and who is a foe, for they must never be allowed to act in any outrageous way toward their fellow citizens. The masses—tradesmen, craftsmen, and the like—will be content to follow the guardians and obey their rule, since they are qualified neither by birth nor by training to govern. Little Christian support is found for Plato's form of government. Rather, Christian principles dictate, as John C. Bennett noted, a government by and for all citizens; that is, a government that has the consent of the governed and in which all citizens participate.[11]

It does not take us long to realize that individual freedom was not Plato's highest value, and much of his philosophy of the state is repugnant to persons reared to believe that democracy is the only healthy form of government. Yet for Plato the only just state is one which is ordered with a view to the good of the whole.[12] This being the case, it follows that the guardians must be first and foremost philosophers because they, more than any other persons, possess the kind of knowledge which has as its province the end or final goal of life. The philosopher, then, was Plato's major hope for a healthy state:

Until philosophers are kings, or the kings and princes of this world have the spirit and power of philosophy, and political greatness and wisdom meet in one, and those commoner natures who pursue either to the exclusion of the other are compelled to stand aside, cities will never have rest from their evils,—no, nor the human race, as I believe,—and then only will this our State have a possibility of life and behold the light of day.[13]

Now we may begin to discern the two kinds of Platonic justice, one centering on the individual, the other on the state; Gregory Vlastos called them, a psychological definition and a social definition of justice.[14] For Plato, the soul contains

Justice

three elements: the rational, the passionate, and the appetitive. The well-integrated personality will be a harmonious mixture of the three. The highest principle of the soul is the rational, and it is the natural role of this principle to rule over the other two. The rational principle and the passionate principle must remain always on guard lest the appetitive soul "no longer confined to her own sphere, should attempt to enslave and rule those who are not her natural-born subjects, and overturn the whole life of man."[15]

As we have noted, in the state there are three distinct elements: the guardians (corresponding to the rational principle of the soul), the auxiliaries (corresponding to the passionate principle), and the masses (corresponding to the appetitive principle). As long as those most fitted to rule hold power, the state need not worry about its enemies, either internal or external, but when the state falls into the hands of those whose natural role is not to rule but to follow, it will degenerate into tyranny and, finally, ochlocracy.

According to Plato, the just man is he who

sets in order his own inner life, and is his own master and his own law, and at peace with himself; and when he has bound together the three principles within him, which may be compared to the higher, lower, and middle notes of the scale, and the intermediate intervals—when he has bound all these together, and is no longer many, but has become one entirely temperate and perfectly adjusted nature, then he proceeds to act, if he has to act, whether in a matter of property, or in the treatment of the body, or in some affair of politics or private business; always thinking and calling that which preserves and cooperates with this harmonious condition, just and good action, and the knowledge which presides over it, wisdom, and that which at any time impairs this condition, he will call unjust action, and the opinion which presides over it ignorance.[16]

Justice, then, was a most profound quality for Plato, for its presence or absence as an attribute of a man's actions can tell us the very condition of that individual's soul, whether it is healthy or unhealthy. Vlastos summarized this condition as follows: "What a man does is for Plato only an 'image' of what he is; his 'external' conduct is only a manifestation of his 'inner' life, which is the life of the 'real' man, the soul. Hence when asks himself in what it is that a man's justice 'truly' consists he feels constrained to look to what goes on inside a man, in a man's soul."[17]

In *The Laws,* Plato clarified his views on justice and injustice. This treatise on the state and its nature is taken up to a large extent with more concrete examples of justice. In this volume, Plato goes so far as to discuss in some detail specific examples of criminal acts and the various types of punishment which should be meted out for them. The citizen who is to be most highly praised, Plato said, is he who acts as a kind of teacher of virtue to the masses.[18] Clearly, he believed that those who make up a state can be educated concerning the true nature of justice. Throughout his writings, he repeated a central theme: the good ruler is also an educator whose responsibility is to lead the people into the paths of virtue.

Plato's view that justice is synonymous with virtue or goodness is found in Christian thought. Furthermore, in Christian thought, God is love and God is just. Paul Tillich draws the distinction even finer: "Justice is that side of love which affirms the independent right of persons within the love relation."[19]

Plato was plainly ahead of his society when he enunciated a theory of crime worthy of the most gifted twentieth-century psychoanalyst: "Let us remember that the unjust man is not unjust of his own free will. For no man of his own free will would choose to possess the greatest of evils, and least of all in the most honorable part of himself."[20] In other words, criminal acts are but manifestations of inner psychic sickness, and the rational part of man's nature can in no way be implicated in them.

Plato's words have an especially relevant meaning for Americans: "A state in which the law is subject and without

Justice

authority is ripe for destruction; but when the law is sovereign over the rulers, and the rulers servants of the law, then, as I see it, the state is secure."[21] It is not too much to say that for Plato it was axiomatic that sick (that is, unjust) rulers, who do not themselves respect the law, eventually will infect the entire populace with their disease as the state itself succumbs. As Alexandre Koyre stated: "Love of justice, devotion to the city, respect for the law: an underlying bond links these things all together. For to be lacking in respect for law, the law which is the very soul of the city, is to put oneself above it, to prefer oneself to the city. Is that not the very height of injustice for a citizen?"[22]

Plato was so concerned with the abuse of power by administrative officials that his ideal state had a special board of examiners to evaluate the behavior of public officials during and after their terms.

Critics of Plato attack him because of the strongly totalitarian flavor of his philosophy of justice and statecraft. Some of his critics maintain that if his theories were to be carried out to their logical conclusions, citizens would find themselves in an atmosphere more than vaguely reminiscent of George Orwell's *1984* and Aldous Huxley's *Brave New World.*

Worthy of honor, too, is he who does no injustice, and of more than twofold honor if he not only does no injustice himself, but hinders others from doing any. And yet more highly to be esteemed is he who cooperates with the rulers in correcting the citizens as far as he can—he shall be proclaimed the great and perfect citizen and bear away the palm of virtue.[23]

At first reading, the critics say, few persons would object to such a statement, yet on further consideration it is plain that it is only a few steps away from situations as those which obtained in Nazi Germany, where each citizen was instructed by the Gestapo to inform on his friends and neighbors. Other critics maintain that Plato also showed his tyrannical bent in a number of passages in *The Republic,* where he is most careful to explain to his auditors the need for censorship in a healthy system of government. Not even Homer, Aeschylus, and Sophocles would escape Plato's busy censors, whose aim is to see that no ideas which might corrupt young learners reach their minds. Even so, Plato provided us with a view of justice that has survived through the ages.

CONSCIENCE AND JUSTICE

"As soon as laws are necessary for men," Pythagoras said, "they are no longer fit for freedom." No one in the history of Western thought would have agreed more with the Greek philosopher than Henry David Thoreau, whose life was devoted to proving, in both word and deed, that the only authority to which men and women should look for guidance in conduct is their own conscience. Thoreau believed that evil and discord arise only when institutions and laws intervene in human relationships, putting an end to the freedom and natural justice which ordinarily prevail when each person's conscience is the sole and final arbiter of his or her actions: "The only obligation which I have a right to assume is to do at any time what I think is right."[24]

Certainly, justice for Thoreau did not consist of what most men say it does, for most men have neither the ability nor the inclination to concern themselves with the question of whether the dictates of government, which supposedly rests on the will of the majority, can be squared with the dictates of conscience. Most citizens of a state are quite content to follow the commands of legislature and court rather than be considered nonconformists. In short, Thoreau believed that the vast majority of people blindly obey authority not because they believe it to be right but because they are afraid to resist and in their acquiescence reduce themselves to a level less than human. "We should be men first," Thoreau wrote, "and subjects afterward. It is not desirable to cultivate a respect for the law, so much as for the right."[25]

Justice, then, for Thoreau consisted in doing what is

Justice

right, and the individual conscience is the one infallible judge of what is right. In fact, he stated quite plainly that conscience is *the* divine voice, superseding even the most hallowed of hieratic and political writings.

They who know of no purer sources of truth, who have traced up its stream no higher, stand, and wisely stand, by the Bible and the Constitution, and drink at it there with reverence and humility; but they who behold where it comes trickling into this lake or that pool, gird up their loins once more, and continue their pilgrimage toward its fountainhead.[26]

Thoreau had little tolerance for those who agree that justice is to be preferred to injustice but who refuse to stand actively in its defense. Believing that conscience is the highest instrument of the Divine, it followed for Thoreau that we must not only think rightly but act rightly as well. Conscience, he concluded, should make us anything but cowards. In this regard, he said, "those who, while they disapprove of the character and measures of a government, yield to it their allegiance and support are undoubtedly its most conscientious supporters, and so frequently the most serious obstacles to reform."[27] Thoreau did not sanction the conduct of persons who would practice an "inner migration." In a letter to Harrison Blake on August 9, 1850, he said: "As for conforming outwardly, and living your own life inwardly, I do not think much of that."[28]

Nor was tilting at windmills Thoreau's favorite pastime. He maintained that minor injustices with no personal involvement should be largely ignored, since they will eventually disappear. But he clearly drew the line at the kind of injustice which requires one to be an agent of injustice to another; such an injustice demands that we break the law. It is for this reason that Thoreau advised his contemporaries not to pay their taxes so long as the federal government tolerated slavery anywhere in the United States. He, of course, was the first to take his own advice and found himself in jail as a result of his defiance of the tax collector.

A Religious Foundation of Human Relations

Going to jail is often the most effective means to protest injustice, Thoreau believed: "Under a government which imprisons any unjustly, the true place for a just man is also a prison."[29] The story is told that upon being informed that Thoreau was in jail, Emerson went to visit him in the hope of paying his fine. He looked at Thoreau and demanded: "What are you doing in there?" Thoreau looked at him sadly and replied: "What are you doing out there?" Thoreau knew that those outside jail might be physically unrestrained but they were really the most imprisoned of all persons because their freedom was illusory and they did not know it. Indeed, Thoreau might have taken for his credo Rousseau's observation when discussing how men were fooled into accepting laws for a society: "All ran to meet their chains thinking they secured their freedom."

Thoreau had no difficulty in perceiving for whom laws worked and for whom they did not work. They worked to the advantage of the affluent, and Justice was never so blind that she could not be bought: "But the rich man—not to make any invidious comparison—is always sold to the institution which makes him rich."[30] Thoreau echoed Rousseau, who also saw that the rich were the only people to profit by laws which gave little protection to the weak and considerable strength to the rich.[31]

"There are a thousand hacking at the branches of evil," Thoreau observed, "to one who is striking at the root." He was one of those striking at the root, and his philosophy of passive disobedience inspired such fighters for freedom as Mahatma Gandhi and Martin Luther King, Jr. He believed that it was not enough simply to oppose injustice; we have to face the consequences which evil imposes on those who follow the commands of conscience rather than those of unjust governments.

Thoreau seldom doubted that conscience will lead each person to right action, but it is on this point that his teachings seem to diverge most significantly from the teachings of Scripture. The Bible teaches us that although the individual has a

Justice

conscience, he also has the freedom to choose good or evil for himself. Man can decide for injustice as well as for justice, and if left to himself, he can easily err. According to the Bible, God's word is the ultimate authority for man, and it must lead conscience. If men follow God's law, justice will be attained. If they do not, only evil and injustice can result, no matter what conscience alone dictates.

In a number of ways, Thoreau and Scripture agree. An examination of Jesus' actions indicates that the methods he followed and those used by Thoreau are similar. The turn-the-other-cheek concept of the Bible indicates nonviolence, and both Jesus and Thoreau recognized that if the state decides a law is broken, it has the authority to render punishment. Thoreau acknowledged this by his willingness to go to jail for nonpayment of unjust taxes; Jesus acknowledged it by his submission in being crucified. It is apparent that they both believed that a higher law eventually will prevail.

CIVIL RIGHTS

"Jesus' work," James H. Cone noted, "is essentially one of liberation. Becoming a slave himself, he opens realities of human existence formerly closed to man. Through an encounter with Jesus, man now knows the full meaning of God's action in history and man's place within it."[32] Indeed, Christian liberation is a condition in which, as Luke 7:22 states, the lame walk, the blind receive their sight, the deaf hear, the dead are raised up, and the poor have the Good News preached to them. Thus Martin Luther King, Jr., joined a long list of persons demanding a just liberation.

For the oppressed, it is counterproductive to speak of love without justice and power. Love without power is a sure way to guarantee subservience. Paul Tillich admonished that "love and power are often contrasted in such a way that love is identified with a resignation of power and power with a denial of love. Powerless love and loveless power are contrasted. . . .

A Religious Foundation of Human Relations

But such an understanding is error and confusion."[33] Writing on the subject of justice and love, Joseph Fletcher concluded:

The main thing to emphasize is that only a misdirected conscience has to wrestle with the "justice" versus "love" problem. It is seen to be a pseudoproblem at once when we drop the traditional systematic habit of separating them as "virtues." ... They are one and the same. To be loving is to be just, to be just is to be loving.[34]

King agreed with Cone, Tillich, and Fletcher.

Behind the nonviolent sit-ins, demonstrations, and marches led by King lay a well-defined philosophy of justice. The winner of the 1964 Nobel Peace Prize stressed time and again that his program against injustice demanded uncompromising commitment from those who wished to participate with him in the venture. It is not difficult to see the similarity between King and Jesus, whom he sought to emulate. In trying to eradicate injustice, King counseled his followers that when one cheek was slapped, the other should be turned, no matter what the circumstances. He asked the oppressed black masses to reply with love when they were spat upon, and it was truly ironic that this apostle of love and understanding among all peoples was himself a victim of violence. Justice for human beings everywhere was his dream, and during his life he was as successful as any man in personally living a just life.

Many persons charged that King showed too great a willingness during his life to break whatever laws he chose to break and to obey only those he felt should be obeyed. He answered his critics by saying that there are two types of laws, just and unjust, and that each individual has a legal and moral responsibility to obey just laws and to disobey unjust ones. The 1954 U.S. Supreme Court decision in the Brown case is a law to be obeyed, King reasoned, because it is a manifestation of justice.

He frequently cited St. Augustine's statement that an unjust law is no law at all. A just law, King often pointed out, is a man-made article which coincides with the law of God;

Justice

conversely, he said, an unjust law is one which is incompatible with the Divine Law. In a similar vein, he referred to St. Thomas Aquinas' remark that an unjust law is a human law that is rooted in neither eternal law nor natural law. Any law that uplifts the human personality is just while any law that degrades man is unjust. This distinction is crucial to an understanding of both King's life and his philosophy.

Almost from the beginning of the 1955 boycott against segregated busing in Montgomery, Alabama, King's opponents equated his campaign with the white citizens councils' resistance to school desegregation. In his book *Stride Toward Freedom*, he set forth his reason for organizing against segregation in Montgomery: "Something began to say to me, he who passively accepts evil is as much involved in it as he who helps to perpetuate it. He who accepts evil without protesting against it is really cooperating with it."[35]

King took pains to point out the difference between his crusade and the destructive tactics of the white citizens councils. He did not advocate evading or defying just laws, as did the rabid segregationalists; that, he said, would lead to anarchy. Rather, he encouraged his followers to break unjust laws and to do so openly, lovingly, and with a willingness to accept a penalty. In this manner, Martin Luther King, Jr., set himself off from the misguided violence seekers and demonstrated to the world that he was a true revolutionary following in the paths of the greatest revolutionary of love, Jesus of Nazareth.

King identified Socrates as one of his philosophical ancestors when he asserted that an individual who breaks a law that conscience tells him is unjust—and who willingly accepts the penalty of imprisonment in order to arouse the conscience of the community over its injustice—is in reality expressing the highest respect for law. When advised by his friend Crito to escape from a death to which he had been unjustly condemned, Socrates replied that neither injury nor retaliation nor warding off evil by evil is ever right.[36] King followed the same route outlined by Socrates when the latter told Crito that by consenting to imprisonment and death, he departed "in innocence, a sufferer and not a doer of evil; a victim, not of the laws, but of men."[37] King repeatedly advised that to suffer at the hands of unjust men was not the same as tolerating injustice, for to accept an unjust system passively is to cooperate with that system and thereby become a participant in its evil. To cooperate passively with an unjust system makes the oppressed as evil as the oppressor.[38]

Justice is a basic issue for each person, for unjust acts do serious damage to the soul of every citizen. Segregation, for example, gives the segregator a false sense of superiority and the segregated a false sense of inferiority. To obey an unjust law was for King a profoundly moral issue: segregation is not only politically, economically, and sociologically unsound, it is also morally wrong and sinful. Segregation creates an I-It relationship of subject and object. King recommended that in order to remove such unjust laws each person must adopt that view toward all other human beings which Martin Buber suggested is the only morally valid one: an I-Thou relationship, the relationship of subject and subject.

One of the major ways of differentiating between a just and an unjust law, King maintained, was to ask who obeys the law in question. An unjust law is a rule which a powerful majority group forces a minority group to obey but does not itself obey. On the other hand, when the majority has the minority follow what it also follows, the resulting sameness is legal. An injustice occurs if a minority is denied the franchise and thus does not participate in creating or enacting any laws. For hundreds of years, the majority group in the South prevented blacks from voting by using such immoral tactics as the poll tax and literacy tests. One major injustice perpetrated in southern cities during the 1950's was an ordinance which decreed that whites could receive parade permits but blacks could receive no such authority in order to protest peacefully the injustices of three hundred years. King demanded to know of the South whether any laws enacted under such circumstances were democratically structured.

Justice

Countless examples drawn from history validate King's views on justice and injustice. He showed us that there was nothing new in his employing nonviolent civil disobedience as a protest against an unjust system. Shadrach, Meschach, and Abednego refused to obey Nebuchadnezzar's laws and made it plain that in not doing so they were merely following the higher law of God. The early Christians willingly faced hungry lions and chopping blocks rather than submit to the unjust laws of the Roman Empire. Protest is far from being an unusual phenomenon in America, since our own great revolution was born in the rebellious gathering known as the Boston Tea Party.

King shook the conscience of the United States when he said that if one took as his sole criterion in judging the moral worth of an act whether the act was done according to man's law, it would have to be said that everything Hitler did was right and everything the Hungarian Freedom Fighters did was wrong. Had he lived in Germany during the Hitler regime, King said, he would have disobeyed the unjust laws of the Nazis and aided the Jews.

King unerringly explained the historical mission of the black civil-rights movement: its final lesson was to be a universal one, a shining example to all men who struggle against injustice:

I had hoped that the white moderate would understand that law and order exist for the purpose of establishing justice and that when they fail in this purpose they become dangerously structured dams that block the flow of social progress. I had hoped that the white moderate would understand that the present tension in the South is a necessary phase of the transition from an obnoxious negative place, in which the Negro passively accepted his unjust plight, to a substantive and positive place, in which all men will respect the dignity and worth of human personality. Actually, we who engage in nondirect action are not the creators of human tension. We merely bring to the surface the hidden tension that is already alive. We bring it out in the open, where it can be seen and dealt with. Like a boil that can never be cured so long as it is covered up but must be opened with all its ugliness to the natural medicines of air and light, injustice must be exposed, with all the tension its exposure creates, to the light of human conscience, and the air of national opinion before it can be cured.[39]

Another oft-raised criticism of King's actions was that they often precipitated violence. He replied that such accusations were

like condemning a robbed man because his possession of money precipitated the evil act of robbery . . . like condemning Socrates because his unswerving commitment to truth and his philosophical inquiries precipitated the act by the misguided populace in which they made him drink hemlock . . . like condemning Jesus because His unique God-consciousness and never-ceasing devotion to God's will precipitated the evil act of crucifixion.[40]

King finally reached the conclusion that each individual must continue every effort to obtain his basic constitutional rights, even though such behavior may precipitate violence.

Time, he felt, plays a neutral role in obtaining justice; progress toward justice is not inevitable but is due to the tireless efforts of men and women willing to work God's will. One cannot, King cautioned, simply consign the end of social injustice to some distant future: there is no time like the present to work for human betterment. His nowness philosophy demands nothing less than an immediate end to racial injustice and a beginning toward recognition of each human being's dignity.

King's philosophy of nonviolence is a middle ground between the do-nothing of quietism and the hate and despair of black separatism. Indeed, he believed that as the black people of the United States move forward to eradicate racial injustice, they must also, at every step of the way, reach a clear understanding of exactly why public demonstrations are taking place. He often said that blacks must march, they must

Justice

make prayer pilgrimages to city hall, they must go on freedom rides in order to achieve justice. Pent-up frustration must be channeled in nonviolent direct action or else it will turn inward and become self-destructive.

When labeled an extremist, King referred to the stirring words of other extremists before him. His philosophy was in exactly the same tradition of other men and women who embodied the Judaeo-Christian ideal. Jesus said: "Love your enemies, bless them that curse, do good to them that hate you, and pray for them which despitefully use you, persecute you." Was Amos an extremist when he said: "Let justice roll down like waters and righteousness like an everflowing stream"? Was Paul a radical witness for the Christian Gospel when he told us: "I bear in my body the marks of the Lord Jesus"?

From King's vantage point, it was not whether we will be extremists but, rather, what kind of extremists we will be. We must choose from the opposite ends of the spiritual continuum—love or hate—for no Christian can be lukewarm in the fight for justice. If we allow injustice to triumph by doing nothing, we are following the philosophy of hate whether we so intend or not. King was fond of saying that the Crucifixion represented the ends of the continuum: the two thieves crucified with Jesus remind us of the worst side of man, while Jesus, an extremist for love, goodness, and truth, represents for us the highest expression of man's finest qualities.

For King, religion was no otherworldly experience; it is a here-and-now spiritual force the mission of which is to bring justice for those who have suffered too long. He went to Birmingham hoping to find allies among that city's religious leaders; instead, he discovered that many ministers were telling their congregations that desegregation should be complied with because it was the law, not because it was morally right. He did not receive Christian love from churchmen who declared that segregation was merely a social issue, not one crucial to the Gospel message of Jesus.

According to King, the role of the church in eradicating injustice is a central and traditional one going back to the

A Religious Foundation of Human Relations

witness of the early Christians, who felt rewarded for suffering for something they believed in. The early saints were no friends of the status quo; every time they entered a town the power structure trembled, and it was mainly through their efforts that such barbarian practices as infanticide and gladitorial contests were stopped. Today, however, church leaders are often the friends of the powerful and wealthy, not the defenders of the weak and the poor. Racial bigots tend to interpret the silence of church leaders regarding moral issues as a sanction for whatever injustices they wish to perpetuate.

On the other hand, many white ministers did support King's campaigns, and some of them subsequently were denied funds and jobs. Community leaders who preferred to hear a safe Gospel message withdrew their backing of ministers who publicly fought against racial injustice. As King so aptly stated, however, these brave men acted in the faith that right defeated is stronger than evil triumphant. Birmingham was a watershed in the struggle for racial freedom in the United States. King believed that if the battle for justice could be won in that city, the rest of our nation would have to follow new paths. He often said that freedom would win out because injustice could never triumph against the heritage of America and the will of God.

King was well aware that the contest for justice could so easily be lost if its adherents allowed themselves to take the easy road to moral compromise. Time and time again, he reiterated that it is wrong to use immoral means to attain moral ends. But he warned those in power that America would have to be cleansed, that it was likewise wrong to use moral means (compromise) to preserve immoral ends. He quoted T. S. Eliot in this regard: "The last temptation is the greatest treason: To do the right deed for the wrong reason."

King found great inspiration in Mahatma Gandhi's application of the philosophy of nonviolence. He saw exactly what Gandhi had seen early in his struggle: that loving commitment to justice can bring strength and courage to those previously counted least among men. Jesus, too, chose his disciples from among the lowly, and it was one of his greatest

Justice

miracles that from these who were despised he fashioned saints.

Injustice anywhere, King said, is a threat to justice everywhere, and those who caution that waiting is the best strategy for blacks in America fail to see that justice too long delayed is justice denied. Like Jesus, he was loving and patient when he encountered human frailties, but also like Jesus, he knew that each time a man compromises with evil, he compromises his soul just that much more. For three hundred and fifty years, black Americans had waited for their rights, both God given and constitutional, and to tell them that by waiting they would overcome was to betray not only a race but justice itself. Jesus and Martin Luther King, Jr., were murdered for their commitment to justice and for their refusal to abandon their divinely ordained ministry on earth, yet in death both men continue to bring disquiet to the mighty and strength to the weak and oppressed.

Commenting on the impact of the civil-rights movement on current theological reflection, Thomas W. Ogletree wrote:

The problem of power also confronts contemporary man with heightened intensity in a political form. Once again, problems relating to political power are not new, nor is the theological analysis of these problems. We need simply call to mind Reinhold Niebuhr's lifelong insistence that responsible ethical reflection requires us to take into account the role of power in adjudicating the conflicting interests of human society. Yet the theological significance of power has more recently been reopened in a new way, primarily through persons previously excluded from the decision-making processes of society who are now showing a profound determination to seize and exercise power in their own right.[41]

DEMOCRATIC JUSTICE

If I had to name a single contemporary American who has consistently championed individual liberty against the tyranny

A Religious Foundation of Human Relations

of majority and government, I would name former U.S. Supreme Court Justice William O. Douglas. Perhaps Douglas characterized himself best when he told Mike Wallace in a 1958 interview that "the great and invigorating influences in American life have been the unorthodox: the people who challenge an existing institution or way of life, or say and do things that make people think."[42] Since his appointment to the U.S. Supreme Court by Franklin D. Roosevelt in 1939, Douglas has been our national legal conscience.

"The Constitution and Bill of Rights were," he said, "indeed, written to accommodate each and every minority regardless of color, nationality, or creed. That is our democratic faith."[43] It is only by ensuring an equal voice to all that America can avoid the perilous gap, suffered by most civilizations in the past, which separates rulers from ruled. Speaking to the Authors Guild on December 3, 1952, Douglas reminded us that restriction of free thought and free speech is the most dangerous of all subversions. It is the one un-American act which could most easily defeat us.[44] He knew, as did Montesquieu, that a nation may lose its liberties in a day and not miss them for a century.[45]

Douglas has never lost sight of the fact that justice is not for the privileged few but for every person. Morality, value systems, and codes of conduct are useless unless a society is willing to grant them to all its citizens. All people need political and spiritual freedoms, as well as economic opportunities. Douglas commented on these rights: "The right to work, I had assumed, was the most precious liberty that man possesses. Man has indeed as much right to work as he has to live, to be free, to own property."[46]

Justice is nothing, Douglas cautioned, if it is not a living, daily reality touching the inner and outer worlds of each citizen. Enshrining justice as some abstract ideal, bloodless at best and tyrannical at worst, is not the way of a true democracy or a free people.

Justice is a way of life, worked out by human hands and brains. No program of justice is therefore perfect. But we know from

Justice

our own experience that it can be workable. Justice as a way of life has proved its efficiency. We have seen it at work at the community level. We have seen it at work on a national scale. In our nation, we have seen programs of justice push back the frontiers of exploitation and narrow the areas of oppression. Ideas of class, ideas of racial discrimination have given way before the powerful drive of democratic justice.[47]

Racial discrimination is a particularly pernicious disease when it attacks a nation supposedly committed to justice for all. Douglas observed that wherever we find racial prejudice, we find a prejudice against any and all ideas which might threaten the entrenched social order: "The worst provincialism of which America can be guilty is the provincialism of prejudice, racial prejudice, prejudice against new and challenging ideas."[48] Preserving the status quo, which so often is little more than codified prejudice, is not justice, Douglas warns, and it is foolhardy to forget that injustice can take many forms in a community: poverty, illiteracy, unemployment, disease.

Men, however, must take care that in their desire to redress injustices they do not emulate those who committed oppression in the past. Wrote Douglas: "For men and for nations alike, the freedom to steal and to exploit today because another stole or exploited yesterday is often falsely labeled as justice. That might makes right, that blood washes out injustices, these too, have also been given the false label of justice."[49] For Justice Douglas, history can never justify the mass crimes of a Robespierre or a Stalin, and those who would build governmental and economic systems based on class, race, or religion remain in the end the ultimate foes of justice.

There will always be those among us, Douglas argued, who would suspend justice in America in the name of protecting the majority. Long before the cases involving Gideon, Miranda, and Escobedo reached the U.S. Supreme Court, Douglas warned Americans that due process is the basic guarantee upon which both our legal system and our freedoms rest and that each attempt by government to suspend due process is one more nail in the coffin of democracy. A real

A Religious Foundation of Human Relations

legal system, Douglas concluded, is not a gift to the people from some legislature or court, no matter how august its membership. The significance of Douglas' caution is implicit in the fact that since 1970 more than one thousand federal, state, and local public officials have been convicted of federal corruption charges.

The basis of Douglas' conception of justice appears to parallel closely the Divine Law of Jesus as set forth in the Golden Rule. This observation is crucial to understanding Douglas' legal philosophy, for his enemies have long sought to depict him as a radical and immoral jurist whose doctrine lacks any real connection with the past. What a shock it must be for those who would vilify him to realize that he has advocated nothing more in his life than the truly revolutionary message which Jesus brought to all mankind! Douglas demonstrates that to respect the rights of all others is to love all others as we are commanded to do by Scripture. Furthermore, he has shown time and again his love for all of the Divine Creation in his lifelong fight to conserve what is God's gift to man: a beautiful and healthy natural environment. Governmental agencies were established to protect the rights of man as a resident of this planet, but all too often, Douglas warns, these very agencies have proved in practice that they are not concerned with protecting anyone or anything except special-interest groups.

Douglas is a supporter of a very old legal safeguard which has come down to us through English common law: standing. It is impossible for all the members of a community to be heard in defense of their environment, but the one individual, or group of individuals, possessing the greatest understanding of the issues in question has standing to speak on behalf of all. Thus Douglas urged that public hearings be held before government bureaus and that persons with standing present their cases. Such a public hearing "would have to operate on the assumption that all life is sanctified and that its sacrifice should not be tolerated except in cases of a clear overriding social need. In other words, let the people help shape

Justice

the policies on which the fate or future of the community depends."[50]

Although Douglas has been involved in much controversy, it is doubtful that he has ever raised the cries of so many Establishment supporters as he did with the publication of a book entitled *Points of Rebellion*. In it, Douglas assessed the meaning of the dissent of the 1960's and concluded that America is in a critical state, not because of the dissenters, but because the nation has failed to meet their challenges. Although the aims of youthful protesters during the past decade were often woefully unclear and their cause frequently misunderstood both by themselves and their critics, Douglas clarified their points of rebellion.

He saw many similarities between the aims of the protesters and their counterparts during the American Revolution of 1776. In fact, he labeled today's Establishment "the new George III" and cautioned that if the Establishment continues its destructive ways, the only conclusion will be another revolution.[51] Douglas saw two distinct sides forming in America: those persons who, because of their positions, control America's destiny (the military-industrial complex, the agribusiness lobby, and the highway lobby) and their victims (the poor, the unemployed, and the disemployed). Sadly, Douglas concluded, the Establishment has managed to buy out the one institution which might have lent its help to the oppressed: the university. Douglas reserved some of his most scathing remarks for the academic community: "When the university does not sit apart, critical of industry, the Pentagon, and government, there is no fermentative force at work in our society. The university becomes a collection of technicians in a service station, trying to turn out better technocrats for the technological society."[52]

He characterized the new American revolution by saying it occurred during a time which was affluent, it was activist and not inflexibly bound to dogma, and its predominantly young leaders did not set destruction as their primary goal, insisting instead that the entire American system become much more humane. Such protest, Douglas said, is perhaps the only way to restore justice to the United States. Tragically, older members of our society cannot accept meaningful change because they have been conditioned to the status quo.

The older generation's failure to guide the young is nowhere better illustrated than in a 1969 letter to Douglas from an American soldier in Vietnam:

Somewhere in our history—though not intentionally—we slowly moved from a government of the people to a government of a chosen few . . . who, either by birth, family tradition or social standing—a minority possessing all the wealth and power—now . . . control the destiny of mankind. . . . You see, Mr. Douglas, the greatest cause of alienation is that my generation has no one to turn to. . . . With all the hatred and violence that exist throughout the world it is time someone, regardless of personal risk, must stand up and represent the feelings, the hopes, the dreams, the visions and desires of the hundreds of thousands of Americans who died, are dying and will die in the search of truth.[53]

Douglas notes that the individuals who are most degraded and unrepresented in America today are the poor; welfare recipients are maligned, jailed, cheated, and written off as wastrels at best and subversives at worst. The American system cannot boast of real justice for all, Douglas asserts, as long as more than half of the six and a half million Americans of Mexican descent in the Southwest live in poverty and their unemployment rate is twice the national average. Nor can we be proud as a nation as long as usury laws and consumer-credit practices wreak such financial havoc on the less privileged members of our society. Douglas denied that the 1968 federal law concerning disclosure of all consumer-credit charges did much for the poor, since the charges for consumer credit are regulated almost entirely by the states. He blames the powerful finance-company lobby for the fact that there has been little real change in laws regulating credit. What we have in

Justice

America, Douglas observed, is welfare for the rich and free enterprise for the poor. To support this claim, he cited large farm subsidies and governmental failure to help poor persons.

The greatest threat to political and economic freedom in our country, Douglas maintains, is the giant military-industrial complex, for this monster is consuming funds which should be used to promote life, not destruction. Douglas summed up well our neglect of human resources in our desire to enlarge what is already the largest military arsenal the world will ever know:

In 1970 we will spend 2 billion dollars for developing the ABM, which is more than we will allocate to community action and model cities programs combined; we will spend 2.4 billion dollars on new Navy ships, which is about twice what we will spend on education for the poor; we will spend 8 billion dollars on new weapons research, which is more than twice the current cost of the Medicare program.[54]

Douglas set forth a program for restoring justice to the American system of government: (1) The Pentagon's budget must be drastically reduced in order to allow for more social-welfare appropriations. (2) Lawyers must be furnished the poor and disadvantaged in order that legal justice may become a reality for all Americans. (3) America's laws must be revised to provide equal redress to all citizens, not just those who are affluent. (4) Federal agencies must allow hearings so that the public may be made aware of just how our resources are being used or misused. (5) We must make the poor the focus of local, state, and federal food programs rather than allow the corporate farmer to dominate our agricultural resources. (6) A much larger sum of money must be allocated each year for employment in the public sector, and such employment opportunities must be increased to include specialists in the whole gamut of human interest. (7) Pentagon, Central Intelligence Agency, and industry control of universities must cease as our educational institutions once again become a major instrument in reshaping society. (8) Widespread equality of

A Religious Foundation of Human Relations

opportunity for all minorities in all areas of American life must become a reality.[55]

Protests and rebellion have not made William O. Douglas pessimistic about its future. On the contrary, he sees hope, not threat, in the fact that America's young realize all is not well with our society:

The dissent we witness is a reaffirmation of faith in man; it is protest against living under rules and prejudices and attitudes that produce the extremes of wealth and poverty and that make us dedicated to the destruction of people through arms, bombs, and gases, and that prepare us to think alike and be submissive objects for the regime of the computer.... The dissent we witness is a protest against the belittling of man, against his debasement, against a society that makes "lawful" the exploitation of humans.... This period of dissent based on belief in man will indeed be our great renaissance.[56]

Throughout his long and distinguished legal career, Douglas has stood up for people against those who would enslave them for power and profit. Freedom of religion, freedom of conscience, freedom of speech, freedom of privacy, freedom to work, freedom of opportunity, freedom to be tried legally in a fair manner—all the most cherished freedoms of this great nation—have found their most tenacious defender in William O. Douglas. Perhaps his courageous faith in democracy was best expressed when he wrote:

The ideal of justice for all people has never been achieved by the grace of a ruler supported by an army. It has come only from people themselves. We must give the peoples of the world that chance. We cannot dictate to them. But we can plead their cause and use our moral leadership to the end that they get that chance.[57]

7
CONTROL

IN BIBLICAL times a man's wealth was measured not only by his flocks and his herds, his ingots of gold, his manservants and maidservants, but also by his offspring: his sons and daughters and their sons and daughters. Today in many segments of the world, particularly the undeveloped nations, the equation for wealth remains basically the same. Consequently, an ancient norm (having many children) has turned into a comtemporary social problem: there are too many people in the world.[1]

At the present rate of growth more than 75 million people are added to the total world population each year. In dramatic terms, every three years more people will be added than now live in America. Unless the trend is reversed, within five or six years the world will have added the equivalent of a new Europe in population. In addition to higher birth and lower infant mortality rates, medical discoveries that extend human life are adding to the population explosion. These conditions compound and complicate the issues of abortion and euthanasia. In an attempt to avoid viewing population control from a selfish, egocentric perspective, I have elected to inject questions of ethics and morality.

Crowded living conditions frequently set in motion a chain of events leading to tensions, hostilities, violence, and crime. During periods of overcrowding, community services—such as public transportation, medical care, electric power, heating, and food distribution—are difficult to maintain. The problems involved in being able to provide adequate housing, recreation, jobs, and schools for an ever increasing number of people are mind boggling. Compounding these conditions is the fact that the deterioration of the environment is such that ecological damage appears to be irreversible. For these reasons, the natural and human resources of a nation merit our attention.

Lynn White, Jr., reviewed ecology-related literature and concluded that today science and technology are so tinctured with orthodox Christian arrogance toward nature that no solution for our ecological crisis can be expected from them alone.[2] Seeking a solution, he suggested that since the roots of our trouble are so largely religious, the remedy must be essentially religious. White did not give credit to religious works which present a positive reading of Scripture and ecology.[3] Even so, his prognosis is not without a considerable theological basis.

ENVIRONMENT

Just as the state must be regarded as an instrument to be used by the people and for the people, so, too, must the economic order, with its technology and vast industrial machines, the riches of the soil and of mineral worth, be regarded as God's gift whereby life shall be more abundant.[4]

Protecting our natural environment has become a crucial national issue. Recognition of the complex problems involved in its deterioration has been slow in coming. Scarcely more than a decade ago, conservationists had the loudest voices of alarm. Now some of the most eminent scientists predict humankind is endangered unless more corrective actions are taken soon; some, in the form of environmental controls, are under way. For the purpose of this chapter, I have chosen to limit the discussion of pollution to that affecting water, one of the natural substances necessary for human survival. And in order to stay within the realm of human relations, I will focus on industrial water pollution, a man-made phenomenon which has affected our environment adversely. Indeed, most water pollution has grown out of the pursuit of material and consumer goods.

Although widespread opinion holds that water pollution can be caused by the addition of any human or industrial waste, a more precise definition is needed for our discussion. Notwithstanding the fact that some researchers measure water pollution by the bacteria count and others consider water to be polluted when anything extraneous is placed in it, I will use Melvin A. Benarde's definition: water pollution is the depletion of oxygen content, with consequent septic conditions, such as offensive odors, floating masses of sludge, and death of fish and other aquatic life.[5] With this in mind, let us examine industrial water pollution and its effect on human beings.

Donald E. Carr's book *Death of the Sweet Water*, especially the chapter entitled "Pollution Is Good Business," offers two basic reasons for pollution caused by industries located near water: the manufacturing plants use large quantities of water and they must have a place to dispose of their dirty water.[6] Thomas G. Aylesworth subdivides industrial pollution into six broad areas: floating matter, such as detergents and oil; colloidal matter caused by polishing compounds and chemicals; settleable solids, such as metal filings and coal dust; dissolved solids, such as mineral salts; toxic substances which poison living things or change the environment in such a way that they cause the death of plants and animals; sludge originating from sewage treatment plants and food processors.[7] All of these pollutants have a serious effect on human and animal lives and can cause problems ranging from relatively minor sicknesses to death.

A Religious Foundation of Human Relations

The hazards of pollution are vividly illustrated by incidents similar to one which occurred in Riverside, California, in the spring of 1965. At that time, an epidemic of gastroenteritis affecting 18,000 people was caused by what was believed to be a chemical poison entering the water supply from industry.[8] Earlier, in 1964, 12.7 million fish were killed nationally by industrial water pollution.[9] When we review these data, the meaning of Isaiah 19:8 becomes clear: "The fishers also shall mourn, and all they that cast angle into the brooks shall lament, and they that spread nets upon the waters shall languish." Public recreation along the waterways will be nonexistent soon if steps are not taken to reduce industrial pollution of our lakes and rivers.[10]

In general, private industries are united against federal regulation of water pollution. Their major arguments revolve around the high cost of preventing it. Those using this argument seem to be too concerned with profits and too insensitive to the needs and sufferings of people. Only a few industrialists define waterways as places of pleasure for the public or as habitats for aquatic life; most define them in terms of how much waste they can assimilate. The assimilation usually stops just short of rendering waters unnavigable for boats. Within this perspective, the thought of protecting and preserving human life has low priority.

Most Americans take water for granted. It has always been here, they reason, and it will never diminish. In reality, when placed within a world-wide perspective, the water problem is worse than the food problem. More than 3 billion people have either an unacceptable quality or an inadequate quantity of water. Oblivious to, or unmindful of this fact, the affluent portion of the world continues to increase its per capita use of water. As more water is polluted, rich and poor nations alike are sharing a common malady: inadequate water for their existing life-styles.

Equally revealing has been the general public's lackadaisical attitude toward pollution. The absence of a mass outcry and protest can be interpreted to mean that the public has been willing to pay the cost of bad health and limited recreation in order to possess the material goods and luxury associated with water pollution. For example, Lake Erie has no unpolluted swimming waters, and only thirty-five miles of New York City's 575-mile shoreline and water front are fit for swimming.

Only recently have we begun to hear a weak protest against the desecration of our water. Slowly, individuals and groups of all ages are joining the campaign to stop pollution, and if they are successful, they will force the federal, state, and local governments to develop programs to control it.[11] Because waterborne disease is most unusual in the United States, it is difficult to mount a crisis campaign. Water-pollution problems in America are not directly associated with health and the spread of disease; rather, they center on fish and wildlife habitat and recreational activities. Much remains to be done. We seem to be only a step away from a condition described in II Kings 3:19: "And ye shall smite every fenced city, and every choice city, and shall fell every good tree, and stop all wells of water, and mar every good piece of land with stones."

POPULATION

"I will make thee fruitful," the Lord said to Jacob in Genesis 48:4, "and multiply thee, and I will make of thee a multitude of people." We could describe these words as characterizing one of Jehovah's emotional periods, marked by large mood swings alternating between expansiveness and fits of irritation. As was typical in that day, the statements set in motion human interactions that surfaced thousands of years later in the form of a human-relations problem. In many ways, the nations of the earth have become like Mother Goose:

> *There was an old woman who lived in a shoe;*
> *She had so many children because*
> *she didn't know what to do.*[12]

A Religious Foundation of Human Relations

As we approach the second millennium, wondering, as some writers say, whether God is dead or just does not want to get involved, we are beginning to see with accelerating clarity the awesome dimensions of our population problem. Perhaps the most graphic illustration of the population-control numbers game, as defined by Paul Ehrlich in his book *The Population Bomb*, is doubling time, the span, in years, of the interval within which a given population replicates itself.[13] The first doubling of the human population, from 2.5 million in 1,000,000 B.C. to 5 million in 8,000 B.C., took almost a million years; current doubling (and now we are speaking of a population well over 4 billion) has required approximately 35 years. Extrapolating from these data, it is likely that before most of us die, we will be surrounded by our contemporaries. Our great-grandchildren will face a world radically different from the one we know today.

Without greater conservation, the dwindling resources of this planet will be stretched beyond their means in trying to support the world's population. The facts of the situation offer a frightening syllogism: Since practitioners in the art of exploiting natural resources offer little hope of radical short-term increases and since a leveling off of the world's population seems improbable within the next fifty years, we are led inexorably to the seemingly unavoidable probability of a rapid and radical increase in the death rate.

A cancer is an uncontrolled multiplication of cells; the population explosion is an uncontrolled multiplication of people. Treating only the symptoms of cancer may make the victim more comfortable at first, but eventually he dies—often horribly. A similar fate awaits a world with a population explosion if only the symptoms are treated. We must shift our efforts from treatment of the symptoms to the cutting out of the cancer. The operation will demand many apparently brutal and heartless decisions. The pain may be intense. But the disease is so far advanced that only with radical surgery does the patient have a chance of survival.[14]

Control

Ecologically, then, nothing is going well. Everyone and everything seems to have let us down:

1. We have been unable to convince the poor and disinherited of the world that procreation, conceivably the only pleasurable and productive activity in their lives, is against their best interests.

2. Our governments, increasingly of late, seem largely to be in the hands of fools and charlatans.

3. The so-called Green Revolution, the agricultural eureka upon which so many people have laid their hopes, is turning brown around the edges. Writes Ehrlich: "Only the naive still have faith that science can pull some kind of technological rabbit out of the hat at the last minute to save us. The more sophisticated are beginning to realize that such rabbits tend to have big appetites and super-abundant noxious droppings."[15]

It seems likely that within the next generation, humankind will suffer a catastrophic nutritional, pestilential, environmental, or nuclear disaster. The loss of a billion people through some failure of our overtaxed ecosystem before the end of the 1980's is a grim possibility. Ehrlich offers plausible scenarios to support his conviction that despite rapid and affirmative action on a worldwide scale, such a cataclysm is a virtual certainty.

One way or another, the human population explosion will probably come to an end well before it reaches the often discussed UN projection of some 6.5 billion people in the year 2000. It would be a miracle if the halt were caused by a precipitous decline in family sizes to below replacement level all over the world. Lacking miracles, the halt will occur in the only other way possible—through the drastic shortening of the lives of enormous numbers of human beings.[16]

No greater blessing could be granted in ancient times than "Increase, both you and your sons." The acute need for large numbers of children, guaranteeing survival of some to child-

A Religious Foundation of Human Relations

bearing age, was related to work power for the family and security for the parents during their old age. Of singular importance was the perpetuation of the family name. In Deuteronomy 25:5, the Israelites are told that when brothers live together and one of them dies without leaving a son, his widow shall not marry outside the family. Her husband's brother shall marry her and the first son she bears shall perpetuate the dead brother's name so that it may not be blotted out from Israel.

The situation has changed. The earth, which was given to all humankind, is unable to satisfy the insatiable appetites of an ever increasing population. This imbalance has caused some writers to question whether there is still a time to be born and a time to die (Ecclesiastes 3:2). Sophisticated medical technology allows us to dictate time of birth, if indeed birth is even considered desirable, and has vastly changed the pattern of life expectancy. The concept of bountiful Mother Earth has been shattered. There is a pastoral poignancy in the concept of life as outlined in Ezekiel 34:25–27, where men and women shall live in peace on the open pastures and sleep in the woods. They will settle in the hills and God will send them rain in due season, blessed rain. Trees in the countryside shall bear their fruit, the land shall yield its produce, and the human beings of the earth shall live in peace of mind on their own soil.

Gordon R. Taylor has noted that 7.5 per cent of the world's population (North America) is consuming 50 per cent of the world's yield of basic resources.[17] By the year 2000, if the rate of procreation continues as projected and resources were unrestricted, North America will be using almost all of the world's resources. Taylor predicts that by 2000 the world population will be seven billion persons, existing in an environment far more industrialized than it is today. There are those who contend that the world could support fifteen billion people, and then there are those who believe that world society will collapse before this point is reached. Time becomes a major determining factor, and no one can say with certainty that there is enough time left.

Control

It becomes imperative to spread word of the population danger; childbearing people are the primary, certainly the most immediate, target. Of considerable importance are those younger people who are not yet affected by the child-producing syndrome. Even young children may be led to a simple, meaningful understanding of the difficulty of feeding everyone in the world if every person capable of doing so reproduces himself or herself. Clearly, more people must be exposed to the realities of dwindling resources as these relate to support of the world's population.

Deuteronomy 4:9-10 admonishes us not to forget the things we have seen with our own eyes, nor let them pass from our minds as long as we live, but teach them to our children and grandchildren. Only through education is there hope for voluntary individual birth control. It makes little difference what sort of contraceptives are available or how easy it may be to secure abortions if people are not willing to produce fewer children.[18] The people of Japan have accomplished this feat; there was no alternative, since space has run out for them. Education, implemented by the communications media, was the primary factor in leading the Japanese people to voluntary birth control. So widely accepted in Japan is the need for birth control that a family of more than three children is the exception rather than the rule of procreation.

Taylor offers solutions in terms of government incentives based on finances. For instance, there might be a tax bonus for every year of married life when a couple does not produce a child; conversely, there could be a tax increase for each child beyond two per married couple. In the seventh chapter of I Corinthians, Paul addressed the subject of alternatives to the production of children as a primary goal for a married couple. He encouraged celibacy, realizing that such condition is not widely appealing. He suggested abstinence from sexual activity temporarily, between husband and wife, to enable them to focus more clearly upon the business of the Lord. Paul seemed to be countering the strength of the sex drive and offering options beyond those in Genesis 3:16: "Unto the woman he said, I will greatly multiply thy sorrow and thy conception; in sorrow thou shalt bring forth children; and thy desire shall be to thy husband, and he shall rule over thee."

If voluntary incentive methods fail to reduce population, the most viable alternative will be government control of the right to reproduce. One can imagine the vast implications, particularly from a religious point of view, of the latter method. For instance, what would happen in those countries, such as Canada and Ireland, in which there is political schism attributable to a Catholic-Protestant struggle for power? Could such countries accept government intervention in the matter of procreation, especially when political power is equated with population (votes)? The same dilemma confronts black and other racial or ethnic minority groups in America.

Even though there are other questions for which we do not have answers, population control seems plausible. Anticipating negative responses, Taylor cautioned that critical steps must be taken immediately. The problem of pollution must be accepted universally as a problem shared to some extent by all people of the world. Top priority must be accorded to research in the various areas of population, environmental, and pollution control; funds must be made available to dedicated, competent experts in these fields. Once the problem areas have been delineated, a massive educational effort must be launched, requiring additional funds and expertise.

In theory, then, if the people of the world are prepared, they can and would launch a concerted attack upon their enemies: the components of pollution and overpopulation. Assuming that the battle would be won by such positively reinforced troops, it would then follow that every effort would be made to keep the world from finding itself in a similar situation in the conceivable future. Can we do it? Taylor concluded: "If he [man] does make a mess of it, at least there will be no one around to say 'I told you so.' It is the future of the human race that we have been talking about."[19]

According to Richard A. Falk, most people agree that there are already too many people in the world and that there will

Control

be many more in the future. Population problems touch on a fundamental issue of human existence: the degree to which individuals should be free to determine the size of their own families, regardless of social and political consequences.[20]

The problem of population pressure dates back to early societies. It is not yet widely appreciated that dramatic increases in world population reflect a falling death rate rather than a rising birth rate. An increasing proportion of the children born reach childbearing age under today's improving public-health conditions, especially with respect to the prevention of infant mortality and the control, by vaccines and insecticides, of lethal diseases, such as malaria and yellow fever, and their carriers. The relationship between falling death rates and static birth rates illustrates the dangerous effects of uneven rates of change. Medical technology, especially epidemiology, has been able to find very effective and rather inexpensive techniques to protect populations against certain kinds of killer diseases. These techniques can be superimposed upon a developing nation's social structure at a low, bearable cost and bring economically underprivileged societies some of the benefits of modern medicine. Birth-control technology, however, is not very easy to disseminate, nor is it very popular in many countries.

Nearly everyone agrees that it is desirable for a government to do what it can to prevent death, but fewer people are prepared to say it is desirable to prevent birth. Falk contends that among poor people everywhere the experience of bearing and rearing children is one of the few genuine pleasures attending an otherwise miserable existence. Moreover, attitudes toward family size are shaped by expectations in earlier generations of much higher infant mortality, often as much as 50 per cent, and these attitudes are retained in the collective subconscious of societies. It takes many generations to reflect a new situation in which 85 to 99 per cent of all infants born survive and have excellent prospects of reaching adulthood. It is not surprising, therefore, that women in Appalachia, central cities, India or Chile continue to want on the average at least three children and generally are not even interested in birth control until after the third or fourth child.

Reducing population growth is not simply a matter of putting the right kind of birth-control pill or intrauterine device (IUD) into the hands of women. The development of a socially constructive attitude toward birth control is just as important as the provision of adequate technology. Falk suggests that the underlying issue of human choice is far more complex than it is with the avoidance or deferment of death by the introduction of better medical facilities or the distribution of better drugs. Rumors and horror stories travel fast in low-income subcultures. Reports that the pill causes cancer of the cervix and the IUD leads to internal bleeding discourage their widespread use and lead women to be more reluctant to practice birth-control. These reports and rumors are likely to be believed, whether true or not, especially in communities and countries where the level of education is low, superstitions are widespread, and many people are generally suspicious about the bad effects of the modern world.

From another dimension, we are burdened with a double level of permissiveness in trying to evolve a rational population policy. World interest depends on the wisdom and conscience of national governments, and national governments depend on the wisdom and conscience of their individual citizens. Former President Richard M. Nixon combined his concern about population pressure with reaffirmation of an individual's right to refrain from family planning and create a family in accord with his religious views, personal interests, values, and preferences. The United Nations Declaration of Human Rights avoids any direct affirmation of such a right, but it does endorse individual freedom to establish and build a family without governmental interference.

The essential point appears to be that neither the pattern of human attitudes nor the structure of national governments seems compatible to the realities of population pressure. The first corrective step is to recognize that population policy is a matter of world interest. The second would be to move national

Control

thinking from a mood of concern into programs of action. Currently, tax and welfare policies subsidize births rather than reward birth control. Some critics caution that progress toward fulfilling the national interest might lead to breaking down the structure of family autonomy that has evolved from earlier views of the relationship between the individual and national government.

Governments are hesitant to interfere with the family or to establish standards regulating family size. Most citizens consider the issue minute in relation to the aggregate problems plaguing local and national governments. In thinking about population policy, several distinct points seem paramount. First, there are fundamental uncertainties about future behavior; these arise from an individual's ability to shape his destiny. Second, there are too many diverse opinions to establish a tolerable world social system. Third, problems associated with world population are aggravated by the distribution of people and by the continued growth of national population in countries with high per capita income. Fourth, the longer we defer effective action to prevent further population growth, the more difficult it becomes to avoid adjustments based on coercion and catastrophe. Fifth, purely voluntary approaches to family planning do not promise to prevent further population growth or reduce the average number of children per family in most national societies.

Quite frankly, the process of fixing population thresholds raises profound issues of life-style and time scale. For example, if the United States adopts a low-population, high-consumption model of accommodation and India adopts a high-population, low-consumption model of accommodation, these two kinds of cultural choices should be protected and understood. At the same time, we need a concept of equality that will not force some parts of the world to endure a disproportionate share of the burden of accommodating overpopulation.

In May 1971 the secretary-general of the United Nations Conference on the Human Environment commissioned an unofficial report dealing with the problems relating to our en-

A Religious Foundation of Human Relations

vironment. A significant portion of the report, written by Barbara Ward and Rene Dubos, deals with the population explosion.[21] According to Ward and Dubos, an interesting phenomenon which occurs in technologically advanced countries is self-imposed birth control. Their citizens no longer need to have a dozen children to ensure that two or three will reach adulthood, they no longer need available manpower to help them raise food and protect the family, nor do they need a large family to ensure they will be cared for in later life. The result is a self-imposed limit on the number of children produced. Technology has replaced the need for large families with medicine, modernized farming, welfare, and social security.

Uncontrolled population growth, then, is concentrated in the so-called primitive and emerging nations. For several reasons, it is not economically feasible for them to achieve technological and cultural advances that bring about self-imposed population control. The most important reason, of course, is the time involved. Natural phenomena, such as famine, will control population before the technological advancements can cause voluntary curtailment.

Emerging societies must concentrate their resources on long-range capital and technological improvements. Rapid population growth requires allocation of the same resources and capital; the result is fragmentation of effort. Eventually, there comes a time when individuals cannot return to society, in labor, skill, and so forth, an equal value for what they drain from society's resources. Each of us reaches the point where he or she is no longer contributing to society but is only a burden.

The range of problems resulting from technology disorients people who depend primarily on the Bible as the ultimate source of reference and authority. Few biblical writers even hinted that technological advancements would prolong life, decrease death and disease, allow the labor of a few to support millions with food, and produce a population that is potentially too large for the earth. The concept of motherhood as a means of women's salvation or the idea of a time for dying were conceived long before technology could interfere with natural population controllers, such as disease and famine.

A person advocating population control espouses ideas contrary to those on which our Judaeo-Christian culture is based. Any attempt to divert destiny from its course, to avoid the natural control of overpopulation by war or famine, is not in keeping with the historical concept of our cultural origins. However, the power to prevent disease or to stave off death probably would have impressed the ancients as much as the power to part the Red Sea.

We have made progress so rapidly that our technology has outdistanced our humaneness. Thus in suggesting solutions to problems, such as population explosion, we must go beyond the traditional reference points of our Judaeo-Christian-based culture and pose solutions that the ancients would have called miracles. Since we have created the problem by technologically tampering with the natural order, it seems right that we must now find our own solutions.

SPATIAL CONTROL

People of varying cultural backgrounds not only speak different languages but also tend to perceive social occurrences differently. This results from selective screening mechanisms that have been learned through associations within their individual cultural environments.[22] Indeed, since the time of the symbolic biblical Tower of Babel, people have been dispersed throughout various regions of the earth, separated by differences in culture and language. Most ethnologists believe that aggression is an inherently animalistic but essential element of the human being's makeup. The need for it results in the proper spacing of animals, thereby preventing them from becoming so numerous that they and their environment are destroyed.

A Religious Foundation of Human Relations

The population of an area is in direct proportion to the number of interactions its residents experience. Drastically increasing interactions, a result of overcrowding, lead to higher levels of stress. Edward T. Hall asserts that as stress intensifies, "subtle but powerful changes occur in the chemistry of the body. . . . Under this (Malthusian) doctrine . . . births drop while deaths progressively increase until a state known as population collapse occurs. Such cycles of buildup and collapse are now generally recognized as normal for the warm-blooded vertebrates and possibly for all life."[23] Citing studies conducted by John Christian and V. C. Wynne-Edwards to support his thesis, Hall asserts that food supply plays only an indirect role in this phenomenon.

Given the high saturation level of poor blacks, whites, Chicanos, and other minorities, it follows that our inner cities are places of considerable frustration and stress. In some instances, stress which exceeds individual tolerance levels is dissipated through socially unacceptable means; crime and violence become commonplace. In order to combat this situation, Hall concluded, and if America is to survive, it is imperative that we rebuild and improve our cities, regardless of cost. Further, the reconstruction should be based on the best available research findings in order to maximize individual need fulfillment. The results of overcrowding are corroborated in biblical history in the fall of Sodom and Gomorrah; even then it led to violent, socially unacceptable behavior. When crowded, most people tend to run or fight.

Among their own kind, animals defend and seem to respect individual areas or territories. Such concepts as *flight distance* (the distance which an animal will permit a perceived or real enemy to approach before it flees) and *critical distance* (slightly less than flight distance, this is the point at which an animal, when cornered, will attack) are readily understood by the experienced hunter or animal trainer. There are species of animals that require physical contact and others that require little or no contact. Essentially, noncontact animals maintain a constant degree of personal distance between themselves

Control

and others of their kind, whereas contact animals stay in close proximity, often sniffing and touching one another. As social animals, humans maintain close distance, but as danger becomes increasingly imminent, it becomes even closer; upon threat of attack, the tendency is to band together into a tightly knit group for common defense.[24] This accounts in part for the crowding together in inner cities of ethnic groups who feel threatened. In biblical times, the cities of refuge illustrate this attempt at coping with danger (see Joshua 20:7–9).

In order to alleviate crowded conditions, the alternative to rebuilding is displacing some of the occupants to other, less crowded communities. This course of action, however, disrupts family and individual life-styles and tends to cause great resentment and psychological distress in the people being moved and residents of the communities to which they are moved. Clearly, the individual cultural needs of the group must be considered carefully.

As we consider Hall's thesis further, it seems insufficient merely to grant another individual or group the care or consideration we would expect to receive under similar conditions (although it would be a good starting point). Rather, in order to assure true community welfare, each person must be placed in a position where he can secure for himself those elements of his environment that are essential to his well-being and continued development. This is not a treatise of segregation or a cancellation of cultural accomplishments, for as humans we have the capacity to transcend racial/cultural problems. The earlier reference to Babel, where the various races and cultures conspired to destroy each other, can be a model for us *not* to emulate. Our choices are few: we can come together and share our limited space in peace or we can create our own Armageddon.

ABORTION

Perhaps no issue of our time involving a religious question has raised so much rancor and recrimination as the problem of abortion. Abortion, an act voluntarily produced with intent to destroy the fetus, usually occurs before the twenty-eighth week of pregnancy. Central to arguments for or against legalized abortion are distinctions between feticide and infanticide. Feticide is synonymous with abortion and implies that the fetus is destroyed before birth; infanticide means destruction of a newborn child by the parents or with their consent.

Neutral observers, unable to understand either the complex matters involved or the intense bitterness generated, might well be excused for thinking that both the proponents and opponents of abortion are indeed worthy philosophical descendants of the medieval Scholastics. "There is no other public issue (not even 'Communism')," observed Howard Moody, "in which *demonology* is so prevalent. If your adversary is the personification of evil and believes only in the destruction of life — whether that of the *fetus* or the *woman* who wants a safe, legal abortion — then there is no ground for conversation or accommodation."[25] The tragedy of the debate is that moral theologians and ethicists on both sides have been overshadowed by extremists.

Without doubt, the immediate reason why the abortion controversy has been rekindled so violently is the 1973 Roe decision of the U.S. Supreme Court, which ruled that "the right of privacy, whether it be founded in the Fourteenth Amendment's concept of personal liberty and restrictions upon state action, as we feel it is, or as the District Court determined, in the Ninth Amendment's reservation of rights to the people, is broad enough to encompass a woman's decision whether or not to terminate her pregnancy."[26] Furthermore, the court concluded:

1. The state has no compelling interest to infringe upon such a fundamental right; thus it cannot regulate or prohibit an abortion during the first trimester of pregnancy. The right to abort or not to abort a fetus during this period belongs to the woman and her physician.

2. The state may "regulate the abortion procedure in ways

Control

that are reasonably related to maternal health," beginning with the second trimester.

3. "If the state is interested in protecting fetal life after viability, it may go so far as to proscribe abortion during that period, except when it is necessary to preserve the life or health of the mother."[27]

Immediately after the decision, the battle lines were tightly drawn, with former Representative Lawrence Hogan and Senator James Buckley unsuccessfully introducing in Congress a constitutional amendment to nullify the court's decision. In 1976 the U.S. Supreme Court ruled that states cannot require a woman seeking an abortion to get consent from her husband, nor force an unmarried female under 18 years of age desiring an abortion to get permission from a parent.

Many persons who are either neutral or biased observers in the abortion debate do not know that there are actually two major historical positions on the issue in the Roman Catholic church. The Greek church fathers generally held that the human soul is present from the instant of conception, hence abortion is always murder. Among the chief theologians holding this view were Gregory of Nyssa, Basil of Caesarea, and Abbot St. Maximus, and it is largely their views on the matter which are now usually held by the clergy and laity of the Roman Catholic church. The issue in question here, of course, is that of hominization, or infusion of the soul. To put it briefly, is the human embryo a person from the moment of fertilization?

The second position, held by St. Thomas Aquinas, is that motion is a principle of life and that abortion is not murder if it is performed before movement by the fetus in the womb has occurred. As did his philosophical master, Aristotle, St. Thomas believed that there is a distinct difference between *potentiality* and *actuality;* although the fetus is potentially human before movement, it is not actually human until after movement has taken place. It must be borne in mind that when St. Thomas was writing (about the middle of the thirteenth cen-

A Religious Foundation of Human Relations

tury), it was generally thought that no movement of the male fetus occurred in the womb before the fifth month of pregnancy.[28] Patrick J. O'Mahony maintains that the exact reason why the position of the Greek fathers, often referred to as the theory of immediate hominization, became the general official position of the Roman Catholic church is open to question; it is possible the church was hesitant to accept St. Thomas' position because it might leave the impression that abortion was favored in some way.[29]

Recent official pronouncements from the Roman Catholic church have tended to follow the inflexible line of the early Greek fathers. Pope Pius XII was explicit in his condemnation of abortion:

The baby in the maternal breast has the right to life immediately from God. Hence there is no man, no human authority, no science, no medical, eugenic, social, economic or moral "indication" which can establish or grant a valid juridical ground for a direct deliberate disposition of an innocent human life, that is a disposition which looks to its destruction either as an end or as a means to another end perhaps in itself not illicit. The baby, still not born, is a man in the same degree and for the same reason as the mother.[30]

The phrase "either as an end or as a means to another end perhaps in itself not illicit" is a significant one for the Roman Catholic and antiabortionists, since it clearly refers to the pronouncement of Pope Pius XI against abortion.

Observing that many people justify abortion because it may save the life of the mother or bring about some good end, Pope Pius XI nevertheless strongly maintained that "the killing of the innocent is unthinkable and contrary to the divine precept promulgated in the words of the Apostle: Evil is not to be done that good may come of it."[31]

Father O'Mahony calls our attention to the teaching of Vatican II: "From the first moment of its conception life must be guarded with great care, while abortion and infanticide are unspeakable crimes." However, he goes on to conclude from this pronouncement that "life from the 'first moment' is

Control

not necessarily equated with infanticide." Finally, he is moved to ask the question: "Does the Council imply that in the early stages of pregnancy the *conceptus* is not *ipso facto* a human person and therefore has not automatically an absolute right to live?"[32]

Father O'Mahony also reviewed a lengthy argument by Father V. Fagone which appeared in two issues of the quasi-official Roman journal *La Civilta Catholica* on June 16 and July 7, 1973. Father Fagone defended the idea that the unborn when hominized, is a human person and that his recognition as a human person does not depend on his relationship with either his parents or his society. Father O'Mahony noted that for him (O'Mahony) the crucial question concerning abortion is: "When is the *conceptus* a human person?" He agrees with the conclusion of Father Fagone: "The fertilized ovum is, from its earliest stages, an ontological, unique individual being. There is a continuity of life from the process of fertilization till the process of death—a point emphasized by all Episcopal conferences."[33]

A 1972 poll of American Roman Catholic church members shows that sixty-seven per cent of the people questioned agreed with the church's traditional position that abortion is immoral.[34] Thus it appears that the majority of American Roman Catholics would take the same position as that of Bishop Walter W. Curtis: "Let me emphasize at this point that abortion—the destruction of the life of an unborn child before or after viability—is morally wrong. Abortion denies the right to life to the unborn child; it affronts human dignity; and it violates God's law prohibiting killing. Neither civil laws nor court decisions are able to change the moral judgment that abortion is wrong."[35] Whether the majority of American Roman Catholics would further agree with Bishop Curtis that an amendment to the United States Constitution is needed is open to question.

It should be noted that all Roman Catholic priests are not committed to the church's traditional position on abortion; a counterposition is being heard more and more from some. This side of the controversy was defined well by an editorial in the Catholic weekly *Commonweal*:

Abortion is a personal and social evil. With a few exceptions—like treatment of a rape victim soon after the attack or the removal of an already gravely damaged fetus (in this case anticipating nature's tendency to abort)—it is difficult to imagine abortions that do not involve varying degrees of moral guilt, personal tragedy and violence to the real or potential dignity of the human person. Abortion is failure: the parents' failure, often because of circumstances out of their control, to assume responsibility for the new life they have begun; society's failure to provide the moral and cultural environment in which each new life would be welcomed, nourished, preserved. But it is also the church's failure. Failure to understand a generation ago that family planning and artificial birth control differed radically from abortion and were not necessarily forms of sexual immorality but potentially positive means of both preserving married love and enhancing respect for life.[36]

Such criticism of the church and its members is becoming more common, for as Robert N. Lynch rather cynically observes: "Parish priests, who must form the forward phalanx in any educational or political efforts, are turned off by the abortion issue in large part because of the cold fact that, too often, today's prolifer is the same person who yesterday was beating the rectory door down on the sex-education program in the parish school."[37]

Gary L. Chamberlain warned that so long as Catholics offer no real alternatives to abortion, their opposition will appear destructive to the quality of life in the modern age. The Roman Catholic church, he charged, "has generally failed to put its money where its mouth is."[38] The more conservative members of the hierarchy and laity surely will feel disquieted when they examine Chamberlain's set of alternatives to abortion because it proposes

a radical questioning of American values and priorities and an enlightened program to change attitudes, for example, toward the stigma of an unwed, pregnant mother. The program would seriously push for child care centers for working mothers, aid

Control

to dependent children, free obstetrical care, full, free counseling for women carrying "unwanted" children and the fathers involved, economic assistance for families suffering the financial burden of another child. There should be funds available for the prevention and correction of defects, and aid for handicapped children and their families.[39]

It is likely that on the issue of abortion, the Roman Catholic church is going to be strained to keep the allegiance of a majority of its members, particularly the younger ones, unless it gives its full support to programs similar to those outlined above.

The argument that God has granted all people the right of self-determination is the basis for an extended defense of abortion by Willis E. Wygant, Jr., a minister of the United Church of Christ. The Reverend Wygant bases his reasoning on Scripture and theological concepts: "Since self-determination is a part of human life, it comes to human beings from the source of all creation, which is God Himself. It is understood that there are always limitations to our human decisions and that we are, therefore, not completely free. However, limited though it is, our freedom is real; it is never license, which implies no limits."[40] It is clear, he continues, that Scripture recognizes the self-determination of man as bestowed by God, for in Genesis 1:1-28 we read that man is told to "fill the earth and subdue it, and have dominion over every living thing that moves upon the earth." The Reverend Wygant maintains that this passage shows man is to have control over God's creation.

Furthermore, Reverend Wygant states, in the New Testament man's right of self-determination from God is shown in Luke 6:12-13, when twelve men chosen out of a group of Jesus' followers freely agree to become his disciples. Nor should we overlook Mark 10:17-22, he says. Instead of berating the young man who rejected eternal life because the price was too high, Jesus allowed him to depart. Reverend Wygant concludes: "These two biblical incidents not only show Jesus' respect for the person's right of self-determination, but point up the fact that Jesus actually could do nothing else, since self-determination is truly in the hands of the individual in question."[41]

The individual can be praised or blamed—that is, be held responsible—for his or her actions only insofar as he or she has the ability and the right to make choices. The Reverend Wygant maintains this is precisely why God has given us the right to self-determination. From this perspective, any antiabortion law, besides violating both God's gift to man and the U.S. Constitution, also is "responsible for the unwanted children that follow, for much of the starvation and poverty problems that we find in our world, and for the deaths of pregnant women who seek medically unsafe abortions."[42] For these reasons, the Reverend Wygant hold that "the parents, particularly the mother, should make the decision relative to abortion on the grounds of self-determination. . . . After all, only the prospective parents know whether or not they want a child, want to be parents, or have the social and economic potential for raising children."[43]

An interesting point raised by Joseph Fletcher is that there may be higher values than the simple perpetuation of life itself, though it appears that the official Roman Catholic argument against abortion denies this:

For those who believe in the metaphysics of substance and accidents, who are convinced that the medieval sacramental theology was a true account of real things, it makes sense to refuse to terminate fetal development. But one more assumption is required for the antiabortion argument. Even if you are willing to revive the medieval notion of the "homunculus" (a miniscule person down in the fetus, maybe even in the sperm or ovum), you still have to assume (judge) that life is the highest good (summum bonum), thus taking priority over all other values—health, quality of life, resources for wellbeing, and so on. This is a vitalistic ethics, and it makes human life sacrosanct, taboo, untouchable.[44]

Fletcher argues further that a large number of knowledgeable individuals are deeply concerned that in our modern world such things as health, quality of life, and resources for well-being may indeed be of higher value than the future value of an embryo. He sees any attempt to write a national anti-abortion law as tyrannical because "it is difficult if not impossible to see how church metaphysics or divine revelations or individual value preferences can be imposed by law on those who do not believe them to be either true or wise."[45]

Certainly, however, it should not be assumed that all representatives of Protestantism automatically reject the Roman Catholic call for a constitutional amendment to prohibit abortion. During a hearing on a proposed antiabortion constitutional amendment before a subcommittee of the U.S. House of Representatives, Eugene W. Linse, Jr., and Jean Garton of the Lutheran Church—Missouri Synod urged "restoration of legal protection for the unborn."[46]

There are at least two controversial Old Testament passages which, depending on one's interpretation, seem to condemn the practice of abortion. The first is Exodus 21:22: "If men strive, and hurt a woman with child, so that her fruit depart from her, and yet no mischief follow: he shall be surely punished, according as the woman's husband will lay upon him; and he shall pay as the judges determine." The second is Jeremiah 20:17: "Because he slew me not from the womb; or that my mother might have been my grave, and her womb to be always great with me." It can be argued here that the prophet identifies himself with the fetus in his mother's womb as if he were more than a simple growth there at the time of her pregnancy. However, during a House subcommittee hearing on a proposed constitutional ban on abortion, Rabbi Balfour Brickner, associate director of the Commission on Interfaith Activities of the Union of American Hebrew Congregations, opposed such a ban. Rabbi Brickner explained that abortion is not equated with murder by Judaism, for his faith does not consider the fetus to be a full human being.

Arguing for a woman's right to terminate her pregnancy, H. Tristram Engelhardt, Jr., asserted that if the fetus is a person, to abort it is murder. He defines a human person as a rational animal, saying: "Only that which is rational, self-conscious, and embodied in an animal organism counts as a human person."[47] Engelhardt pointed out that St. Thomas Aquinas agreed with Aristotle that the fetus is only potentially a person until it begins to move: "At most, the fetus is an animal with great promise of becoming more than just an animal. One speaks more of what the fetus will do or will be as a person, rather than what it is."[48] According to this view, the council question is how, exactly, to define the term *human*. According to Engelhardt, although a being in early infancy cannot be said to be fully a human person, "the child is appreciated socially as an individual to whom one has actual—not potential—obligations in a fashion quite different from the fetus in the mother-fetus relationship."[49] Thus in this argument a crucial question is resolved: There are not two persons concerned when a pregnancy is terminated or not terminated; there is only one: the mother.

And the debate goes on. So too does abortion. In 1974, for example, there was one legal abortion for every four live births in America.

EUTHANASIA

Euthanasia, which means "good death" or "happy death," refers to either the commission of some act that shortens a person's life or the omission of an act that would prolong it. Legally, euthanasia, like suicide, is not permitted by American law. Efforts to legalize euthanasia came to the fore in 1938, when the Euthanasia Society of America was organized. The three areas of focus by most proponents are: compulsory euthanasia for the aged, incurably diseased, and the insane; compulsory euthanasia for monstrocities and defectives in the early stages of life; and voluntary euthanasia for the dying.

Certainly these are not new concepts. Aristotle, for example, felt "there should be a law that no *deformed child* shall be reared."[50] Listen to Seneca: "If one death is accompanied by torture, and the other is simple and easy, why not snatch the latter? Just as I select my ship, when I am about to go on a voyage, or my house when I propose to take a residence, so shall I choose my death when I am about to depart from life."[51]

In order to illuminate the issues, Earl C. Dahlstrom poses several questions:

Is life defined by those factors, such as respiration and circulation, with which the medical examiner or coroner is concerned? Can life be said to continue after its psychological values have disappeared? If there is only the "whole person" so that body, mind, and spirit are basically inseparable dimensions of the whole, can life be said to continue in only one of these dimensions? If death occurs only when the cells of the body die, if death occurs at different times in different cells and organs, and if biological death can be postponed by the action of machines, is there any objective way of defining when human life ends except as its vital functions are unable to manifest themselves spontaneously without the help of artificial processes? . . . If death may be legally or morally preferred to intense suffering, may it be preferred to drugged stupor? If drugged stupor may be legally or morally preferred to great pain, why then cannot death?[52]

Whatever its formal interpretation, euthanasia, or facilitating death either by commission or omission, is forbidden by moral tradition, by law, and by the Hippocratic oath that governs medical practice, yet it is currently receiving increased public support. When asked in a Gallup Poll, "If a person has an incurable disease do you think doctors should be allowed by law to painlessly end a patient's life, if his family requests it?" fifty-three per cent of the respondents answered affirmatively.[53] "Yet this trend runs directly counter to the emphasis which the Jewish and Christian tradition place upon life as God's gift, not to be disposed of by human hands," Thomas C. Oden observed. "According to Jewish and Christian Scripture, God alone is the author of life and no human being has the right to end the life of another."[54]

So urgent has consideration of a definition of legal death become that the 187th General Assembly of the United Presbyterian church was petitioned thus: "Therefore, the Presbytery of Des Moines, in its Stated Meeting on April 22, 1975 at Williamsburg, Iowa, requests the 187th General Assembly (1975), meeting in Cincinnati, Ohio, to enact a special committee to study the subject 'Determining when death occurs,' and report at the succeeding meeting of the General Assembly."[55]

As the earth becomes more crowded, as life-sustaining devices become more sophisticated and as the demand for organs for transplants increases, new definitions and decisions concerning euthanasia will be required. For twentieth-century men and women, euthanasia poses a complex problem that is certain to proliferate rather than diminish:

It is even medically conceivable that the lower level of vitality of a comatose patient could with mechanical assistance permit his survival for a much longer time than would normally be possible for a person in good health. Suppose that were the case. Is it reasonable, is it ethically reasonable, to maintain such a dependent population which would increase and become longer lived with every technical improvement—in the face of the enormously expensive survival needs of the relatively healthy population and the scarcity of the means by which those needs may be met?[56]

Theology, which has long been consulted for ultimate answers to ultimate problems, is most conspicuous in the euthanasia debate but without consensual consistency, for a broad disparity of perspectives is set forth by Jewish, Catholic, and Protestant leaders in response to this increasingly significant problem. A sampling of their views will suggest the degree of complexity.

A characteristic of Judaic ethics is to translate, whenever possible, abstract moral generalizations into specific legal obligations. Jewish ethics are most clearly found in Jewish law. Therefore, to determine Judaism's position on euthanasia, we ought to consult Jewish legal literature. As is the case with all problems in Jewish law, euthanasia can be posed properly only by exploring the obligations attending a decision concerning it, for basic Jewish law is not predicated upon rights, but upon obligations. To facilitate matters, the following questions may be posed with specific regard to euthanasia:

1. What is an individual dying of a terminal disease obliged to do? What is he permitted to do?

2. What is a physician treating a terminal patient obliged to do? What is he permitted to do?

3. If the life of a terminal patient is ended by the patient himself or by someone else, is the killer a murderer?

4. Are one's obligations toward a terminal patient being kept alive aritifically different from those toward one not being kept alive artificially?

5. Is there any permissible alternative to euthanasia or death for the terminal patient?[57]

There is unusual consensus among rabbinic authorities representing the orthodox, conservative, and reform Judaic approaches in contemporary literature on euthanasia. This situation obtains because of the clear and unequivocal position taken by classical Jewish sources on the subject: "According to Jewish law, 'a dying man is regarded as a living person in all respects.' Active euthanasia—causing or accelerating death in any way—is considered murder."[58]

According to Jewish law, each moment of human life is considered intrinsically sacred. However, according to one Talmudic view, although a physician is admonished not actively to cause a terminal patient's death, he is obliged to attend the patient's illness. It is sometimes the case in the treatment of a patient that drugs prescribed to alleviate unbearable pain may, in fact, accelerate the death process.

From the Jewish perspective, a minority argument for euthanasia is presented in the analogy of a terminally ill patient and a criminal condemned to be executed. It is argued that in instances where a criminal is condemned, there is substance in the law providing that a sentence (for example, death by stoning) may be reduced in both time and degree of affliction. From this premise it is generalized that the terminally ill at least should be accorded treatment equal to that given the condemned criminal—which would allow for reducing the time and degree of their physical affliction.

There is vigorous dispute among Roman Catholics on euthanasia. Those who consider the Catholic position a reflection of the Vatican's pronouncements through a variety of popes cite the guidelines of Pope Pius XI, who proclaimed: "What could ever be a sufficient reason for excusing in any way the direct murder of the innocent?"[59] They also quote Pius XII, who condemned the "deliberate and direct disposing of an innocent human life."[60] In these interpretations, "the innocent" is the key concept, for church members are permitted to kill in self-defense and in war but are prohibited from committing abortions or mercy killings.

Catholics who have other interpretations of the ethical defensibility of euthanasia remind us that this tradition is quite nuanced and advanced regarding the indirect termination of life, which may be defined as an action or omission having some other immediate effect in addition to the death of a person. Such a death, even when predicted to follow an act, need not be intended in itself but merely can be permitted. Writing in *Christian Century*, Merle Longworth said: "On this issue the churches are ahead of other social institutions, perhaps because Christians do not view life as the greatest good, or death as the greatest evil. Moral theologians in general have not argued for the simple prolongation of life. An early and landmark pronouncement was the encyclical promulgated by Pope Pius XII *in 1957*, stating that extraordinary means of prolonging the life of those in coma need not be taken."[61]

Closely related to this pronouncement is the Catholic teaching, papally endorsed, which provides that only ordinary means need be used to prolong life. Any means that involve a grave burden for either the patient or the one who attends him could be classified as extraordinary means. Concerning the latter, Cardinal Jean Villot, Vatican secretary of state, made the

Control

following statements in a 1970 address to the International Federation of Catholic Medical Associations:

A medical man does not have to use all the techniques of survival offered him by a constantly creative science. In many cases would it not be useless torture to impose vegetative resuscitation in the final stages of an incurable sickness? The doctor's duty here is rather to ease the suffering instead of prolonging as long as possible, by any means whatsoever and in any condition whatsoever, a life no longer fully human and which is closing to its natural end. . . .[62]

Discussing the Karen Ann Quinlan case, Thomas C. Oden presents an opposing view:

Regrettably, the majority opinion in American pastoral care and theology jumped too hastily to the side of offering immediate relief to the family without thinking much about precedential consequences. . . . All this is not surprising, however, since American pastoral care and theology both Protestant and more recently Catholic have come too much to rely on a restricted and normless situation ethic which often amounts to sentimental immediacy and emotive concern without attention to normative obligation or long-range social consequences.[63]

Joseph Fletcher discusses the right to live and the right to die from the Protestant perspective. He says there are two major emphases regarding the priorities of man; one gives precedence to rights, the other to needs. The first characterizes the legalistic or moralistic temper, and the second is the overflowing-love or agapistic temper that accords precedence to needs. Delineating his own position as it relates to euthanasia, Fletcher concluded: "As in the balance of rights and needs, needs should come first, so in the balance of biological life and human life being a man or a person is of more value than simply being alive. Martyrs know this and heroes know it; I take it to be the meaning of the Cross."[64]

Contrary to much common sentiment that to employ every possible artificial life-support system in terminal illness is the

A Religious Foundation of Human Relations

benign thing to do, Fletcher argues that modern man must decide whether such tactics are not merely the prolongation of dying rather than the prolongation of living. He also postulates that with the advent of modern technology, death has changed its shape and many older persons now are beginning to fear senility more than death. Fletcher is not alone in his belief that death has ensued when brain function is lost irreversibly, no matter whether heartbeat or blood circulation or breathing persists. The traditional criteria for the determination of death are being replaced by the concept of brain death, as confirmed by retina and deoxygenation tests.

Whatever position we take, it is important to maintain communication with persons who are terminally ill, for "if the patient is to reach a stage of active acceptance of the inevitable, the lines of communication must be maintained and developed, however embarrassing it may be for the healthy ones, staff or relatives who watch and who will be left behind."[65] One dying patient left this sad poem behind for the living to think about:

I huddle warm inside my corner bed,
Watching the other patients sipping tea.
I wonder why I'm so long getting well,
And why it is no one will talk to me.
The nurses are so kind. They brush my hair.
On days I feel too ill to read or sew,
I smile and chat, try not to show my fear,
They cannot tell me what I want to know.
The visitors come in. I see their eyes
Become embarrassed as they pass my bed.
"What lovely flowers!" they say, then hurry on,
In case their faces show what can't be said.
The chaplain passes on his weekly round
With friendly smile and calm, untroubled brow
He speaks with deep sincerity of life,
I'd like to speak of death, but don't know how.

Control

> *The surgeon comes, with student retinue*
> *Mutters to sister, deaf to my silent pleas*
> *I want to tell this dread I feel inside*
> *But they are all too kind to talk to me.*[66]

Despite all philosophical arguments to the contrary, "we see death as the offender, the enemy. With Dylan Thomas we rage against the dying of the light."[67]

AND WOMEN, TOO

As a prelude to the feminist movement in the Church, Jeanne Richie wrote:

It is my conviction that the problem of women's status in American society is urgent, that it cannot be postponed while we attend to apparently more pressing matters—race, youth, war, inflation, the pollution of our air and water. I believe that the systematic subordination of women in America must be ended before these other problems we face will yield to attack. I believe also that this is a question which should be of particular concern to our churches, since they are so heavily dependent on the support of women and since few institutions so systematically deny women full participation.[68]

Many people find it impossible to relate the feminist movement to the Bible in a positive manner. Somewhat dejected, Kate Millett concluded that "patriarchy has God on its side. One of its most effective agents of control is the powerfully expeditious character of its doctrines as to the nature and origin of the female and the attribution to her alone of the dangers and evils it imputes sexuality."[69] Beginning with the Creation, the Bible places women in a subordinate role. When Eve took the blame for tasting the forbidden fruit, the stage was set for centuries of female subjugation. Thus God declares in Genesis 3:16: "I will greatly multiply your pain in child-

A Religious Foundation of Human Relations

bearing, in pain you shall bring forth children yet your desire shall be for your husband, and he shall rule over you." From the earliest pages of the Bible, woman is relegated to second-class citizenship. Analyzing the role of the Christian wife, Rosemary Haughton wrote:

The Christian wife, then, goes to church in her capacity as a wife. She goes decked in her best clothes, not to show off, or because "everyone does," but because her contribution to the sacrifice of thanksgiving is derived from her success as a wife and a mother. The clothes she wears in church will naturally be suited to the occasion, but they should be as feminine and as beautiful as her income allows. They are the symbol of her vocation. . . . Whether her taste and income dictate pretty cottons or gaudy silks or a more sober elegance, she is proclaiming the fact that she worships God as a woman, that she is not ashamed of her femininity and all that that implies. She shows that it is by her feminine qualities, including her power of attracting the opposite sex, that she is trying to fulfill her vocation, and so do her part in building the Kingdom of God on earth.[70]

In Proberbs 31:10-31 we find the belief that the worthy woman is far more precious than jewels, that she does good and not harm for a man all the days of her life. Commenting on the prevailing stereotype of a wife's roles, Judy Syfers noted that most men say: "I want a wife who will take care of my physical needs . . . keep my house clean . . . keep my clothes clean, ironed, and replaced when need be . . . take care of the details of my social life . . . remain sexually faithful . . . understand that my sexual needs may entail more than strict adherence to monogamy. My God, who wouldn't want a wife."[71] In a similar vein, Kate Millett noted that "what requires further emphasis is the responsibility of the female, a marginal creature, in bringing on this plague, and the justice of her suborned condition as dependent on her primary role in this original sin. The connection of women, sex, and sin constitutes the

Control

fundamental pattern of western patriarchal thought thereafter."[72]

In a sympathetic vein, David Riesman mused: "I think what I would ideally like to see in our society is that sex become an ascribed rather than an achieved status. That one is simply born a girl or a boy and that's it. And no worry about an activity's de-feminizing or emasculating one."[73] Riesman will get his wish if the prediction that the family of the future won't even be based on sex or sexual relationship is fulfilled. Until then, however, historical attitudes of woman's place will remain deeply ingrained in institutions influencing employment, income maintenance, marriage, sex relations, maternity, civil rights, housing, divorce, political affairs, and mental health.

Caroline Bird's theory of gradualism describes the stand of the new masculinists within contemporary American life: "It's right for you to have a job . . . but your job, which may bring in a fair amount of money, is to serve the family's menage and not to compete in any way with your husband."[74] New masculinism requires that women work for men. The particular feminine duties are not specified but require individual females to find tasks that men need done from time to time. Women may be liberated in that they may fulfill a man's job as long as they do it in the name of someone else and not for their own power and prestige.

Richie points out what she describes as the debilitating aspects of the Church's sex caste: almost all ministers are males; only outside the mainstream of Protestantism are clergywomen found in relatively large numbers.[75] A woman desiring to make a career of religious work is generally restricted to religious education, where she will assist the minister. This condition obtains even though church membership and attendance are predominantly female, Sunday schools are mainly staffed by women, and church social committees are overwhelmingly female. The exception to this pattern is found in the composition of lay boards which make church policy;

these are predominantly male. Denial of ordination to women is especially offensive to Margaret N. Maxey:

The unsuitability of women themselves for ordination can no longer appeal to genetics for support of social prejudices. The emotional quality of objections to ordaining women was recently epitomized in the question of one horrified reactor: "Pregnant priest?" Anatomy, of course, destines women to be pregnant just as inescapably as it destines men to be celibate. Nevertheless, anatomy and celibacy have been major reasons for excluding women both from having positions with political decision-making power in Christian churches, and from having mutual bonds with those who do.[76]

The ordination issue gained national attention in 1975, when the Reverend L. Peter Beebe of Christ Episcopal Church in Oberlin, Ohio, and the Reverend William A. Wendt of St. Stephen and the Incarnation Church in Washington, D.C., were brought before Episcopal ecclesiastical courts and admonished for allowing women to conduct communion services in their churches. The Reverend Allison Cheek celebrated communion in the Reverend Wendt's church, and the Reverend Carter Heywood conducted a communion service in the Reverend Beebe's church. The Reverends Cheek and Heywood were two of eleven women ordained to the Episcopal priesthood in 1974. However, the Episcopal Church's House of Bishops passed a resolution shortly after the ordinations declaring them invalid and forbidding the women to function as priests. In 1976 the House of Bishops and the House of Deputies reversed the resolution and narrowly voted to permit women to be priests and bishops.

The old masculinists believe that a woman is limited by her anatomy. Although the new masculinists support updating of women's roles, old masculinists—sometimes referred to as the backbone of the nation—prefer the status quo; that is, women should be preoccupied with finding husbands and raising children. Clearly, the ideas of the new feminist are counter to those of the old masculinist. The new feminist feels that sex roles have no place in the world of work, and the old masculinist feels that few women have any place in the world of work.

There are many biblical references to the roles of husband and wife: "Wives, submit yourselves unto your own husbands, as unto the Lord. For the husband is the head of the wife, even as Christ is the head of the church. . . . Therefore as the church is subject unto Christ, so let the wives be to their own husbands in every thing" (Ephesians 5:22-24). "The aged women likewise, that they be in behaviour as becometh holiness, not false accusers, not given to much wine, teachers of good things; that they may teach the young women to be sober, to love their husbands, to love their children, to be discreet, chaste, keepers at home, good, obedient to their own husbands, that the word of God be not blasphemed" (Titus 2:3-5).

The wives depicted in the historical writings exhibit a wide variety of characteristics, yet a coherent picture is not difficult to obtain. The good (ideal) wife is well illustrated by Abigail, wife of Nabal (and later of David) (I Sam. 25:2-42), with supplementary traits drawn from other examples. She is intelligent, beautiful, discreet, and loyal to her husband (despite his stupidity and boorish character in the case of Nabal; see Jer. 2:2). Prudent, quick-witted and resourceful, she is capable of independent action, but always acts in her husband's behalf. The good wife does not attempt to rule her husband, nor does she openly oppose him. She defers to him in speech and action, obeys his wish as his command, and puts his welfare first. She employs her sexual gifts for his pleasure alone and raises up children to his name.[77]

At best, the women's liberation movement is not an activity designed to force women to abandon their role as housewives but a concerted drive to provide equal opportunities in work situations outside the home for women who do not want to be primarily a wife or mother. A few overzealous feminists make the mistake of minimizing the importance and rights of those women who enjoy being wives and mothers.

Paul required that women refrain from fulfilling leadership roles in the church: "Let your women keep silence in the churches: for it is not permitted unto them to speak; but they are commanded to be under obedience, as also saith the law. And if they will learn any thing, let them ask their husbands at home: for it is a shame for women to speak in the church" (I Corinthians 14:34–35). Feminists have leveled sharp criticism at Paul for this and other views he expressed about women. Criticism is especially sharp for his view that woman was created expressly for man and that women should play a subservient role. In fairness to Paul, we should note that other passages attributed to him support women's equality. His insistence upon fidelity in marriage for both men and women renders a biblical injunction against double standards in sex morals. In fact, Paul's statement that "there is neither male nor female . . . in Christ Jesus" (Galatians 3:28) has been quoted frequently to support women's equality.

Just as white males used paternalism to keep blacks in their place during slavery, chivalry is being used to keep women in their place. The old masculinist places women on a pedestal so that he knows where they are at all times. Women in the world of work step down from this pedestal. When Garda Bowman interviewed business executives, she uncovered a great deal of hostility toward female executives. Most of the males queried felt that women were "temperamentally unfit for management."[78] Bowman points out that when male executives become angry, they are admired by other males for their manly anger, but when women executives display the same behavior, they are considered emotionally unstable.

Generally, women who elect to leave their protective pedestals encounter problems in being accepted by men as equals. This is true even when women clearly illustrate their competence. Consequently, many women are criticized when their behavior parallels that of their male counterparts and again when it does not. Even appearance can become an issue, as were the flat-chested, bobbed-hair female styles of the 1920's and the pantsuits of the 1960's and 1970's: "The woman shall not wear that which pertaineth unto a man, neither shall a man put on a woman's garment: for all that do so are abomination unto the Lord thy God" (Deuteronomy 22:5).

An altering and meshing of sex roles will not occur easily. However, Caroline Bird is correct that "sex roles based on a division of labor between men and women are not inevitable just because they have been universal in the past."[79] Yet because sex roles are tied into the Judaeo-Christian ethic, change in this area is likely to be slow, and we should not be surprised if such change is accompanied by discord for several generations. In the end, the conservation and proper use of our human resources, female and male, will be the key in our efforts to save the earth's natural resources.

Like a Bob Dylan song, things are changing, albeit slowly. In 1976 a task force established by Reform Jewish synagogues in the New York City area proposed demasculining the liturgy, dropping the masculine words "Father" and "king" and substituting "community," "unity," or "kinship" for "brotherhood" and "fellowship." Among Christians the National Council of Churches, an umbrella organization of Protestant and Eastern Orthodox churches, has agreed to drop from the next edition of the Revised Standard Version of the Bible all masculine words that are not in the original Greek text.

8
THE HELPING RELATIONSHIP

IN *Church Dogmatics,* Karl Barth outlined four levels of humanity on an ascending scale: the eye-to-eye relationships, mutual speech and hearing, mutual assistance, and all of the three foregoing levels plus a spirit of joy.[1] Looking someone in the eye refers to acknowledging his existence. Mutual speaking and hearing are important because we do not become fully human until we tell others who we are and hear them tell us who they are. And the opposite is true: we do not know who we are until we have heard from others who we are. Next, we need counsel when we are in trouble, food when we are hungry, recognition when we achieve, and so forth. Thus our mutual dependence requires mutual assistance. Finally, Barth observed, human beings cannot really be human without helping each other in a spirit of genuine loving concern.

A successful helping relationship has four characteristics found in Gospel messages of the Bible: universalism, individualism, equality, and freedom. These characteristics are interrelated; in the words of Ernest Troeltsch, "they require each other."[2] The ethical foundation of universalism is individualism, and the subtle implication of individualism is

The Helping Relationship

universalism. Likewise, in the eyes of God, all people are equal in value and status. The equal value given to each person by God does not negate our uniqueness and, consequently, freedom of response.

I-THOU

"How may I understand my experience of a relation with God?"[3] Thus did Martin Buber, the great Jewish philosopher and theologian, characterize the supreme goal of his life, a life marked by deep compassion and profound thought. He grew up with a desire to contribute to modern theology in a world that was rapidly becoming savage, unloving, and uncaring. Until forced by Nazi racism to emigrate to what is now the state of Israel, Buber taught at the University of Frankfürt. As much as any thinker of this century, he has tried to lead modern man away from the feelings of alienation, which he believes produced the holocaust of the Nazi state.

What Buber understood as the helping relationship, the relationship which replaces our sense of alienation, can best be understood only if Buber's philosophy of an I-Thou relationship is grasped in its fullest meaning. He makes it clear that an I-Thou relationship is not completely comprehensible, at least not in the traditionally rational way, because thought alone will not reveal to us the nature of the helping relationship. In Buber's words: "The world is not comprehensible, but it is embraceable through the embracing of one of its beings."[4] It would appear, then, that understanding, if it comes, must grow out of an act which annihilates our sense of feeling apart from both ourselves and others. Not only does the I-Thou relationship erase our feelings of alienation, it also reveals to us the true nature of others: "If I face a human being as my Thou and say the primary 'I-Thou' to him, he is not a thing among things, and does not consist of things. Thus a human being is not he or she, bound from every other he or she, a specific point in space . . . but all else lives in his light."[5]

A Religious Foundation of Human Relations

Thus such a relationship becomes a focal point for experiencing the world as a totality through recognition of the other. But humans find even more than this through the I-Thou relationship, for, as Buber stated, "creatures are placed in my way so that I, and fellow creatures, by means of them and with them find the way to God."[6] It would appear that the I-Thou relationship reveals to us, in some mystical fashion, the entire universe in microcosm. Buber delineated three spheres in the human world of relationships: our relationships to nature, our relationships with other people, and our relationships with spiritual beings.[7] According to Buber, spiritual identity is the key to establishing our humanity: "Every true deed is a love deed. All true deeds arise from contact with a beloved thing and flow into the universe."[8]

The opposite to the loving, revealing I-Thou relationship is the I-It relationship, which is dehumanizing and destructive. Ironically and sadly, almost every I-Thou relationship will eventually become an I-It relationship, for once the I-Thou relationship is established, the Thou tends to be treated as an object, not a subject. Buber stressed that we can overcome this paradox. He classified I-It relationships as being purely intellectual and experiential. "The development of the function of experience and using," he wrote, "comes about mostly through decrease of man's power to enter into relations."[9]

I-It relationships can lead us into error because they create a false picture of exactly who we are in the universal system. If we are the I, this causes us to define ourselves as superior to all others, and with such a perception, it is impossible for us to enter into mutual relations with others. Therefore, it is only through the concept of the Thou that we can become truly and humanely an I. Buber spoke of a primal world which precedes form, out of which we are born. Each newborn infant is not yet the personal, actualized being that he or she has the potential to become. The I can develop out of this primal world only gradually, by entering into meaningful human relationships.

It is by entering into and developing relationships with others that we can come in contact with the Thou and thus

The Helping Relationship

become a person in the fullest sense. Every real relation with another person, Buber asserted, is exclusive. From this interaction, the Thou is freed, steps forth, and confronts us. And, according to Buber, the Thou is realized only in relationships which are truly helping ones. At this point, Buber parted company with traditional theology. He maintained that even if one does not directly accept God as a being, one does relate to God if he enters into a relation with a Thou in which actions and thoughts are not limited by any consideration other than humanity. One of man's greatest mistakes, Buber believed, is his historical attempt to turn God into an I by understanding or categorizing him, when in actuality man's relationship with God is established only through his relationship with other people.

The only way to help ourselves is by helping others, for, as Buber cautioned, "he who calls forth the helping word in himself experiences the world. He who offers support strengthens the support in himself. He who effects salvation to him salvation is disclosed."[10] This can be interpreted to mean that those persons who claim to have faith in God and to glorify him have entered into a false, inauthentic relationship with the Creator if they fail to help others, for it is only in helping others that we can truly display our love for God. Buber saw hope for modern men and women only if they regard their religious obligations as human obligations.

Buber rejected the idea that religion is merely a closed, mystical experience between one man and some transcendent being called God. "Religion," he wrote, "is not the mystical flight to a realm transcending the everyday; rather, it is an attitude of openingness and expectancy amid the opportunities of each mortal hour."[11] He defined God as one who gives meaning to personal life, the being who makes persons capable of meeting, associating, and helping one another. For Buber, God can only be described as the absolute person who is derived from each of us or from our relations with each other. Buber's I-Thou construct has been used with varying degrees of clarity and success by theologians Karl Heim,[12] Karl Barth,[13] and Emil Brunner.[14] For example, Brunner wrote:

A Religious Foundation of Human Relations

Every human "I," is in the last resort a being who seeks himself. This self-seeking may be refined, but is indissolubly bound up with our present existence. In this sense the harsh saying of Grisebach, "The Self is the Evil," is absolutely true. Our life—even though we may be very "socially-minded" and friendly towards other people—ultimately circles round ourselves as the central point. We only absorb our neighbor as it were into our circle, but no effort avails to enable us to break through this charmed circle of self-interest.[15]

Buber believed that in seeking to shut God out of worldly affairs, humans have increased their feelings of alienation, thereby destroying what is most precious within them. From this perspective, God is within humans and they within him, and the two are forever inseparable. This belief provides us with the reason for hope in an otherwise irrational world inhabited by cynical and selfish people. "The only basis for affirming the meaningfulness of life in the face of the insurmountable evils of human existence," Lowell D. Streiker observed, "is the recommendation that man's sufferings are also the sufferings of God."[16] Man's failure before God and man, the theme on which Buber based his philosophical position, is characterized well in Franz Kafka's remark that "we are sinful not merely because we have eaten of the Tree of Knowledge, but also because we have not eaten of the Tree of Life."[17]

Meaningful existence, however, brings with it an awesome sense of responsibility. Once we enter into an I-Thou relationship, we cannot again deny the possibility of such a relationship. Yet if we enter into no relationships except those which are impersonal or are I-It relationships, we are not free in any true sense of the word. For as long as we ascribe our actions to external causes, refusing to take responsibility for them, we are living in a world of destructive manipulations. As Buber put it: "Causality has unlimited reign in the world of It."[18]

Often in the Bible we are told that people do not do the good they want to do; instead, they do the evil they do not want to do. Here, too, it would appear that there exists some

The Helping Relationship

contradiction between Scripture and Buber's message, for if we do what we do not really want to do, then we are not personally responsible for our own lives. A basic premise of Buber's philosophy is that our lives are authentic only if we have entered into I-Thou relationships, and if we have entered into such relationships, we are free and we are responsible for our actions.

It is in the realm of freedom and responsibility that a major point of difference appears between Buber's writings and certain passages in the Bible. Some of the latter call for restrictions of helping activities: "Do not try to work together as equals with unbelievers, for it cannot be done. How can right and wrong be partners? How can light and darkness live together? How can Christ and the Devil agree?" This type of helping relationship may seem unduly divisive of mankind because such admonitions would seem to drive people apart, not only in the religious sphere, but in social, political, and moral matters as well.

Buber rejected the eye-for-an-eye philosophy found in the Old Testament, and it might also be said that he would consider the teaching of the Golden Rule as ultimately springing from an ethic built on selfishness and personal gain. Such a command seems to imply that others are objects, not subjects. Buber's commandment to us might be simply: "Do good unto others." Clearly, Buber's teachings parallel various New Testament messages in their strong emphasis on love and mutual helping. Humans, in their relationships with others, and thus with God, are quite in the center of creation for Buber. Therein lie both the tragedy and glory of humankind.

THE SELF-ACTUALIZED PERSON

Although the number of practitioners in the fields of psychology and psychotherapy has grown enormously since the pioneering work of Sigmund Freud, relatively few have stood out from their colleagues as truly creative forces—individuals who have added new dimensions to the study of personality. When a history of twentieth-century psychology is written in years to come, there is little doubt that a special place in it will be allotted to Abraham H. Maslow, the father of humanistic psychology. Some have referred to Maslow's contribution to psychology as a "third force," but he preferred to speak of his psychology of transcendence as a "fourth psychology."[19] Unlike those who believed that only the so-called sick have need of psychotherapy, Maslow chose to stress the positive side of mental health. No individual could be called whole, Maslow said, unless he had fulfilled the genuinely human need for something to aspire to, however well he might have satisfied his other, more obvious needs.

Maslow described what he called a hierarchy of needs peculiar to the human organism. As was noted earlier, the most basic needs are the physiological ones that sustain the body, such as food and sleep. When these are satisfied, the human organism begins to concentrate on fulfilling a need for safety, which usually is accomplished best in an environment which is structured in an orderly and secure fashion. Not until the basic physiological and safety needs are satisfied does the human turn his attention to fulfilling his need for affection, love, and belonging. Maslow warned, however, that we must not confuse the biological sex urge with the desire for tenderness and intimacy between persons. The former is physiological and the latter is primarily psychological. At this point in the development of the person comes the realization of a need for self-esteem and for the esteem of others. With the satisfaction of these needs, the individual can turn his attention to his highest need: self-actualization.

For Maslow, the need for self-actualization in the individual means that he now strives to do what he, as a unique person, is fitted to do. Man, Maslow concluded, cannot be content being less than himself, for he must be what he can be; otherwise he will be untrue to himself.[20] Only those whose basic needs are gratified will be motivated by higher values. All such individuals are devoted to some task, call, vocation,

The Helping Relationship

or beloved work outside themselves. Albert Einstein saw this need as well as anyone when he said: "The satisfaction of physical needs is indeed the indispensable precondition of a satisfactory existence, but in itself it is not enough. In order to be content, men must also have the possibility of developing their intellectual and artistic powers to whatever extent accords with their personal characteristics and abilities."[21] One of the key observations made by Maslow was that in order to satisfy needs at each step of the hierarchy, the person will have to change or modify his behavior, and no need is ever completely gratified.

What are the characteristics of these rare self-actualizing people whose needs are as gratified as possible? How can we recognize them? What kind of behavior do they manifest? Maslow gave us an almost poetic description of them:

Self-actualizing people are, without one single exception, involved in a cause outside their own skin, in something which fate has called them to somehow and which they work at and which they love, so that the work-joy dichotomy in them disappears. One devoted his life to the laws, another to justice, another to beauty or truth. All, in one way or another, devote their lives to the search for what I have called the "being values" ("B" for short), the ultimate values which are intrinsic, which cannot be reduced to anything more ultimate. There are about fourteen of these B-values, including truth and beauty, and goodness of the ancients and perfection, simplicity, comprehensiveness, and several more.[22]

Maslow cautioned that the B-values are not the same as our personal attitudes toward them or our emotional reactions to them. The B-values induce in us a kind of "requiredness feeling" and also a feeling of unworthiness.

The gratification of basic needs in the modern world, an indispensable accomplishment on the path to self-actualization, can be brought about only through the intervention of other human beings. Maslow referred to the gratification of such needs as food, safety, belongingness, love, and respect as being basic therapeutic medication.[23] A particular source of help in fulfilling basic needs are interpersonal relationships, and every individual who is kind, helpful, decent, psychologically democratic, affectionate, and warm is a psychotherapeutic force, albeit a small one sometimes. Such an individual pursues, it seems, a special way of being rather than, perhaps, a way of thinking. Archibald MacLeish described it: "Man can live his truth, his deepest truth, but he cannot speak it. It is for this reason that love becomes the ultimate human answer to the ultimate human question."[24]

Obviously, we should expect self-actualized individuals to be the most expert at establishing meaningful interpersonal relationships, for they have deeper and more profound personal relationships than those of any other adult, although not necessarily deeper than those of children. According to Maslow, such persons are capable of more fusion, greater love, more intense identification, and a greater obliteration of ego boundaries than most other people would consider possible.

Another prominent psychologist, Robert R. Carkhuff, has developed a profound characterization of the helping relationship which supplements Maslow's philosophy:

In a real sense then, the helping process is a process of rehabilitation as well as a process of personal emergence and/or re-emergence. It is a process in which each barrier looms higher than the last, but one in which the rewarding experiences of surmounting previous hurdles increases the probability of future successes. If the helper is not committed to his own physical, emotional, and intellectual development, he cannot enable another to find fulfillment in any or all of these realms of functioning.[25]

According to Carkhuff, an effective helper is one who is devoid of dysfunctional growth patterns and who has become both paternal and maternal in nature by combining both the responsive and assertive elements. Because such a helper can sensitively comprehend both the internal and external realms of the physical, emotional, and intellectual, he can act to modi-

The Helping Relationship

fy these realms in a manner that is creative and responsible. The individual being helped can comprehend himself and others to the extent that the helper can empathize with the former's world. In order to empathize with another person, however, the helper must have a deep personal awareness of himself or herself. Thus the self-actualized person comes closest to approximating the ideal helper. In short, the more self-actualized the helper, the more effective and healthy will be the interpersonal relationships which he or she establishes.

What parallels can we find in the Bible? Does Scripture give us examples of the helping relationship? Without doubt, the New Testament provides the paradigm for human behavior in the deeds and teachings of Jesus. Luke relates many instances of Jesus' kindness, love for sinners, acts of forgiveness, and compassion for the poor, and James, in his Letter to the World, furnishes us with rules for communicating with people.

The ultimate act of love for one's fellow man is dying for him, as is shown by the crucifixion of Jesus. The next most vital way of helping another is the commandment of the Lord to love our neighbors, but Jesus' lesson would have been incomplete if he had not told us who our fellow man or neighbor is. In Luke, Jesus relates the parable of the good Samaritan and in doing so tells us that our neighbor is everyone in the world who needs help, care, and love. Jesus made it plain that next to giving up our life, helping our neighbor is the highest calling. The good Samaritan satisfied other persons' physical needs, as well as their need for safety and love. Thus, Maslow's idea that a person's basic needs are fulfilled by another through interpersonal relationships has definite confirmation in the teachings of Jesus. It is certainly not going too far afield to say that the good Samaritan in the story told by Jesus is a model of the self-actualized individual.

Throughout the New Testament, Jesus' actions are guided by the philosophy of helping one's neighbor. In Matthew 10:40, Jesus says: "He that receiveth you receiveth me, and he that receiveth me receiveth him that sent me." Likewise, in Jesus' reply to Satan's attempt to seduce him with worldly goods

A Religious Foundation of Human Relations

("Man shall not live by bread alone"), we realize that humans have a higher need than merely satisfying those which are physical. Here we see confirmation for the emphasis which Maslow's psychology places on our higher nature.

Jesus' appeal to man's higher nature, to his needs for safety, love, feelings of worth, belongingness, and self-esteem, are well illustrated in Luke 6:20-22: "Blessed be ye poor; for yours is the Kingdom of God. Blessed are ye that hunger now; for ye shall be filled. Blessed are ye that weep now; for ye shall laugh. Blessed are ye when men shall hate you, and when they shall separate you from their company, and shall reproach you, and cast out your name as evil." Jesus' promise to soothe these hurts is exactly the kind of relationship Maslow called therapeutic.

In the parable of the prodigal son (Luke 15:11), which should more accurately be called the parable of the loving father, Jesus described the behavior of a father who forgave his son and accepted him back into the family relationship with a moving interpersonal exchange between the two. The father rushed out and kissed his son before the son could speak. (This demonstrates vividly that all our needs are not satisfied by the use of verbal communication.) The father also satisfied the needs of the son who stayed with him and could not understand why his returning brother was being so well received. With a few words the father satisfied this son's needs for esteem, love, and belongingness.

James's espistle provides us with definite guidance in helping and caring for others. Indeed, James affords us an excellent example of the motivation of the self-actualized individual. A compendium of rules for establishing the helping relationship can easily be drawn up, such as "happy is the man who remains faithful under trials" and "do not fool yourselves." James also gives examples of dysfunctional behavior and warns against them: "Do not criticize one another, my brothers. Who do you think you are to judge your fellow man?" "But now you are proud, and you boast, all such boasting is wrong." The latter behavior is nontherapeutic and would not be practiced by the self-actualized individual.

The Helping Relationship

Just as Jesus had doubts on the Mount of Olives about accepting the will of God, Maslow cautioned that the self-actualized person will not find an easy road through life: "It would convey the wrong impression to say that they are self-satisfied. What we must say rather is that they can take the frailties and sins, weaknesses and evils of human nature in the same unquestioning spirit with which one accepts the characteristics of nature."[26]

Quite clearly, the teachings of Scripture and Maslow are compatible in their respective explications of the helping relationship, for each source stresses the positive aspect of satisfying the needs of others by caring. Both sources place great emphasis on the importance of interpersonal relationships in satisfying basic human needs, and each maintains the significance and need for a higher calling in man's life. While the Bible states that man can achieve eternal life by serving God, Maslow believes that by serving others and helping them find need satisfaction, both the helper and the person helped grow and are happier. By helping and caring for others as Maslow recommended, each of us carries out Jesus' commandment "to love thy neighbor as thyself." The theoretical foundations which Maslow has bequeathed to the field of human relations are secure and offer rewards for the social practitioner, both in personal growth and salvation of the soul.

Thus far I have done considerable talking about helping. Now I shall turn my attention to specifics of the helping relationship.

THE NATURE OF THE HELPING RELATIONSHIP

The helping relationship is created when a person turns outward to satisfy a need for another. In order for such a relationship to exist, two basic ingredients are necessary. First, the helper must possess a quality or asset which is desired by the individual seeking assistance. Second, the helper and the client must be willing partners.

A Religious Foundation of Human Relations

In a helping relationship, someone with a need seeks out another individual who can satisfy that need, and when the helper agrees to assist, the helping relationship is established. The helping relationship is not necessarily formed between two persons, however, for the individual in financial need might find money, the sick man might possibly heal himself, one who is lost could use a map, and a student could get knowledge from books in a library. In such cases, the helping relationship is established between a person and some source, not necessarily human, outside oneself.

When an individual suffers from a personality dysfunction, it is necessary that he get help from someone who is fully functioning and who has both a positive self-image and a strong, healthy identity. Furthermore, the helper in such a case, usually a psychotherapist, cannot remain a cold and distant individual; he or she must be a willing and empathetic other person in the relationship. Carl R. Rogers has contributed much to our understanding of the helper's role in the helping relationship.

For nearly a half-century, Rogers has been involved in helping relationships with a wide range of individuals: children, adolescents, and adults with educational, vocational, personal, and marital problems; normal, neurotic, and psychotic individuals; those who seek help and those who are referred for help. Rogers summed up his myriad of personal experiences by saying: "I regard it as a deep privilege to have had the opportunity to know such a diverse multitude of people so personally and intimately."[27] He described the end result of the helping relationship in Socratic terms: "I rejoice at the privilege of being a midwife to a new personality—as I stand by with awe at the emergence of a self, a person; as I see a birth process in which I have had an important and facilitating part."[28] There can be no finer description of the helper's role in a true helping relationship.

What can we learn from Rogers about the nature of the helping relationship? How does he exemplify the genuine helper in his own psychotherapeutic practice? It is evident that he possesses the two major characteristics needed by a genuine helper. Above all else, he is a willing participant, for he regards the helping relationship as a professional challenge: "To be faced by a troubled conflicted person who is seeking and expecting help has always constituted a great challenge to me. Do I have the knowledge, the resources, the psychological strength, the skill—do I have whatever it takes to be of help to such an individual?"[29]

The goal of Rogers' treatment is helping his clients to become strong and healthy personalities in their approach to life. He describes such a personality as fully functional or fully integrated. These descriptions are not unlike Maslow's description of the self-actualized person. For Rogers, the journey to good psychological health is a "process, not a state of being. It is a direction, not a destination. The direction which constitutes the good life is that which is selected by the total organism when there is psychological freedom to move in any direction."[30] He set forth three characteristics of the individual as he moves toward the good life: an increasing openness to experience, a way of living that is increasingly existential, and an increasing trust in his own organism.

Rogers described the beginning of the process for making full use of one's faculties:

I should like to draw together these three threads describing the process of the good life into a more coherent picture. It appears the person who is psychologically free moves in the direction of becoming a more fully functioning person. He is more able to live fully in and with each and all of his feelings and reactions. He makes increasing use of all of his organic equipment to sense as accurately as possible the existential situation within and without. He makes use of all the information his nervous system can thus supply. He is more able to experience all of his feelings and is less afraid of any of his feelings. He is his own sifter of evidence and is more open to evidence from all sources. He is completely engaged in the process of being and becoming himself, and thus dis-

covers that he is soundly and realistically social. He lives more completely in his moment but learns that this is the soundest living for all time. He is becoming a more fully functioning organism and because of the awareness of himself, which flows freely in and through his experience, he is becoming a more fully functioning person.[31]

A successful helper, one who guides his client to a fully functioning or self-actualized state, must himself have reached such a point, else his goal for another will remain only partly fulfilled. By helping so many persons, Rogers has shown that he has a fully integrated personality. Here are some of the most significant of his beliefs:

In my relationship with persons, I have found that it does not help in the long run to act as though I were something that I am not.

I find that I am more effective when I can listen acceptively to myself and be myself. One way of putting this is that I feel I have become more adequate in letting myself be what I am.

I have found it of enormous value when I can permit myself to understand another person.

I have found it enriching to open channels whereby others can communicate their feelings, their private, perceptual worlds, to me.

I have found it highly rewarding when I can accept another person.

The more I am open to the realities in me and the other person, the less I do find myself wishing to rush in and fix things.

It has been my experience that persons have a basically positive direction.

Life at its best is a flowing, changing process in which nothing is fixed.[32]

How does such a man, who has successfully entered the helping relationship literally thousands of times, view it? How does he characterize it? In his book *On Becoming a Person*,

The Helping Relationship

Rogers elaborated the process at length, detailing the manner in which he has helped so many individuals. He perceives his task as a psychotherapist to be that of serving as a facilitator, establishing with his client a relationship in which the individual will discover within himself the capacity to use the relationship for growth and change, the indispensable ingredients of personal development.

The relationship which I have found helpful is characterized by a sort of transparency on my part, in which real feelings are evident by acceptance of this other person as a separate person with a value in his own right and by a deep empathetic understanding which enables me to see his private world through his eyes. When these conditions are achieved, I become a companion to my client, accompanying him in the frightening search for himself which he now feels free to undertake.[33]

Therefore, the helping relationship, as Rogers defines it, is one in which the helper facilitates personal growth by way of a deep empathetic understanding and a total acceptance of the client. Only in this way, Rogers concluded, is growth achieved. The helper also grows in the relationship, for the successful helping relationship is never one in which only one person benefits. In fact, Rogers maintains that possibly the greatest measure of just how much the helper has succeeded in helping another is the growth of the helper:

The degree to which I can create relationships to facilitate the growth of others as separate persons is a measure of the growth I have achieved in myself. In some respects, this is a disturbing thought; but it is also a promising or challenging one. It would indicate that if I am interested in creating helping relationships, I have a fascinating lifetime job ahead of me stretching and developing my potentialities in the direction of growth.[34]

In short, the helping relationship is one between two individuals. One is psychologically mature—a fully functioning or self-actualized person—and the other has not yet reached psychological maturity. During the course of the relationship, both persons achieve personal growth, for in it the helper is not sapped in his strength by the weaker but, rather, promotes growth while realizing a further refinement of his psychological development. Thus the relationship is as helpfully symbiotic as any in the entire world of nature.

When one compares the helping relationship, as defined by Rogers, with the Christian ethic, one sees some striking parallels. While Rogers seeks to become a fully functioning person, the Christian seeks the state of grace and, through it, salvation: "By grace we are indwelt by God. . . . God's indwelling means God making himself at home in us and depends on our invitation. When we are infants the sponsor extends the invitation to him on our behalf. When we reach the use of reason, we confirm the invitation. We can withdraw it at any time and so lose God's indwelling."[35] It is grace which allows the Christian to become filled with God and thus to become more like God, just as the more closely one emulates Carl Rogers, the more one becomes a fully functioning person. Rogers urges us to value other persons, to prize them with unconditional acceptance, because by doing so we take on added value ourselves; Christians are taught to honor and value other persons because we are all valued by God.

As was noted earlier, interaction between two human beings is not required for the establishment of a helping relationship, since the person can sometimes find whatever he is seeking in a nonhuman outside source. An example of just such a relationship is that between the believing Christian and God. When the Christian genuinely seeks salvation and is willing to grow spiritually, God, an outside nonhuman source, stands ready to give help. Dietrich Bonhoeffer observed: "It is becoming clearer every day that the most urgent problem besetting our Church is this: How can we live the Christian life in the modern world?"[36] Free will has resulted in many Christians' behaving very much like J. Schoneberg Setzer's tropical fish:

The Helping Relationship

> *Because God is a Father who wants children who are true persons, he has given us a small amount of independent power in our self-conscious free wills. . . . I have the same relationship with my tropical fish that God has with man. I have total power and responsibility over them in their fragile aquariums. . . . But even these little fish have a type of free will, a power to cooperate or not to cooperate with me.*[37]

A quote from Joseph A. Leighton makes this point:

> *The freest man is he who is able to look at his own possible choices in the light of a good for others, or of a good for the family, the national community and for the larger human community. The free man must have sympathetic imagination, the ability to put himself in the place of others and to put others in his place.*
>
> *The individual cannot become morally free if he is a creature of strong, narrow, egoistic passions or of purely sensual nature. On the other hand, if he is sympathetic and socially minded he becomes freer the more his feelings for and with others are enlightened by thoughtfulness, by the imaginative foreshadowing and reflective comparison of* values *for persons.*[38]

Certain assumptions must be made in comparing the relationship between humans and God with that between the client and Carl Rogers in the helping relationship. God possesses all attributes that are required for achieving a state of grace and he willingly gives them to human beings. To the Christian, these assumptions are undeniable truths and thus are part of the deep faith which underlies the Christian ethic. The parallel between Rogers' theories and Christian doctrine is easily drawn. Psalms 37:39–40 makes reference to God as a helper: "The salvation of the righteous is of the Lord; he is their strength in the time of trouble. And the Lord shall help them and deliver them; he shall deliver them from the wicked, and save them, because they trust in him."

In the New Testament, John describes God's willingness to help his earthly children: "For God so loved the world that

A Religious Foundation of Human Relations

he gave his only begotten Son, that whosoever believeth in him should not perish, but have everlasting life. For God sent not his Son into the world to condemn the world; but that the world through him might be saved" (John 3:16–17). Scripture contains many more references to the way in which God has helped and is always willing to help us in our quest for grace and salvation. Psalms 121:1–2 suggests that because the Christian knows God is a willing helper, he has faith: "I will lift up mine eyes unto the hills, from whence cometh my help. My help cometh from the Lord, which made heaven and earth."

Thus in the Bible it is easy to see that God is a willing participant in a helping relationship with humans, since by definition they possess that which all people seek: grace and salvation. Even more so than Carl Rogers, who in his relationship with his clients becomes a loving companion and accompanies them in the frightening search for themselves, God is with us each step of the way to salvation. This is summed up in Psalm 23:

The Lord is my shepherd; I shall not want. He maketh me to lie down in green pastures: he leadeth me beside the still waters. He restoreth my soul: he leadeth me in the paths of righteousness for his name's sake. Yea, though I walk through the valley of the shadow of death, I will fear no evil: for thou art with me; thy rod and thy staff they comfort me. Thou preparest a table before me in the presence of mine enemies: thou anointest my head with oil; my cup runneth over. Surely goodness and mercy shall follow me all the days of my life: and I will dwell in the house of the Lord for ever.

DRUG ADDICTION

For thousands of years, human beings have turned to drugs of various sorts, with or without a particular religious ritual, to find some experience which would either put them in contact with the supernatural or at least make their existence on earth a more pleasant one. Thus a crucial point concerning the use of drugs, of whatever kind, is that throughout man's journey on this planet, such usage has been primarily motivated by a desire to escape or transcend a reality which the users feel is either too painful to bear or too limited in affording them access to some more universal knowledge. Understandably, then, organized religion, by its very nature, has come to regard drug addiction as a major threat to its assertion of God's authority in human affairs. Few persons adopt the model suggested by Carl G. Jung:

If the doctor wants to offer guidance to another, or even to accompany him a step of the way, he must be in touch with this other person's psychic life. He is never in touch when he passes judgment. Whether he puts his judgments into words, or keeps them to himself, makes not the slightest difference. To take the opposite position, and to agree with the patient offhand, is also of no use, but estranges him as much as condemnation. We can get in touch with another person only by an attitude of unprejudiced objectivity. This may sound like a scientific precept, and may be confused with a purely intellectual and detached attitude of mind. But what I mean to convey is something quite different. It is a human quality—a kind of deep respect for facts and events and for the person who suffers from them—a respect for the secret of such a human life. The truly religious person has this attitude.[39]

Howard J. Clinebell, Jr., defined the classic Judaeo-Christian argument against drug addiction, of whatever kind, as follows: "For the Christian, life is a gift and a trust, to be lived to its fullest under the rule of love. This love expresses itself in deep respect for oneself as a child of God and in respect for and service to, others. Damaging one's body, the instrument of loving service to others, is incompatible with the stewardship of life, respect for self and others, or affirmation of the basic goodness of creation (i.e., reality)."[40] Another Protestant writer, Kenneth W. Mann, maintains that drug addiction often may spring from a person's attempt to deal

A Religious Foundation of Human Relations

with the knowledge that he is incomplete as an individual in the highest sense. He may have good love relations, his economic and social needs may be met, and he may have adjusted reasonably well to his job. In short, his primary gratifications have been relatively well satisfied. Yet such individuals "may feel deficient in the fuller expression of their personalities because they have never undertaken the kind of unselfish social responsibility of which they know they are capable—because to do so would require sacrifices for others that they may be afraid of, or too self-preoccupied to make. But underneath there may be the gnawing sense that, to this extent, their lives are devoid of meaning, and their drugs behavior may be an expression of this concern."[41]

Drug dependency reduces the addict's ability to adjust to the blows and misfortunes that inevitably are a part of everyday life. As countless pastoral counselors have discovered, tranquilizers and barbiturates can be used to mask powerful feelings (both positive and negative) which must be faced and worked through if an addict is to grow toward fuller personhood. The final judgment on whether the use of drugs is destructive to the person must rest on the question of whether the particular use of drugs facilitates or replaces constructive coping. Father John T. Servodidio, a Roman Catholic priest who has enjoyed a great deal of success in working with young drug addicts, agrees that the addict finds it extremely difficult to deal constructively with life: "Certainly in dealing with people, you realize that the biggest problem is the low value they place upon themselves. This is particularly true of people in trouble with life. They have come out feeling as though they are nobody. They need to realize that because of their relationship with Christ, they are—each of them—someone. If we believe that man is made in the image and likeness of God, an individual cannot be a nothing, a *no-good.*"[42]

It is precisely because drug addiction takes the person away from his relationship with Christ that Christian theologians argue that it takes him away from his genuine relationships with other persons as well. The drug replaces both the

The Helping Relationship

love of a Supreme Being and love for other human beings. In the words of Clinebell:

There is also something frightening about the thought of synthetic human relationships, held together only by the artificial bond of psychoactive drugs. Christian insight and psychological research agree that personhood can find its true fulfillment and continuing wholeness only in genuine relationships — i.e., relationships which strengthen mutual trust, integrity, and affection. Generally speaking, chronic drug dependency not only fails to strengthen these qualities in relationships, but it also tends to foster their opposites — mutual distrust, dishonesty, self-rejection, and self-centeredness. Defining Christian love as "sensitivity and responsiveness to the needs of others," we would have to say that the entire process and inner dynamics of drug dependency tend to work against it. The person tends to center his world more and more on his magical chemical and his own subjective needs, relating to others mainly as means of satisfying these needs."[43]

Christian love is the one thing which the drug addict is unable to experience, for he is unable to take full responsibility upon himself and thus cannot allow himself to feel responsibility for another single human being. Monsignor William B. O'Brien draws this portrait of the young drug abuser:

A drug addict is an extremely immature person emotionally. He has never grown up, he has never transformed from the boy to a responsible, mature adult. He cannot cope with the difficulties one encounters in the transition from child to man. He chooses to run; and what he runs from are all the feelings and responsibilities that are unpleasant and hard to deal with. The way he runs is by using the security of heroin or any other drug which will provide a temporary relief from reality — the reality of hurt, loneliness, frustration, fear and work. A drug addict feels these pressures but will refuse to admit that they are even present. By successfully removing himself from the pain of reacting to stress, he detaches himself and spends his energy reinforcing his isolation to what he feels is a non-painful state. Of course, he becomes increasingly withdrawn from society, indulging more and more in his own hopeless and suicidal existence.[44]

On the other hand, Edward Wakin refuses to admit that the young drug abuser is weak in the usual sense: "You've got to be strong to survive in the drug field. You've got to be able to get the money and the resources. You've got to get what you want. So is it a question of a weak will, or is it a question of the way you see yourself, of your image of yourself?"[45]

Even granting the assertion that some mystical experiences can be drug induced, many theologians would agree with Huston Smith that the crucial question is not answered by such experiences: "Drugs appear able to induce religious experiences; it is less evident that they can produce religious lives. It follows that religion is more than religious experiences."[46] In short, a large number of theologians would maintain that a religious experience, mystical or otherwise, must be reflected in a radical transformation of the individual's life—a transformation which leads the individual to dedicate his life to God—or it is not a true religious experience.

There is little agreement among theologians about why drug addiction has reached such widespread proportions in the United States in recent years. Some writers assert that too many middle-class American parents have given their children little or no meaningful direction. Many theologians zero in on parents' irresponsibility in allowing their children to assume complete proprietorship over their own growth process. The Church, they maintain, should stand with parental authority on this point. To do otherwise is to do young people a disservice, for when we deny them a loving authority, we do not prepare them for life. Rather, we prepare them for individual, spiritual, and social destruction.

Young people are the victims of an outmoded, inhumane educational system in the United States, Wakin charges:

The Helping Relationship

My personal opinion is that society is creating addicts. First of all, look at the schools. Next to parents they have children the most, and the school system cracks the kids. I don't care whether it's a ghetto or a suburban school; the young face a negative image of themselves. We never let them develop from within, never let them be what they want to be. They are always being compared and tested, being put into dumb and smart categories, backward or advanced categories. The word, education, means to draw out, but our whole educational structure is out to stuff in. All kids suffer the pain of the comparing and judging and of being put down. It's built into the educational system.[47]

Few readers will be surprised that many theologians are impressed with the program of Alcoholics Anonymous (AA) in helping those addicts who really want to be cured. AA's basic approach is heavily oriented toward traditional religion. Joseph H. Fichter, a noted Roman Catholic sociologist, compared AA meetings with those of Catholic and Protestant charismatics: "The recovered alcoholic is usually humbly ready to admit to previous guilt feelings. This appears to be the case also with charismatics, all of whom say that they 'know how it feels to repent and to experience the forgiveness of sins.' Their mystical *metanoia* is, therefore, generally preceded by repentance—and, after all, this is what Peter preached to the people of Jerusalem at the first Pentecost. He told them to 'turn away from your sins' and promised that 'you will receive God's gift, the Holy Spirit.'"[48] Fichter observed that when he attended AA sessions, he found a gigantic revival meeting: speakers encouraging everybody to stay converted and members greeting one another joyfully, all in an over-all spirit of religious fervor.

Although most clergy of all faiths would strongly resist the legalization of narcotics in the United States, the governing board of the National Council of Churches went on record in March, 1973, as favoring the decriminalization of the simple possession of marijuana.[49] Several writers have advocated the legalization of heroin, pointing out that for organized crime, this would effectively take the profit out of drug dealing. Writers supporting this view argue that "the Puritan ideal of building a holy commonwealth in which socially and individually harmful practices are banned underlies our national mind-set and our laws. In this century, however, that ideal is clearly unattainable. In trying to achieve it, we have created a body of unenforceable laws."[50]

Persons trying to help drug addicts should memorize the well-known prayer attributed to Reinhold Niebuhr: "Lord, grant me the patience to accept what cannot be changed, the courage to change what must be changed, and the wisdom to know one from the other."

Finally, a successful helping relationship is, as Ralph Waldo Emerson observed, a precious moment: "We mark with light in memory the few interviews we have had, in the dreary years of routine and of sin, with souls that made our souls wiser; that spoke what we thought; that told us what we knew; that gave us leave to be what we only were."[51] In the words of Karl Menninger:

The world is made up of people, but the people of the world forget this. It is hard to believe that, like ourselves, other people are born of women, reared by parents, teased by brothers, . . . consoled by wives, . . . flattered by grandchildren, and buried by parsons and priests with the blessings of the church and the tears of those left behind. . . . It is easier to speak of fate, and destiny, and waves of the future than to see the ways we determine our own fate, right now and in the immediate past and future.[52]

Henry Guntrip succinctly captured the pain involved in caring about other people: "Is what I am seeing really in him or is it in me; or, if it really is in him, does it affect me so much because it is in me also? . . . I am a group of different persons, seeing and reacting to you who also seem to be a group of different persons, some of whom are probably really in you, and others of whom I project into you."[53]

THE SEARCH FOR BALANCE

Man's curiosity about himself and the world in which he lives has led him to give high priority to order, understanding, and predictability, the hallmarks of cognitive activity. These three elements are manifested in man's development of internal controls and in his apparent need to preserve the consistency and stability of his frames of reference. In order to satisfy the latter need, it seems necessary for most persons to screen and interpret all new experiences in relation to their already existing assumptions. Early in the helping relationship, the helper finds that a major source of difficulty within the person being helped is that the latter has come to recognize the difference between the self that he believes he is and the self that he thinks he should be. In other words, the client cannot make important new experiences fit his already existing assumptions about himself. Such a conflict can lead, not unnaturally, to psychological imbalance.

Psychologist Leon Festinger suggests that when new information contradicts already existing assumptions, we experience *cognitive dissonance* and remain psychologically uncomfortable until we can somehow reconcile the differences between the two or at least convince ourselves that such differences do not exist.

In the modern world, with its numerous and conflicting sets of values, the individual is daily forced to make decisions which often contradict his professed morality. Dissonance arises and produces tension, which in itself can be a strong motivating force. Recognizing this salient fact, Festinger posited two basic hypotheses concerning dissonance: the existence of dissonance, being psychologically uncomfortable, will motivate the person to try to reduce it and by so doing achieve consonance; when dissonance is present, the person will, in addition to trying to reduce it, actively avoid situations and information which would be likely to increase the dissonance. Thus dissonance (that is, the existence of nonfitting relations among cognitions) is a motivating factor in its own right. "Cognition," according to Festinger, is "any knowledge, opinion or belief about the environment, about oneself, or about one's behavior."[54]

For example, if a person believed himself to be a practicing Christian, he would deem it necessary to keep the Ten Commandments, one of which is "Remember the Sabbath day, to keep it holy." If this person went swimming on Sunday, he might experience some dissonance, since he would be committing an act not strictly in keeping with the Fourth Commandment. However, the dissonance he experiences would be much greater if he broke the Sixth Commandment, "Thou shalt not kill," for this commandment is valued more highly by both himself and his society. Although both rules in question are biblical commandments, it is obvious that the breaking of one is a much more serious breach of morality than would be the breaking of the other.

Consideration of the role of action in shaping thought or of behavior in molding the "inner life" leads directly to an interpretation of Christian existence as worldly responsiblity. Heidegger's own contention that the self is always "self-in-world" (In-der-Welt-Sein) lays a foundation for unfolding the meaning of selfhood in terms of worldly responsibility. Yet Heidegger so emphasized the inauthenticity of life in the public sphere and the existential significance of those experiences which "individualize" man and thrust him back upon himself, that he was never able to explore the connection of his own insights to life in society. Bonhoeffer forces us to recognize that patterns of thought which attend simply to "private" matters, such as death, guilt, and meaninglessness, involve flight from the realities of the world. As such they are little more than contemporary versions of the old pietistic concern for individual salvation in the world to come. In contrast, our present task is to bring to awareness the processes by which the fundamental issues of Christian existence confront us in the midst of social and political struggles of contemporary life.[55]

We may safely assume that it is most unusual for an individual to be dissonance free, since for any action he might take, it is possible that at least one cognitive element will be dissonant with the behavioral element in question.[56] There is a parallel for this condition in the wisdom expressed of Ecclesiastes 7:20: "For there is not a just man upon earth, that doeth good, and sinneth not."

As has been noted, the presence of cognitive dissonance within the individual gives rise to pressures on him to eliminate or at least reduce it. The strength of the pressure will correspond to the magnitude of the dissonance, as will the strength of the desire to avoid future situations that will increase or renew it. According to research, there are three major ways to reduce dissonance: reduce the importance of the dissonant elements, add consonant elements, or change one of the dissonant elements so that it is no longer inconsistent with the other or others.[57] The more disturbing a particular decision proves for an individual, the more he will strive to justify that decision: "The decision can be justified by increasing the attractiveness of the chosen alternative and decreasing the attractiveness of the rejected alternative. One would expect a post-decision cognitive process to occur that accomplishes this spreading apart of the attractiveness of the alternatives."[58]

When an individual finds himself engaged in behavior that is contrary to his convictions, beliefs, or principles or when he finds himself committed to actions which promise no rewards, a state of dissonance will exist and he will attempt to reduce it. This premise led Festinger and James M. Carlsmith to design a study in which the subjects were offered either one dollar or twenty dollars for telling a fellow student that a boring and tedious task which they had just performed was really quite interesting. In the experiment, the subjects who were offered the smaller reward expressed greater interest in the task than the subjects who were offered the larger reward. The seemingly surprising result was explained by the assumption that one dollar was an insufficient reward for the false statement; hence there was dissonance between the subjects' knowledge that the task they had just finished was extremely boring and their knowledge that they were nevertheless expressing great enthusiasm about it. One way the lower-paid subjects could reduce such dissonance was to believe that the task was not really that boring.[59]

The conclusions we can draw from the above study offer keen insights into the nature of our society. The persons who took the one-dollar reward felt more dissonance in lying than did those who took the twenty dollars. Although it probably disturbs most of us to lie, we do it at least sometime during our lives. Perhaps the dissonance produced by lying may be determined by the situation in which we find ourselves at the time. But the study does seem to show that, at least in some cases, if we are rewarded enough, our conscience will not bother us and we can find many reasons for justifying our action. The individual who is not rewarded sufficiently, we might assume, suffers from serious dissonance and thus must make himself believe that the facts were really as he had pictured them to someone else. We might also note that in some cases individuals believe it is permissible to lie if the reward is sufficient. Perhaps the cynicism embodied in the term *conscience money* is not wholly without foundation.

One crucial application of the dissonance theory is in acts of aggression. When an individual aggresses against another person who he believes is a really good person, he is likely to experience dissonance, particularly if there is little reason for his aggressive behavior. Some experts have found that as dissonance increases, the aggressor's postaggression attitudes toward his victim become increasingly negative. Festinger summed up the results of experiments dealing with the phenomenon of cognitive dissonance:

If a person is induced to do or say something which is contrary to his private opinion, there will be a tendency for him

The Helping Relationship

to change his opinion so as to bring it into correspondence with what he has done or said. The larger the pressure used to elicit the overt behavior . . . the weaker will be the . . . tendency. The results strongly corroborate the theory.[60]

The theory of cognitive dissonance is a way of describing the mechanics of guilt feelings suffered by many persons reared in the Judaeo-Christian tradition, especially those who believe they have transgressed the moral laws embodied in such a tradition. Although the Ten Commandments remain among the highest standards for conduct ever set forth, for many persons they also represent an improbable set of goals for total fulfillment. In trying to live according to the Ten Commandments, many Christians are in dissonance. This is to be expected in our worldly environment, which is not supportive to the practice of sainthood. Realizing this to be true, we must accept the challenge to resolve our dissonance in ways that will neither destroy us nor injure others.

9
THE FUTURE

OUR contemporary society is described by some writers as being characterized by bewilderment, tension, and chaos. Others describe it in glowing terms. Although they may disagree about the condition of our society, most writers agree that our present store of information is vast. It is estimated that ninety per cent of all the scientists who have ever lived are our contemporaries and that the majority of all the scientific literature of the world has been produced in the past fifty years. In fact, our technological progress has proliferated the options we may exercise almost to the point of rendering us disoriented.

At a time when we are uncertain what tomorrow's society will be like, we must prepare to fill a responsible niche in that society. It is disquieting to know that we cannot wait until a completely reconstructed order has been established before we formulate our answers to questions raised by a growing technology. Specifically, we are haunted daily by the prospects of a horrendous worldwide misery implicit in nuclear war, of extinction by ecological disruption, of a population explosion that presages famine, and of the political problems that attend governing the peoples of the world during periods of momentous crises. In our modern age of atomic warfare, Jeremiah 4:27 ("For thus hath the Lord said, The whole land shall be desolate; yet will I not make full end.") is prophetic. The hope—and there is hope— rests in the minds and deeds of today's generation.

LOOKING AHEAD

A new science called futurology may be able to assist us in establishing the values that are relevant for the future. Bertrand Russell posed this question:

So far as physical conditions are concerned there seems to be no good reason why life, including human life, should not continue for many millions of years. The danger comes, not from man's physical (potential) or biological environment but from himself. He has survived, hitherto, through ignorance. Can he continue to survive now that the useful degree of ignorance is lost?[1]

It was because man has become godlike in terms of knowledge, creativity, and destruction that Russell raised the question of survival: "Assuming that men remain capable of scientific techniques, what ways are possible by which they might escape from total destruction? We are now asking a narrower question than can man survive? We are now asking 'can scientific man survive?'"[2]

One of the most imminent problems that haunts our dreams with a frightening regularity is a nuclear war. If such a holocaust is to be avoided, it is incumbent upon men and women of vision to act decisively now.

We do not want to look at this thing simply from the point of view of the next few years; we want to look at it from the point of view of the future of mankind. The question is simple: Is it possible for a scientific society to continue to exist or must such a society inevitably bring itself to destruction? It is a simple question but a very vital one. I do not think it is possible to exaggerate the gravity of the possibilities of evil that lie in the utilization of atomic energy. As I go about the streets and see St. Paul's, the British Museum, the Houses of Parliament and other monuments of our civilization; in my mind's eye I see a nightmare vision of those buildings as heaps of rubble with corpses all around them. . . . It is not enough to make war rare; great and serious war has got to be abolished, because otherwise these things will happen.[3]

In 1955, deeply concerned about the potential destructiveness of nuclear power and the moral frailty of national leaders, Russell sent a statement, which contained what he believed was an alternative to human destruction, to the leaders of the so-called Great Powers. The statement, also signed by some of the most knowledgeable persons living at that time, pointed out that if human beings are to survive, we must abolish war and choose instead happiness, knowledge, and wisdom:

Here, then is the problem which we present to you, stark and dreadful and inescapable: Shall we put an end to the human race; or shall mankind renounce war? . . . There lies before us, if we choose, continual progress in happiness, knowledge and wisdom. Shall we, instead, choose death, because we cannot forget our quarrels? We appeal, as human beings, to human beings: Remember your humanity, and forget the rest. If you can do so, the way lies open to a new Paradise. If you cannot, there lies before you the risk of universal death.[4]

To bring about consensual restrictions, Russell advocated the establishment of a world government. Remaining cognizant of past wars, he asserted it is unlikely that any nation would survive unless all the major weapons of war and all the means of mass destruction are in the hands of a single authority, which would have irresistible power and, if challenged to war, could wipe out any rebellion within a few days. Anticipating his critics' reactions to this plan, Russell further

The Future

asserted that the most desirable way of securing world peace would be by a voluntary agreement among nations to pool their armed forces and submit to an agreed-upon international authority. Far ahead of his time, Russell listed the following initial prerequisites to secure peace between East and West:

1. There must be a different atmosphere in debates between East and West.

2. The United States and the Soviet Union, and as many other powers as possible, should make a solemn declaration that a nuclear war would be an utter disaster to both East and West and also to neutrals and that it would not achieve anything that East or West or neutrals could possibly desire.

3. A temporary moratorium should be declared for a period of two years, during which time each side would pledge itself to abstain from provocative actions.

4. There should be a reform and strengthening of the United Nations.[5]

Bertrand Russell ended his book with an uneasy hope, not because the future of man is reassuring, but because there is always the possibility of hope: "I am writing at a dark moment [July 1961], and it is impossible to know whether the human race will last long enough for what I write to be published, or if published, to be read. But as yet hope is possible, and while hope is possible, despair is a coward's part."[6] Looking into his crystal ball, Russell concluded:

If our present troubles can be conquered man can look forward to a future immeasurably longer than his past, inspired by a new breadth of vision, a continuing hope perpetually fed by a continuing achievement. Man has made a beginning creditable for an infant—for, in a biological sense, man the latest of the species is still an infant. No limit can be set to what he may achieve in the future. I see, in my mind's eye, a world where minds expand, where hope remains undimmed, and what is noble is no longer condemned as treachery to this or that paltry aim. All this can happen if we will let it happen. It rests with our generation to decide between this vision and an end decreed by folly.[7]

A Religious Foundation of Human Relations

Most futurists take wide-ranging and speculative literary excursions into the dangers that grow out of what men and women may do to each other: the daily and hourly risk of total destruction of all that humans have achieved since they stood upright and employed their hands, their minds, and their hearts to clear away obstacles to their environment. Some of the books focusing on the future are invitations to reflect on urgent issues. The better literature provides readable accounts of what some very wise and concerned persons see as solutions to our survival. We may not accept the solutions of Bertrand Russell, but what he offers should put us on the alert and encourage us to inquire earnestly: "Have scientific men and women a future?"

The Bible contains a concept of a warless world which can be secured only through wise decisions. The concept first appears in God's promise to Abraham as found in Genesis 12:1–3: "Get thee out of thy country, and from thy kindred, and from thy father's house, unto a land that I will shew thee: And I will make of thee a great nation, and I will bless thee, and make thy name great; and thou shalt be a blessing: And I will bless them that bless thee, and curse him that curseth thee: and in thee shall all families of the earth be blessed."

The hope for world peace surfaced first as a confident belief that at some time in the indefinite future God would take a stronger hand in the affairs of his people, delivering them from oppression and danger and crowning them with prosperity and happiness. In Isaiah 2:2–4, we find the following prophecy:

It shall come to pass in the last days, that the mountain of the Lord's house shall be established in the top of the mountains, and shall be exalted above the hills; and all nations shall flow unto it. And many people shall go and say, "Come ye, and let us go up to the mountain of the Lord, to the house of the God of Jacob; and he will teach us of his ways, and we will walk in his paths": for out of Zion shall go forth the law, and the word of the Lord from Jerusalem. And he shall judge among

The Future

the nations, and shall rebuke many people: and they shall beat their swords into plowshares, and their spears into pruninghooks: Nation shall not lift up sword against nation, neither shall they learn war any more.

Isaiah's focal point was the city of Jerusalem, which to him and other devoted Jews was the center of creation. He predicted the end to war and its sinful waste of lives and materials.

Isaiah's prophecy must have meant much to people living in Jerusalem, for God had placed them in a situation of extreme urgency and danger. When an army of conquest marched from Egypt, Babylonia, Assyria, or Syria, it was likely to pass the gates of Jerusalem. Costly defense preparations had to be made, even during times of peace. In the last days, according to prophecy, all this will be changed. There will be time and material for the manufacture of plowshares and pruning hooks and no further need for swords and spears.

In Deutero-Isaiah 65: 17–18, 24–25, we find the following:

For, behold, I create new heavens and a new earth: and the former shall not be remembered, nor come into mind. But be ye glad and rejoice for ever in that which I create: for, behold, I create Jerusalem a rejoicing, and her people a joy. . . . Before they call, I will answer; and while they are yet speaking, I will hear. The wolf and the lamb shall feed together, and the lion shall eat straw like the ox: and dust shall be the serpent's meat. They shall not hurt nor destroy in all my holy mountain, saith the Lord.

How much later these words were written after the first passage, we cannot ascertain, but the authors' visions of peace seemed to grow more mature with the passing years. They projected their hopes into the more distant future, when war would be a nightmare of the past and man would have the spirit and the knowledge to live together as children of God.

To those who argue that the prophets were not realistic, that their hope to see wolves and lambs feed together is contrary to natural law, religious scholars point out that many of

God's workings transcend the material limitations which man places upon himself and his world. The authors, however, with all their vision, could not even begin to entertain the concept of a world of war waged by twentieth-century men whose blatant disregard for the limitations of nature threatens to annihilate all life forms.

The rule of God as outlined by Deutero-Isaiah finds concrete expression in future predictions of the birth of the Prince of Peace, Jesus. The prophecy concerning the Messiah was indispensable to Deutero-Isaiah's vision of the glorious days of the future. Scripture had predicted a time when God would clothe himself in human form. John 1:14 reflected the fulfillment of this prophecy: "And the Word became flesh and dwelt among us."

Bertrand Russell's prognostications are fraught with graver import when one considers that, according to Christians, true to the word of the prophets, a savior did come as a gift of peace to mankind and subsequently was crucified. Coming at God's command and by a miracle of grace, the Messiah was to have a voice in the affairs of men. From a Christian perspective, such a prophecy was amply fulfilled in the facts of Jesus' life.

The ancient words of wisdom were forgotten in the awesome resolve of Western man to make the A-bomb and the H-bomb and enter the nuclear age. A frightening loss of restraint resulted at Hiroshima and Nagasaki. The type of nuclear device dropped there was labeled—and certainly not unjustly— *the hell bomb*. The flippant quip "Now all men are cremated equal" violates both the dignity of man and any pretense of reverence for life. The frantic search by men and women for more potent powers capable of mass murder merits the somber jest "The road to hell is paved with good inventions." Paul Tournier suggests that we take the Christian road to tomorrow:

There is less faith put in reason as a guide for humanity today than was the case in the last century. The atomic bomb has something to do with this. Those scientists who are in the

The Future

van for scientific progress are themselves afraid of the dangers inherent in it. After having made a public apology to the Japanese people, Professor Robert Moon, one of the nuclear physicists who helped to create the atomic bomb, declared to the Moral Rearmament Assembly that this mortal danger would only be removed if we began to listen to what God was saying to us: "In our time," he added, "the Holy Spirit must take first place, and the intellect must come second." . . . It is characteristic of Christianity that choice is made not of principles but of a person, of the living God, of Christ. It does indeed bring with it all the moral principles that can be discovered by reason. But it makes us more than mere machines applying principles: it makes us persons. It brings us a personal relationship, a current of life springing from the very source of all life, and true liberty.[8]

Those who still have the temerity to conjecture about the future agree that the hope for a future secular society in which there is no war is rooted in a concept of dedicated world government. By contrast, the Christian's hope for a world of peace is anchored in the transforming power of Jesus Christ as the Lord. Skeptics say it is unlikely that world peace can be achieved through either a world government or Christ's reigning in the hearts of men and women. Yet the dream of a warless world appeals to citizens of all nations, particularly to nations burdened with an obligation of billions of dollars each year for the maintenance of military might. If these nations no longer must expend such a great portion of their resources to support a defense machine, perhaps they can allocate more to develop their educational systems and beautify areas that have been scarred by the progress of technocracy.

HIGHER EDUCATION

Seekers of peace and human betterment must pin a large portion of their hopes on the field of education, where there is already much speculation regarding the future. In considering

A Religious Foundation of Human Relations

the future as regards education, it seems appropriate to review the traditional purpose of universities. The common one has been to prepare a select minority to practice one or more of the so-called liberal professions. The three areas to which Muslim and Christian universities first catered were religion, law, and medicine.

The original purpose of universities was not to provide a higher education for the general population as a whole or even for a majority. Rather, it was to select a small circle of elite whose personal temperament and ability qualified them to be trained to practice certain particular professions which their societies considered relevant.[9] The inadequacy of such a concept to serve a democratic form of government, where an educated constituency is a requisite, is at once apparent.

The elite concept of higher education remained relatively constant for centuries. However, in the seventeenth century a revolt against accepting Christian dogma on faith began, and the decision to make rational inquiry and independent examination part of higher education led to experimental science. The eighteenth and nineteenth centuries saw the application of experimental science to technology. The nineteenth and twentieth centuries have seen progressively greater specialization than ever before. This specialization and its human effects must be taken into account as we chart the course of education in the future.

The unprecedented expansion of knowledge has led to greater specialization by both teachers and students. Consequently, many students now complete their education with very little exposure to the philosophical and social foundations which persuade students to introspection and appraisal or reappraisal of their values. Too often, modern education and training prepare students to function well, but only within a particular specialty. In short, subject areas that tend to humanize students have been neglected.

However complicated or precise it may be, knowledge alone will not suffice for future education. Nathan M. Pusey, former president of Harvard University, lamented "the failure of recent

The Future

educational practice to prepare men in terms of heart and will and mind to prevent the strife, misunderstanding and willfulness that now arise, or resolutely to cope with them once arisen."[10] More than twenty years later, little had changed.

The federal government has exerted a profound influence on higher education, mainly by granting or withholding funds. Contracts and grants have had considerable impact in the past and are likely to do so in the future. It should be noted, however, that no master plan or coherent set of principles has been formulated for such expenditures. Despite federal legislation, local controls have in most cases remained predominant, at least in spirit.

In our society, most college and university students are encouraged to transcend the subcultures in which they were born and reared, and students are offered the mobility that education provides. The exposure to fellow students and professors, as well as books, tends to free students from the boundaries of a particular culture.[11] Future education must build upon foundations that deemphasize the unnatural barriers of race, color, sex, and social class.

Within higher education, the demands for publication and research have increased. In some academic circles they have been pushed to detrimental limits where professors must virtually publish or perish. This has led many teachers to place less emphasis on teaching and more on research and publication. How will this ultimately affect future students? Currently, it is not uncommon for a student to sign up for a course listed as being taught by a senior professor and never have any contact with him or her during the entire course. The gap is bridged by an assortment of graduate assistants and, in some cases, teaching machines.

Such depersonalization of education, where no student-teacher bond is cemented, has had adverse effects on student bodies and the quality of their instruction. In a few cases, courses are almost totally depersonalized. For example, a science course at an Oklahoma university is self-administered; the professor has committed his lectures to cassette tapes, and his classroom and exhibit room are arranged by a graduate assistant who merely writes on the chalkboard an instruction to start the tape and allows the students to take it from there. The future in education must be planned to ensure that the human relationship between teacher and student is not attenuated or lost. If this is not done, our educational legacy to posterity will contain only the dead letter, void of the spirit of interaction.

An increasingly large number of students are attending two-year community or junior colleges, and one must ask what effect this will have on the future of education. One negative factor that will develop is lack of the mixture of people from different regions and backgrounds needed to cross-fertilize minds and facilitate understanding. The two-year schools tend to focus on vocational-technical programs determined by community needs and frequently offer courses of study suited to students who for one reason or another do not meet the higher standards of four-year colleges and universities. Most community colleges seek to give all of their students a sound general education. A few progressive institutions are trying to give students skills and knowledge that will enable them to think effectively, express themselves clearly, and function in a responsible and mature manner. The high degree of alienation in America demands increased emphasis on activities that can assist students in gaining values by which they can live and thereby serve more effectively in our increasingly complex society. Great care must be exercised so that planning of the future does not make of education merely a vocational apprentice mill that trains human robots to operate industrial machines.

Values that help the student learn to give as well as take, to contribute as well as consume, would have the effect of modifying traditional attitudes toward the poor and disadvantaged. Indeed, there is need for programs of significant interpersonal worth to both students and their communities. Such an idea is not new. Proverbs 3:13–14 provides this guidance: "Happy is the man that findeth wisdom, and the man that

The Future

getteth understanding. For the merchandise of it is better than the merchandise of silver, and the gain thereof than fine gold." In Proverbs 15:4 the instruction on interpersonal communication may well serve as a basis for educational guidelines of the future: "A wholesome tongue is a tree of life: but perverseness therein is a breach in the spirit." Additional thoughts on the benefits of wisdom, as opposed to mere technical information, are found in Proverbs 27:11: "My son, be wise, and make my heart glad, that I may answer him that reproacheth me."

If future education is to meet the technological demands of our nation and the psychological and sociological needs of citizens, improved methods and techniques are essential. A major goal of college education should be the fullest possible development of each student's personality. It has been predicted that future students will be more heterogeneous in ability, value orientation, and personality than students of today. It is also predicted that only one out of twenty students from affluent homes will be concerned with finding himself or herself or reexamining society's purpose; the majority will be concerned with acquiring a vocation and getting ahead in the world.[12] If such conditions dominate the future, we will become self-contained cocoons of silk spinners that provide people insulated existence but deny them essence. William Barclay urges us to prepare students to become instrumental in moving the nation toward specific goals instead of letting it drift without purpose:

In life we need to know our goal. One of the distressing things in life is the obvious aimlessness of the lives of so many people. They are drifting anywhere instead of going somewhere. Maarten Maartens has a parable like this. "There was a man once, a satirist. In the natural course of time his friends slew him, and he died. And the people came and stood around his corpse. 'He treated the whole round world as his football; they said indignantly, 'and he kicked it.' The dead man opened one eye. 'But,' he said, 'always towards the goal.'" Someone once drew a cartoon showing two men on Mars looking down at the people in this world scurrying here, there and everywhere. One said to the other, "What are they doing?" The other replied, "They are going." "But," said the first, "where are they going?" "O," said the other, "they are not going anywhere; they are just going." And to go just anywhere is the certain way to arrive nowhere.[13]

In striving to meet the challenge of future education and its diverse demands, the long-held idea of a campus and its facilities may be obsolete. People talk about going to college as if it were an escape from life—which in many cases it may be. The concept of a campus should be more than simply a place; in reality, it is a system, and too often a contrived architectural community is imposed upon college students. And too often the lives of students and teachers are directed inward to an irrelevant campus life that only reputedly facilitates learning.[14] Future planners may need to place greater emphasis on the relevance education must have to the cultures it would perpetuate. Several major city universities exist and function effectively without an elaborate campus and its trappings. With an eye toward cost and efficiency, can we afford or do we need to continue building schools based on the campus model? Can we and should we use the new media of communications and computer technology for improvement of teaching? Would it be possible to facilitate learning without dehumanizing the students and the learning environment?

Modern technology might possibly help students with different abilities to arrive at the same level of competence in basic skills by different routes and at different times. This kind of instruction could free the faculty from routine tasks and allow more time for individualized help that could inspire students to achieve their full potential. Many other questions need to be posed and answered and much reevaluation undertaken if future human needs are to be met.[15]

The future holds unlimited challenge for practitioners in the field of education. The need for ingenuity and creativity is greater than it has ever been; certainly money is needed to train faculty, build facilities, and acquire and maintain equipment. Proper management of educational facilities is being aided by technology, but technology must serve, not enslave.

The Future

The need to strive for wisdom must be a part of future planning, and proper values must be stressed therein. This idea is not new.

CORRECTIONAL INSTITUTIONS

In 1948, James H. Robinson wrote:

Justice for minorities is seldom equal and evenhanded. In cases of crime by the majority against the minority, law is often accommodated to the advantage of the majority. In case of crime on the part of the minority against persons or property of the majority, the law is frequently too harsh. Nor is decision equitable when crime is committed by minorities of the same group; it is usually too lenient. Obviously this widespread practice in all parts of the nation, though it varies in degree from section to section, is a great obstacle blocking the path of equal opportunity and responsibility of individuals and groups. Unfortunately, few churches do more than pass resolutions condemning these wicked practices.[16]

This section of my book was written for persons who want to do more than pass resolutions.

In planning for the future, no area is in greater need of reform than correctional institutions. Prisons, jails, juvenile training schools, and probation and parole machinery are the parts of our criminal-justice system that the public sees least and knows least about. Unless there is a jailbreak, a prison riot, or a sensational scandal involving corruption or brutality, little attention is devoted to correctional policies and practices. The institutions housing approximately one-third of the corrections population are situated for the most part in remote rural areas or in the basements of police stations and courthouses. The other two-thirds are on probation and parole, invisibly dispersed throughout American communities. In this instance, "out of sight, out of mind" is an appropriate saying.

A Religious Foundation of Human Relations

The invisibility belies the correction system's size, complexity, and crucial importance. Corrections consists of scores of different kinds of institutions and programs of great diversity in approach, facilities, and quality. It has been said that corrections facilities on any given day are responsible for more than one million offenders. In the course of a year, they handle more than two million admissions and spend more than a billion dollars doing so. If our corrections system could restore all or even most of these people to the community as responsible citizens, America's crime rate would drop significantly.[17] As it stands today, a substantial percentage of offenders become recidivists; that is, they go on to commit more serious crimes.

In view of current circumstances, *corrections* does not seem a proper term for this process. Indeed, criminologists are increasingly beginning to feel that the conditions under which many offenders are handled, particularly in institutions, are a detriment to rehabilitation. However, there are hopeful signs that far-reaching changes can be found, and if society is to escape a return to the rule of club and claw, they must be implemented. A nation on the verge of famine, energy shortages, and a deficit trade balance cannot afford to let a large segment of its population remain unproductive.

In only a small proportion of correctional staffs are treatment and rehabilitation the primary functions. Approximately one-fourth consist of probation and parole officers working in communities and educators, social workers, psychologists, and psychiatrists working in institutions. By contrast, to three-fourths of the nation's correctional manpower is assigned the major responsibility for such functions as custody and maintenance.[18] A common attitude toward offenders is described in Job 18:16-19: "His roots shall be dried up beneath, and above shall his branch be cut off. His remembrance shall perish from the earth, and he shall have no name in the street. He shall be driven from light into darkness, and chased out of the world. He shall neither have son nor nephew among his people, nor any remaining in his dwellings."

The Future

Whatever the difference in type and quality among correctional institutions—from large maximum-security prisons to open forestry camps without guards or fences; from short-term detention homes for juveniles to penitentiaries where men and women spend most of their lives; from institutions of physically brutal and mentally stultifying routine to those with a variety of rehabilitative programs—there remains an inherent sameness about places where people are imprisoned.[19] This results partly from restraint per se, whether symbolized by walls and guns or by the myriad of more subtle restrictions on personal liberty. It also results from the institutional community's isolation from the outside world and from the alienation and separateness of the inmate society. It is fed by the strangeness of living apart from families, with no choice regarding place of residence, selection of intimate associates, or type of occupation; all are crucial values that are taken for granted in the outside world.

Restraints have advantages and disadvantages, and both must be weighed when future plans are formulated. On the one hand, they serve to punish and deter, and they prevent dangerous offenders from committing more crimes in communities while serving their sentences. Then, too, by keeping inmates away from the conditions of community life and subjecting them to a special environment that can be artificially controlled twenty-four hours a day, prisons sometimes afford opportunities for rehabilitative treatment that cannot be duplicated in the community.

On the negative side, an artificial environment that works against self-reliance and self-control often complicates and makes more difficult the reintegration of offenders into free society. Sometimes, institutions foster conspicuously deleterious conditions, such as idleness, corruption, and burtality. Proverbs 3:27 offers guidance to effect change: "Withhold not good from them to whom it is due, when it is the power of thine hand to do it."

A model penal institution should be relatively small and located as close as possible to the areas from which its inmates

A Religious Foundation of Human Relations

are drawn. Although a model institution might have a few high-security units for short-term detention under unusual circumstances, difficult and dangerous inmates should be sent to other institutions for longer confinement. Penal reformists suggest that a model institution resemble, as much as possible, a normal residential setting. For example, rooms would have doors rather than bars, inmates would eat at small tables in an informal atmosphere, and there would be classrooms, recreation facilities, and dayrooms as well as shops and libraries. Primarily, however, education, vocational training, and other activities would be conducted in the community or would draw into the institution community-based resources. Like probation and parole officers, its staff would be active in arranging for offenders to participate in community activities and in guiding and counseling them.

Other proposals for corrections practices suggest that some offenders might be released after an initial period of detention for diagnosis and intensive treatment. The model institution would permit corrections officials to invoke short-term detention — overnight or for a few days — as a sanction or discipline. Even if initial screening and classification indicated that long-term incarceration was required and an offender was therefore confined to another facility, the community-based institution could serve as a halfway house or prerelease center to ease an inmate's transition to community life. It could indeed serve as the hub for a satellite network of separate group homes and residential centers to be used for some offenders as a final step before complete release.

If supported by sufficiently flexible laws and policies, future corrections policies and practices like those cited would permit institutional restraint to be used only for as long as necessary and in carefully graduated degrees rather than as a relatively bland and inflexible process. A final advantage of such concepts is that institutions that are small and close to metropolitan areas and highly diversified in their programs provide excellent settings for research and experimentation

The Future

and can serve as proving grounds for needed innovations. Not only are they accessible to university and other research centers, but their size and freedom foster a climate that is crucial to academic inquiry and to the implementation of changes suggested by it.

Even in institutions committed to longer-term custody, many steps could be taken to improve their functioning. The most fundamental might be the creation of a collaborative regime in which staff and inmates work together toward rehabilitative goals and in which unnecessary conflict between the two groups is avoided. This style of management is more readily achieved if the institution staff is augmented by persons from the free community with whom inmates can identify.

In creating change, the nation's correctional institutions cannot perform their assigned work by merely tinkering with faulty machinery. A substantial upgrading of services and a new orientation of purpose toward integration of offenders into community life is a necessity. To achieve this end, there should be new divisions of labor, cooperative arrangements between federal, state, and local governments, and a better balance between institutional and community programs. The future must provide a wide variety of techniques for controlling and treating offenders in an arrangement that allows the techniques to be used flexibly and interchangeably. A strategy of research and validation must be substituted for the present random methods of determining how correctional resources should be used.

Many criminologists agree that the following principles should govern correctional operations:

1. Correctional operations should be located as close as possible to the homes of the offenders.

2. Reciprocal arrangements between governments should be developed to permit flexible use of resources. Regional sharing of institutional facilities and community programs should be greatly increased.

3. Large governmental units should take responsibility

for a variety of forms of indirect service to smaller and less financially able units, helping them to develop and strengthen their correctional services.

Because the federal government is best equipped to assume a large share of responsibility for providing impetus and direction for needed changes, it should take increasing responsibility for the future planning necessary to help upgrade the correctional programs of state and local governments. In the future, the federal government can stimulate action by providing financial and other assistance to state and local governments. Federal financial support is of crucial importance in developing the capacity to secure, analyze, and disseminate information concerning which treatments prove most successful with different classifications of offenders; in assisting state and local agencies to recruit and train the many kinds of personnel needed to staff new programs; and in providing funds for research, demonstration, and curriculum development projects.

Ultimately, however, state governments should develop and administer correctional services, involving local governments as much as possible and decentralizing operations through regional offices. Future planning should take into account the fact that no single pattern of organization has been designed to fit the variety of conditions that exist. Certainly, needs in the correctional field are a challenge to imaginative intergovernmental problem solving.

In the future, some correctional roles can be filled by established community organizations. Currently, several nongovernmental organizations are trying to improve corrections practices; operating independently of vested interests and of the limitations imposed by public office, they can play an important role in bringing about needed changes. They can conduct surveys, provide consulting services, and help with information exchange. Above all, they can inform the public about identified needs and problems and mobilize the grassroots support required for major changes. If public funds are made available to help private agencies perform these func-

The Future

tions, it is imperative that they maintain their perspective from outside the system in order to be constructive critics and monitors.

Education also can make a contribution. At present, most university curricula ignore the field of corrections despite the fact that many disciplines and professions—psychology, sociology, public administration, human relations, law, social work—have expertise that could do much to improve corrections. Clearly, universities have an indispensable role in filling the knowledge gap. Two things come to mind immediately: We must not foster vocational programs which supposedly answer questions about how to perform meaningful jobs but do not address the complexities of keeping a job. We must overcome the reluctance of scholars to address specific problems faced by institutional staffs charged with the perplexing task of controlling and rehabilitating offenders.

If we take no action conerning corrections, the negative consequences for the future are staggering. No doubt it would be more impressive to have available a quantitative statement of societal costs and consequences over the decades ahead if we maintain the present faltering correctional system, plus a statement of the gains that could be achieved through implementation of improvements. Unfortunately, it is impossible to provide such a balance sheet. Fortunately, the ineffectiveness of the present system is no longer a subject of controversy. True, the costs of action for the future are substantial, but the costs of inaction are immensely greater. Inaction would mean, in effect, that the nation would continue to avoid, rather than confront, one of its most critical social problems. If so, we will accept for the next generation a huge if not immeasurable burden of wasted lives. Decisive action, on the other hand, could make a difference that would matter significantly, and within our own time.

A humane penal reform system can be provided only by people with humane intentions. One of our greatest current wastes—and one we must avoid in the future—is that of human resources. Without effective attention to this matter, we may possibly survive even our own potentially destructive technology only to become victims of one another.

POVERTY

Based on current demographic trends, the world population will double in the period 1975 to 2000. However, even if we double the world food production during this period, more people would be starving and malnourished in 2000 than there were in 1975. The hunger gap will be abolished only by trebling food production. The additional one billion people demographers expect in the next twelve years are the biological equivalents of five billion people. Currently the biological feeding burden of the planet Earth is not 4 billion people but, counting pets and livestock, twenty billion population equivalents. For example, the feeding population of the United States is approximately 1.7 billion, this figure includes more than 200 million people and 150 million pets. The United Nations Food and Agriculture Organization has calculated that doubling food production (through added food acreage and increased yield per acre) would require investments of more than a trillion dollars. The cost would be considerably higher to treble food production.

Because of disproportionate animal production, Westerners consume two to six times more grain per day than do their counterparts in the Third World: Africa, Latin America, and China. Furthermore, Western countries have three times more tilled land available to feed each individual. Consequently, most persons in the Western portion of the world have yet to experience food and population pressures that are confronting the rest of the world.

Bruce G. Birch concluded: "The stark realities of the world food crisis have made hunger a priority item on the agenda of American churches."[20] However, in any consideration of poverty and hunger from the Judaeo-Christian perspective, it is well to recognize that "the fundamental problems confronting our

The Future

nation are not primarily technical, economic, or political; they are basically ethical and spiritual."[21] The Church can either fulfill its proper role and become a part of a world solution or assume an ostrich posture, head in the sand, and contribute to the perpetuation of poverty, an increasingly critical problem that contains the seeds of wholesale human destruction. Indeed, the Church is the only institution in society that has a divine mandate to probe basic questions of human values and the human spirit. It has a long tradition of altruism that stresses God's concern for the poor and oppressed.

The problems of poverty are manifested in the interlocking crises of hunger, energy, the population explosion, and an inequitable distribution of resources which will require prompt changes in the life-style of the developed countries if large segments of the world's people are not to suffer and die. "We have been called to alter our habits of diet and driving, to decrease our use of mass transit," writes J. Oscar McCloud. "All of this is good, because it requires us to face the fact that any solution of our present worldwide problems necessitates *permanent* change in many areas of our life habits, not just an emergency relief response."[22] Poverty is not a transient, intermittent problem; it is one that must be approached from a global perspective, and Christians have been called upon to take the lead in defining and shaping new and more responsible life-styles. It is well to remember this statement attributed to Confucius: "In a country well governed poverty is something to be ashamed of. In a country badly governed wealth is something to be ashamed of."[23]

The total number of Americans with incomes below the federal poverty line increased to 25.9 million in 1975. During this period, the annual income poverty line for an urban family of four was $5,500. A growing number of the poor are persons over sixty-five years of age. Although black Americans comprise a large proportion of the poor, poor whites are the numerical majority. Because our national norm is affluence, to be poor in America is to be one of the poorest persons in the world. As recently as 1976 the U.S. Department of Agriculture refused to distribute funds allocated by Congress to provide high-nutrition food for low-income nursing or pregnant women, infants and children under five years of age who are deemed nutritional risks. Withholding funds and telling poor Americans about deplorable living conditions of citizens in other countries does nothing to relieve their suffering. Action is needed to prevent and abate poverty.

Edward M. Huenemann asserts that "the doctrine of creation clearly implies that we are to assume systemic responsibility. It also assumes that we are free to affect the whole of creation. We are given a certain 'power of dominion.' Some sort of response to the whole of creation is inevitable. . . . Response to the hunger issue is so clearly a mandate for Christians that only the most deceptive rationalization could enable us to evade the demand."[24] In *New Catholic World*, Charles W. Maynes suggests that if poverty and its attendant problem of hunger are to be alleviated and widespread ravages of war averted, it is urgent that the developed and developing nations enter into some kind of prolonged, professional, nonideological, ministerial-level discussions with one another on the issues of world development.[25] It is apparent that a new international economic order must be formulated as a means of alleviating poverty here and abroad and that this task will require great spiritual insight.

Most persons seeking solutions to poverty make no distinction between it and hunger; the terms are used interchangeably. Moreover, in most commentary, solidarity of action is stressed. From a theological perspective, Denis Goulet says, "solidarity is the primary ethical value to which we must appeal in dealing with the hunger problem; it is a more fundamental moral category than either justice or charity."[26] However, genuine solidarity is difficult to attain because of the world's uneven development of both human and material resources.

Commenting on poverty in the United States, Frederick J. Perella states that in contemporary society, analogous to flesh on bones, hard times and shrunken economies reveal basic shapes in our country: the grotesque features of chronic

The Future

economic inequality.[27] Today the entire world is looking in the mirror of its own morality as these problems force basic value decisions. The present viewers see too many victims of poverty. Slowly, more and more of the world's people are challenging this degradation that stems from economic inequality and pseudodemocratic principles.

In our modern world, nearly five hundred million persons, most of them children, are close to starvation; countless thousands die each week. Before the crisis resolves itself, millions — perhaps as many as one billion — of people will die. And as Aristotle so aptly commented, poverty is the parent of revolution and crime. In the wake of such problems, is it any wonder that the world is looking to responsible spiritual guidance for methods to alleviate such a degree of present and projected suffering and needless death? In order to stop the catastrophe in the developed and underdeveloped world, important moral choices must be made immediately. Belief in the basic right of existence for all human beings is a manifestation of scriptural love. But in the United States and in other countries that exhort humans to display compassion and take positive steps, we have defied our prophets. We defy them even though we have been bombarded through the media with the stark facts of the world's poverty and hunger. For some incomprehensible reason, most people still lack the motivation to act on that information. Richard A. Hoehn suggests: "There is a simple exercise to bring home at the first-person emotional level a small part of what it means to be, if not starving, at least deprived. It is based on creating the conditions in which one feels to some extent what the poor and hungry feel."[28]

Discussing child starvation, Stewart Hiltner says: "There ought to be a Christian eschatology for this situation, with some strong guidelines for present practice. I wonder what Nathan would say."[29] In considering the ultimate extremity of global famine and the formulation of policy to deal with it, some experts have advocated triage:

The classical triage criterion, developed during wartime, is that of "maximum benefit." Wounded soldiers were divided into three groups: those who would survive without treatment, those who would die regardless of treatment, and, finally, those who would die unless treated immediately. Maximum medical benefit was attained by treating members of that third group as priority cases. . . . When one begins to apply this procedure to the problems of allocating scarce food resources on a global scale, the size differential—and accordingly the lack of control of the situation, the unpreditability of the results, and the resulting uncertainty of the final outcome—render inaccurate any comparison of this with the medical situation. Both situations represent problems of distributive justice to be sure. But the difference in scope between the immediate consequences of medical triage and the vast, unforeseeable consequences of a global food triage would seem to invalidate any further analogy between the two.[30]

Joseph Fletcher recognizes that in the exercise of global triage should widespread famine occur, ulterior motives might very well be used in selecting aid recipients. Most decisions concerning poverty, he suggests, are made in terms of enlightened self-interest rather than disinterested love, which love he believes any Christian situationist would advocate.

The food crisis prompts three responses: first, meet the present emergency situation, which, it is hoped, will soon ease; second, meet the medium-term problem of raising production in the developed countries in order to store reserves against emergencies; third, launch a long-term campaign to increase food production in the developing countries so that they may become self-sufficient. It will be necessary for those seeking reforms to demand changes. A unique Canadian group is doing just that:

GATT-Fly is an inter-church project which delves into trade issues affecting the welfare of the less-developed countries. It is sponsored by the Anglican, Lutheran, Presbyterian, Roman Catholic and United Churches. The group conducts studies on the food, energy and monetary crises and suggests policy alternatives for Canada. The Canadians argue that though the churches have long been involved in providing food aid, and

The Future

funds for agricultural development, now, besides that, they should help to make their government more sympathetic to Third World demands for a just international economic order. They realize that this involves a vast educational program, which must be directed both at government and at the man (and woman) in the pew.[31]

Ralph Waldo Emerson was correct when he said poverty demoralizes. One of the most insidious evils of poverty is that for too long it has been equated with laziness, inferiority, and lack of virtue. These epithets add humiliation to the other burdens of people who find themselves in this state. Many writers feel that although there are many biblical admonitions concerning care for the poor, those persons with the capability to assist often have been remiss in their obligation mainly because they do not truly empathize with the poor. To empathize is to know that "poverty leads to loss of dignity, freedom and security, and it is easy to lose sight of the simple fact of poverty in concern for those values, and all the other values that elude the poor. . . . They are denied a rightful claim to subsistence, to existence. Their existence depends on the whims of others. The world denies them dignity, integrity, security, freedom and justice."[32]

Although economic justice as a political force is less than 150 years old, it has gained increasing prominence as the problem of poverty has become a central issue in international affairs. In 1948 the United Nations Declaration of Human Rights affirmed the "equal and inalienable rights of all members of the human family." Specifically concerning poverty, this principle of human rights is applied to economic justice: "Everyone has the right to a standard of living adequate for the health and well-being of himself and of his family, including food, clothing, housing and medical care and necessary social services, and the right to security in the event of unemployment, sickness, disability, widowhood, old age and other lack of livelihood in circumstances beyond his control."[33]

In analyzing biblical material germane to this subject, hunger and poverty cannot be separated. Although it has been

A Religious Foundation of Human Relations

recorded many times that famine struck an entire nation, rich and poor alike, it was mainly the poor who went hungry, for people of affluence were able to buy food from other nations. Bruce C. Birch has observed: "In both the Old and New Testaments hunger is linked with other terms describing those who have been forced by societal conditions into a marginal existence—the poor, the needy, the widow, the orphan, the oppressed."[34] Despite all admonitions in both Jewish and Christian scriptural literature, the poor remain with us. This appears to be a paradox, for there are many accounts that God especially loves and administers to the poor. Psalms 12:5 records: "Because the poor are despoiled, because the needy groan, I will now arise, says the Lord; I will place him in the safety for which he longs." In both Psalms (9:12, 17-18, 10:12) and Isaiah (41:17), we are assured that God will not forget or forsake the poor or needy.

From a theological perspective, since God has so clearly identified himself with the poor, there is an incumbent responsibility upon the more privileged to exercise special concern for the less fortunate. The rights of the poor are delineated most clearly in the legal codes of the Old Testament, where concern for the poor is taken out of the realm of voluntary charity. The clearest statement appears in Deuteronomy 15:

There will be no poor among you . . . if only you will obey the voice of the Lord your God. . . . If there is among you a poor man, one of your brethren, in any of your towns within your land which the Lord your God gives you, you shall not harden your heart or shut your hand against your poor brother, but you shall open your hand to him, and lend him sufficient for his need. . . . You shall give to him freely, and your heart shall not be grudging. . . . For the poor will never cease out of the land; therefore I command you, You shall open wide your hand to your brother, to the needy and to the poor.

It is abundantly clear here that God's chosen are commanded to care for the poor. To conform to his will is part of what it

The Future

means to be the elect of God, and the exhorted activity is obligatory, not optional.

The people of Israel are reminded by God that they were once slaves in Egypt. The prophets of the Old Testament also bore witness to the rights and privileges of the poor. The poor were accorded the right of gleaning in the fields, and the owners were admonished, for the sake of the poor, not to be so thorough in their harvesting that those in poverty be denied sufficient leavings. In Nehemiah 5:6–11, an extensive reform is launched to return to the poor the land taken from them in payment of debts and the goods taken to pay interest.

It is plain in the Old Testament that the world's land belongs to God and has been bestowed upon humans as a gift; humans are stewards, not owners; the profits of the land should be spent for good services toward the poor, for this is the desire of God, the rightful owner of the land; and wealth is regarded at best as an impediment to righteousness, with the potential to motivate the exercise of great evil:

The prophets repeatedly characterize wealth as leading to indifference or to complicity in oppression: "Woe to those who lie upon beds of ivory, and stretch themselves upon their couches, and eat lambs from the flock, and calves from the midst of the stall; who sing idle songs to the sound of the harp, and like David invent for themselves instruments of music; who drink wine in bowls, and anoint themselves with the finest oils, but are not grieved over the ruin of Joseph."[35]

A large portion of New Testament perspective regarding the poor and hungry is an extension of the tradition of Israel. Some writers even suggest that Jesus radicalized that tradition, for it is clear from the beginning of his ministry that he identified with those in circumstances of poverty. Jesus spoke often of the poor and singled them out as especially blessed by God. Jesus makes it quite clear that he is identified with the poor and the needy to the extent that acceptance of him is equated with ministering to their needs: "The witness of both Old and

New Testaments makes clear that concern for those forced to live a marginal existence is not an optional activity for the people of God, nor is it only a minor requirement. Identification with those persons is at the heart of what it means to be of the community of faith."[36]

RACISM

Ponder these thoughts of Robert A. Bennett:

The black experience in America is not the Jewish-Christian experience in ancient Palestine. But as the tale of sorrows of a people awaiting deliverance, the black narrative has a message consistent with the biblical witness though not to be found in that witness. It is a testimony of its own, distinct from Scripture even as it would proclaim its word to us in biblical images and in categories of scriptural revelation. In this interplay of the new and old, of the familiar and the unique, the black experience partakes of religious experience as it attempts to speak and thereby mediate to us something of God's intentions for us. Though not of canonical status, the story of the black man in America is a self-validating account of faith which when heard and heeded, helps black and white respond more creatively to the divine word for our present situation.[37]

This passage is not cited to suggest that blacks are missing in Scripture. Indeed, the Bible makes several references to blacks, including Joseph's trip to Africa and Solomon's transplanting an African court to rule his empire. What we can deduce is the historically low status of blacks—and other nonwhites—as a people.

Considering the past and the present, one of the surest things about future American society is that it will continue to be made up of many races. For those who want to plan a democratic future, racism is a problem of urgent priority. An African folk tale from Kenya illustrates some of the feeling that separates black and white people:

The Future

> *After God had made men, the first ancestor of the Europeans tried to imitate Him and to create a man too. And so he did. He built many men who looked exactly as they should, on the outside. But in the end, when he tried to make their hearts beat, he did not succeed. He had to give up. Therefore, until this day, people say the white man is mighty. He can do everything, even build people. If only he could make their hearts beat!*[38]

Biblically, we can build a case for a one-family view of the earth. Genesis 10:32 is an attempt to show that Hebrews descended in a few generations from one common ancestor: Noah. The chronology divides the earth's population into racial families derived from Noah's three sons: Shem the progenitor of the Semites, Ham of the Africans, and Japheth of the Indo-Europeans. This accounting gives credence to the belief that people are related racially and spiritually, but Christian racists choose not to accept it.

While Christian racists never appeal to the notion of the Demiurge to account for the nature of the existence of out-races, the doctrine of the second fall is explicitly enunciated in some naïve and obscurantist circles. The usual form of this theological proposition is the assertion that God himself has condemned Negroes to be the "hewers of the wood and drawers of the water now, henceforth and forever" under the curse of Ham. A variation of the doctrine is the notion that Negroes are the descendants of Cain's union with an ape whom Cain, the first criminal, saw fit to marry "in the land of Nod." This means that while the Negro shares the universal condemnation of the human race in Adam, he also bears the added condemnation of God in a special, racial fall.[39]

In 1968 the United States Commission on Civil Disorders warned the president of the United States that we were on the verge of becoming permanently two separate and unequal societies, one black and the other white.[40] The race schism has been described by many scholars as the most serious domestic crisis since the Civil War. Recently, the national focus has begun to change. Writes Matthew Holden, Jr.: "For many observers, the milieu now is one of social conservatism rather than social change, one in which the severest domestic economic fear is not of unemployment but of inflation in which perhaps the most fundamental issue being discussed is the purported conflict between environmental protection and economic growth."[41]

Disillusioned by the obstacles placed before them and the general neglect accompanying the obstacles, a growing number of blacks no longer advocate religious or racial integration. As they see it, the only solution is to establish and maintain the integrity of black people by establishing their own unique black culture. This need not be negative, however. Acklyn and Alma Lynch believe the shock of the sordid past accorded blacks by whites is beginning to heal; that the black people have healed, and that new dynamisms are being released that will thrust them into the future with greater energy and force than ever before.[42] Mark 12:10 offers a basis of hope for this theory: "Have ye not read this scripture; The stone which the builders rejected is become the head of the corner."

Addressing their black compatriots, the Lynches wrote: "You are overcoming the corruptive influences of Western civilization which excluded you from the activation of your conscious mental achievements of the past four centuries. You will throw off the burden that enslaves you, for it is erected within you."[43] According to the Lynches, the future growth of blacks will materialize only if they cut the umbilical cord that binds them subjugatingly to Western society. The Lynches say Third World countries are moving toward socialism and away from the exploitation that attends colonization.

In *The Pillage of Third World*, Pierre Jalee contends that the Western bloc (Canada, the United States, Europe, Japan, Israel, and Australia) exploits the economies of African and Latin American countries for the benefit of monopolistic capital and influences or controls the policies of those countries to that end.[44] In America, the Lynches assert, white exploiters concentrate on playing black politicians against the black masses in urban and rural areas in an attempt to divide

The Future

and conquer those who are most intent upon justice: blacks who retaliate against brutal attacks and jailings and other forms of unethical behavior.

In order for blacks to survive in the future, the Lynches conclude that it will be necessary for them to establish a national and international black political structure:

Our guidelines should be freedom with responsibility. What do we mean when we refer to freedom? First, there is the freedom of black people to determine their own destiny. Second, there is freedom from exploitation, hunger, and disease. Third, there is personal freedom to live in dignity and harmony with other men. Fourth, there is freedom from alienation. Fifth, there is freedom of creative thought and development as people consistently express their cultural, moral and spiritual sensibilities.[45]

For the future to bring the long-awaited equality sought by nonwhites, improved education and leadership must be initiated to facilitate equality. It must make them aware that they are kept as consumers rather than as producers and that this prevents them from controlling their economic destiny: "When one man controls the means by which another obtains food, clothing and shelter which are essential to life, then there is no equality. The man whose means of living are controlled by another, must serve the interests of this other regardless of his own desires or his own needs."[46] Emil Brunner supports this position. "Man can hardly be expected to subdue the earth unless some fragment of it belongs to him," he writes. "Over the space he must have full power to do all that the measure of his creative gifts allow."[47]

It seems reasonable that nonwhites in general and blacks in particular must plan for economic self-sufficiency if they are to throw off their bonds and improve the quality of their lives. Such a movement might include collective purchases of land for the development of an agricultural base; development of banking and insurance industries that can finance and sustain economic growth; development of a communications industry to educate blacks about their civil rights and responsibilities; development of an industrial sector to meet consumer needs; development of an efficient transportation system; development of a mechanism to deal with trade relationships between black people on the Continent and black people in the Americas; and, finally, creation of an exchange program of technical and scientific expertise among black people to meet developmental needs.

These and other programs might allow nonwhites to have a quality of life comparable to that of their white counterparts. In any case, it is abundantly clear that if resegregation is to be avoided, it is incumbent upon those in authority to build a true nation of brotherhood, love, and respect. W. E. B. DuBois posed a question that is of special significance to persons in positions of authority:

I sit with Shakespeare and he winces not. Across the color line I move arm in arm with Balzac and Dumas, where smiling men and welcoming women glide in gilded halls. From out of the cages of evening that swing between the long-limbed earth and the tracery of stars, I summon Aristotle and Aurelius and what soul I will, and they come all graciously with no scorn nor condescension... wed with Truth, I dwell above this veil. Is this the life you grudge me, O knightly America? Is this the life you long to change into the dull red hideousness of Georgia? Are you so afraid lest peering from this high Pisgah, between Philistine and Amalekite, we might see the promised land?[48]

COMPUTERS

In *Man and the Computer*, John G. Kemeny cautions:

The computer is the most patient and obedient servant that man has ever found. As long as it is well cared for, so that its physical well-being is assured, it will serve him well. The computer's sole goal in life is to carry out instructions given to it by human beings.... Computers are so obedient that,

A Religious Foundation of Human Relations

he construction of the robot managers is in Kemeny's
he easiest part of the whole schema. The miniaturization
ponents now called LSI (large-scale integration) could
ossible the construction of a powerful computer the
human brain. The robot could then be provided with
gans and means for locomotion and thus could react
and sound stimuli.[57]

problem of reproduction by computer-manager robots
cult one, but Kemeny claims it is theoretically pos-
uild a self-reproducing machine. Thus a robot could
a new robot and, in biblical terms, "breathe life into
When it had physically assembled the new machine,
nsfer to it the contents of its own memory, thereby
man's own valued need to transfer ideas and con-
the self-reproducing robot has been perfected, only
will be man made; the others will be created by
ts" and programmed so that each offspring differs
its parents, or even a few improvements could be
an evolutionary process could take place. If one
ng were destroyed, perhaps the robot could be
to cry out as David did in the Old Testament:
Absalom would God I had died for thee!" But
od of the Bible or the Koran or the Talmud in
rolled society?

rgued that human beings act much like insuf-
they perform repetitive, mind-dulling tasks,
r implications of personal needs, and become
ess. How much simpler to turn all the social
esses over to a machine! If we can love tele-
s, cars, and membership in restricted clubs,
to love robots, too? As is said in John 14:23:
he will keep my words: and my Father will
the robots will keep the words or values we
. In fact, they are likely to do so more faith-
God's words.

lready conditioned or programmed to base
ns on information and behavioral patterns

The Future

even if the instructions you give them are completely nonsensical, the computer will carry them out to the letter.[49]

Kemeny argues that the Orwellian picture of a cradle-to-grave existence governed by automated and regimented lifestyles need not grow out of a computerized society. In the future, he says, value systems may have to be turned over to a gigantic computer complex set in motion by a totalitarian world government unable to cope with terrestrial starvation, overpopulation, and the proliferation of atomic weaponry.[50] But, Kemeny continues, the global managers—robots who watch, process, and manipulate our needs—will be what we program them to be.

The danger is that automation, a new god, is just around the corner waiting to be enthroned, just as Zeus and Athena were worshipped in ancient Greece. Remember, however, that the Bible admonishes: "I am the Lord thy God, which have brought thee out of Egypt land, out of the house of bondage. Thou shalt have no other gods before me." Will the new god correct the dehumanized prison system, bring equality to our educational establishment, free ethnic minorities, and solve Lord Russell's need for a world government? Is such synthetic Caesarship, in fact, possible?

In Genesis 1:26, we are told: "God said let us make man in our image, after our likeness: and let them have dominion over the fish of the sea, and over the fowl of the air, and over the cattle, and over all the earth, and over every creeping thing that creepeth upon the earth." Kemeny contends that by the year 2000, man will have exercised this dominion and computers will become a new species.[51] In essence, man will have created a new life form—and very likely in his own image if our past pride is any criterion.

This argument is based on several assumptions. A species is a distinct form of life, and computers are distinctive. Thus it is not ridiculous to compare a machine to a living being. The traditional distinction between living and inanimate matter may be important to a biologist, but it is unimportant and possibly dangerously misleading for a philosophical system of

A Religious Foundation of Human Relations

values in the twenty-first century.[52] But Exodus 20:4 cautions: "Thou shalt not make unto thee any graven image, and shalt not bow down thyself to them, nor serve them: for I the Lord thy God am a jealous God."

What distinguishes living from inanimate matter? Since there is no universally accepted definition of life and since our lawyers and doctors are currently engaged in a debate over just what actually constitutes death, Kemeny presents these criteria for life:

1. Metabolism: the ability, and not necessarily the chemical ability, to perform a change in matter to generate energy.

2. Locomotion.

3. The ability to reproduce.

4. Individuality.

5. Intelligence: the ability to manipulate and use symbols in the brain.

6. The view that life is natural as opposed to an artificial state of being.[53]

Kemeny concedes that we tend to shape our definition of living to fit those species that have developed through the evolutionary process. Since the highest species tend to have all the characteristics of lower species, plus additional ones, our definitions put particular stress on lower living forms in order to be as inclusive as possible.[54] And since metabolism is common to all species but intelligence is not, the former is considered an essential trait for life, the latter a luxury. In Kemeny's classification, there is no provision to include species that demonstrate some of the higher qualifications but not the lower ones, since examples of such species are not found in the evolutionary chain.[55] In fact, Kemeny surmises that extraterrestrial exploration will discover species that biologists will be forced to classify as living even though they do not fit the standard definition.

Kemeny points out that traditional definitions and values of life are already in a great deal of flux because of recent developments in biochemical laboratories which portend the creation of life types (test-tube babies made from the very

The Future

nuclei of RNA and DNA). Considering
would computer-manager robots fit th
living? Kemeny offers cogent argume
they would fit quite well.

Robots definitely could exhibi
show the ability to think and to c
tifically testable sense, the least of
and verbal tasks plus a sophis
arguments. They could ask a
rapidly, and remember perfectl
robots also could manipulate
teresting to note that Kemeny
philosophical mind-body qual
robot spirit or feeling as they
sense.

Robots could display a
same sense that human be
playing of programmed e
stimuli. In fact, they coul
of neurotic or psychotic
appear to foster in hum

There is no way to rer
partly because no one
his situation or the
also because the app
innovate, to give ri
comprehended in t
There is an imp
points to a proce
who questions h
other, both bec
and because w
no act can be
come to term
to what mig
role they ac
movement

book
of con
make
size of
sense o
to sight

Th
is a dif
sible to b
assemble
its dust."
it could tr
satisfying
cepts. Onc
the origina
their "parer
slightly fron
made so tha
of its offspr
programmed
"Oh, my son
where is the (
this robot-con

It can be a
ficient robots:
ignore the deep
sick in the proc
problems and st
vision sets, hous
couldn't we learn
"If a man love me
love him." Surely
program into then
fully than we keep
Since we are a
our values and nor

The Future

disseminated by the mass media, especially television, it will not be a difficult transition for us to accept computer-controlled robots. After all, how many human managers can preserve an ethic focusing on justice, wisdom, and impartiality? The attractions of such a future society are many. We could, for instance, let the robots make war for us, lay down their lives for us: "Greater love hath no man than this, that a man lay down his life for his friends" (John 15:13).

However, there remain two nagging questions: Will the robot managers be any more our friends in this brave new world than the human leaders are in today's world? Will the robots assist us in creating a humane future? Tomorrow's future lies imprisoned in the enslaved minds of the present. We can only hope that a slumbering Michelangelo will awaken among us to loosen the bonds of beauty that have inspired humans to reach their noblest heights. Surely a humane society will need to be made up of men and women who will have the proper value system to integrate their overwhelming knowledge within humane priorities. Human relations without a religious foundation will be nothing more than a game of insensitive manipulation for selfish ends. That is not my dream.

NOTES

CHAPTER 1

1. Robert N. Bellah, "Civil Religion in America," in William G. McLoughlin and Robert N. Bellah (eds.), *Religion in America* (Boston, Houghton Mifflin, 1968), 6.
2. Samuel Beckett, *Proust* (London, J. Calder, 1965), 3.
3. Archie, J. Bahm, *The World's Living Religions* (New York, Dell, 1964), 16.
4. *Ibid.*, 17.
5. *Ibid.*, 32.
6. *Ibid.*, 36.
7. *Ibid.*, 40.
8. *Ibid.*
9. Homer W. Smith, *Man and His Gods* (New York, Viking Press, 1932), 15.
10. George Henderson, *Human Relations: From Theory to Practice* (Norman, University of Oklahoma Press, 1974), 59.
11. Bahm, *op. cit.*, 239.
12. Edith Hamilton, *Mythology* (Boston, Little, Brown, 1942), 7.
13. *Ibid.*, 8.
14. *Ibid.*, 9.
15. *Ibid.*, 14.
16. This section is based in part on an unpublished paper, "The Helping Relationship," written by Norma Banks and Ellen Feaver Blyden at Norman, Oklahoma, July 24, 1975. It is revised and reprinted with their permission.
17. Langdon Gilkey, "Sources of Protestant Theology in America," in McLoughlin and Bellah, *op. cit.*, 160.
18. *Ibid.*, 162.

19. Wilbur G. Katz and Harold P. Southerland, "Religious Pluralism and the Supreme Court," in McLoughlin and Bellah, *op. cit.*, 260.
20. Franklin H. Littell, "The Churches and the Political Body Politic," in McLoughlin and Bellah, *op. cit.*, 42.
21. Bryan Wilson, "Religion and the Churches in Contemporary America," in McLoughlin and Bellah, *op. cit.*, 80.
22. Thomas Carlyle, "Past and Present," in Gordon N. Ray (ed.), *Prose in the Victorian Period* (Boston, Houghton Mifflin, 1958), 138.
23. Karl Menninger, *Love Against Hate* (New York, Harcourt, Brace & World, 1942), 293.
24. Donald Meyer, "Churches and Families," in McLoughlin and Bellah, *op. cit.*, 230.
25. Karl Menninger, *The Human Mind* (New York, Alfred A. Knopf, 1930), 3.
26. Paul Tournier, *The Meaning of Persons* (New York, Harper & Row, 1957), 32.
27. Carl G. Jung, *Civilization in Transition*, Vol. 10 in *Collected Works* (Princeton, N.J., Princeton University Press, 1959–68), 64–65.
28. Anthony Storr, *The Integrity of Personality* (New York, Atheneum, 1961), 41–43.
29. Carl G. Jung, *The Undiscovered Self* (New York, Mentor, 1957), 16–20.
30. Jung, *The Undiscovered Self*, 68–69.
31. Ludwig A. Feuerbach, *Die Philosophie der Zukunft* (Stuttgart, Fromann, 1922), 41.
32. Robert W. Miller (ed.), *The New Christianity* (New York, Dell, 1967), 78.
33. M. Esther Harding, *The 'I' and the 'Not-I'* (Princeton, N.J., Princeton University Press, 1965), 75.
34. Maurice Nicoll, *Psychological Commentaries* (London, Vincent Stuart & John M. Watkins, 1964), I, 149–50.
35. Jung, *The Undiscovered Self*, 117–18.
36. Desmond Morris, *Intimate Behavior* (New York, Random House, 1971), 11.
37. *Ibid.*, 243–44.
38. Pitirim A. Sorokin, "The Powers of Creative Unselfish Love," in Abraham H. Maslow (ed.), *New Knowledge in Human Values* (Chicago, Henry Regnery, 1959), 11.
39. Kurt Goldstein, "Health As Value," in Maslow, *op. cit.*, 182.
40. Rollo May, *Man's Search for Himself* (New York, W. W. Norton, 1953), 174–79.
41. Jess Lair, *I Ain't Much Baby—But I'm All I've Got* (Garden City, N.Y., Doubleday, 1969), 162.
42. W. Gordon Ross, *Companion of Eternity* (New York, Abingdon Press, 1961), 182.
43. *Ibid.*
44. Sren Kierkegaard, *The Works of Love* (New York, Harper & Row, 1962), 22.
45. Claude Steiner, *Games Alcoholics Play* (New York, Ballantine Books, 1971), 122.
46. Goldstein, "Health As Value," *loc. cit.*, 184.

Notes

47. William Glasser, *Reality Therapy* (New York, Harper & Row, 1965), viii.
48. *Ibid.*, 9.
49. *Ibid.*, 14.
50. *Ibid.*, 6.
51. *Ibid.*, 60.
52. Eric Berne, *Games People Play* (New York, Grove Press, 1964), 48.
53. *Ibid.*, 62.
54. Theodore Roszak, *Where the Wasteland Ends* (New York, Doubleday, 1972), 62.
55. Naomi Brill, *Working with People* (Philadelphia, J. B. Lippincott, 1973), 48.
56. Felix P. Biestek, *The Casework Relationship* (Chicago, Loyola University Press, 1957), 3.
57. *Ibid.*, 17.
58. *Alcoholics Anonymous* (New York, Alcoholics Anonymous World Services, 1955), 17.
59. O. Kohner and J. Lebman, *Hope for Man* (New York, Simon & Schuster, 1966), 72.
60. George C. McCauley, "Values of Jesus," *New Catholic World*, Vol. 217 (January–February, 1974), 103.
61. *Ibid.*
62. Marc Tanenbaum, "Major Issues in the Jewish/Christian Situation Today," *New Catholic World*, Vol. 217 (January–February, 1974), 30.
63. Eva Fleishner, "The Religious Significance of Israel: A Christian Perspective," *New Catholic World*, Vol. 217 (January–February, 1974), 19.
64. *Ibid.*
65. McCauley, *loc. cit.*, 108.
66. Maureen Joy, "Kohleberg and Moral Education," *New Catholic World*, Vol. 215 (January–February, 1972), 14.
67. "Toward a New Humanist Manifesto," *The Humanist*, Vol. 33 (January–February, 1973), 13.
68. George F. Thomas, *Christian Ethics and Moral Philosophy* (New York, Scribners, 1955), 389.
69. Earl C. Dahlstrom, *Helping Human Beings: The Ethics of Interpersonal Relations* (Washington, D.C., Public Affairs Press, 1964), 109.
70. Albert Schweitzer, quoted in George Seldes (ed.), *The Great Quotations* (New York, Pocket Books, 1967), 155.
71. Roy B. Chamberlin and Herman Feldman (eds.), *The Dartmouth Bible* (Boston, Houghton Mifflin, 1950), xxix. In this book I have used the King James Version and the Revised Standard Version.
72. See Ernest Troeltsch, *The Social Teachings of the Christian Churches*, trans. by Olive Wyon (London, George Allen & Unwin, 1931), Vol. I.

CHAPTER 2

1. Henri Bergson, *The Two Sources of Morality and Religion* (Garden City, N.Y., Doubleday, 1935), 78.

A Religious Foundation of Human Relations

2. M. K. Gandhi, *The Story of My Experiments with Truth* (Washington, D.C., Public Affairs Press, 1948), 79.
3. *Ibid.*, 378.
4. *Ibid.*, 615.
5. Martin Luther King, Jr., *Why We Can't Wait* (New York, The American Library, 1963).
6. Whitney M. Young, Jr., *Beyond Racism* (New York, McGraw-Hill, 1972).
7. Rudolf Dreikurs, *Social Equality: The Challenge of Today* (Chicago, Henry Regenry, 1971).
8. John H. Holmes, *My Gandhi* (New York, Harper & Row, 1963), 59.
9. Don A. Torgersen, *Gandhi* (Chicago, Children's Press, 1968), 238.
10. Adlai Stevenson, quoted by Arthur P. Davies, *Saturday Review*, Vol. 42 (February 7, 1959), 11.
11. C. Eric Lincoln (ed.), *Is Anybody Listening to Black America?* (New York, Seabury Press, 1968), 280.
12. Dreikurs, *Social Equality*, xiii.
13. Holmes, *op. cit.*, 69.
14. *Ibid.*, 71.
15. Gandhi, *op. cit.*, 337.
16. Martin Luther King, Jr., "Love and Civil Disobedience," *New South* (December, 1961), 6.
17. Richard Shaull, "Christian Faith As Scandal in a Technocratic World," in Martin E. Marty and Dean G. Peerman (eds.), *New Theology No. 6: On Revolution and Non-Revolution, Violence and Non-Violence, Peace and Power* (New York, Macmillan, 1969), 132.
18. Holmes, *op. cit.*, 132.
19. Quoted in Beatrice Pitney, *India: A World in Transition* (New York, Frederick A. Praeger, 1967), 77.
20. Holmes, *op. cit.*, 58.
21. *The Interpreter's Dictionary of the Bible* (Nashville, Abingdon Press, 1962), 716.
22. Gandhi, *op. cit.*, 307.
23. *Ibid.*, 92.
24. *Ibid.*, 96.
25. Holmes, *op. cit.*, 130.
26. *Interpreter's Dictionary*, 47.
27. Holmes, *op. cit.*, 109.
28. Gandhi, *op. cit.*, 249.
29. Holmes, *op. cit.*, 31.
30. Herbert W. Richardson, "Martin Luther King—Unsung Theologian," in Marty and Peerman, *New Theology No. 6*, 180.
31. Martin Luther King, Jr., "Bold Design for a New South," *The Nation*, Vol. 196 (March 30, 1963), 260.
32. Martin Luther King, Jr., "Letter from Birmingham Jail," *Christian Century*, Vol. 80 (June 12, 1963), 767–73.
33. *See* Martin Luther King, Jr., *Where Do We Go From Here: Chaos or Community?* (New York, Bantam Books, 1968).
34. George Brietman (ed.), *Malcolm X Speaks* (New York, Grove Press, 1966), 12.

Notes

35. George Celestin, "A Christian Looks at Revolution," in Marty and Peerman, *New Theology No. 6*, 100.
36. Harvey G. Cox, *The Secular City* (New York, Macmillan, 1965), 107. See also Jacques Ellul, *Violence: Reflections from a Christian Perspective*, trans. by Cecilia Gikings (New York, Seabury Press, 1969).
37. Young, *Beyond Racism*, 2.
38. *Ibid.*, 11.
39. *Ibid.*, 22.
40. *Ibid.*, 62.
41. *Ibid.*, 132.
42. *Ibid.*, 133.
43. William A. Clebsch, "American Churches As Traducers of Tradition," in Martin E. Marty and Dean G. Peerman (eds.), *New Theology No. 9: Theology in the Context of New Particularisms* (New York, Macmillan, 1972), 73–74.
44. Young, *op. cit.*, 225.
45. Rudolf Dreikurs and Loren Grey, *Logical Consequences* (New York, Meredith Press, 1968), 6.
46. Alvin Toffler, *Future Shock* (New York, Random House, 1970).
47. Alfred Adler, *Social Interest: A Challenge of Mankind* (London, Feber & Feber, 1938), 17.
48. Henderson, *op. cit.*, 38–39.
49. Dreikurs, *Social Equality*, 175.
50. *Ibid.*, 189.
51. Richard McKeon, "The Practical Use of Philosophy of Equality," in L. Bryson, *et al.* (eds.), *Aspects of Human Equality* (New York, Harper & Row, 1957).
52. John Donne, cited in Seldes, *op. cit.*, 630.

CHAPTER 3

1. Havelock Ellis, *Studies in the Psychology of Sex* (New York, Random House, 1936), 310.
2. Plato, *Symposium*, trans. by B. Jowett, in Louise Ropes Loomis (ed.), *Plato* (New York, Walter J. Black, 1942).
3. *Ibid.*, 165.
4. *Ibid.*, 167.
5. *Ibid.*, 198.
6. *Ibid.*, 200.
7. Aristotle, quoted in Seldes, *op. cit.*, 407.
8. Aristotle, *Nicomachean Ethics*, trans. by Martin Ostwald (New York, Bobbs-Merrill, 1962), 260.
9. *Ibid.*, 255.
10. *Ibid.*, 252.
11. *Ibid.*
12. *Ibid.*, 219.
13. *Ibid.*, 229.
14. *Ibid.*, 239.

15. Anders Nygren, *Agape and Eros,* trans. by Philip Watson (Philadelphia, Westminister Press, 1953), 232.
16. *See* Karl Barth, *Church Dogmatics,* ed. by T. F. Torrance and G. W. Bromiley (Edinburgh, T & T Clark, 1960), Vol. III.
17. Jacques Maritain, *Moral Philosophy* (New York, Scribners, 1964), 81.
18. Bernard Häring, *The Law of Christ* (New York, Newman Press, 1963), II, 98 ff.
19. Erich Fromm, *The Art of Loving* (New York, Harper & Row, 1956), 7.
20. Erich Fromm, quoted in Seldes, *op. cit.,* 631.
21. Sigmund Freud, quoted in Erich Fromm, *The Anatomy of Human Destructiveness* (New York, Holt, Rinehart & Winston, 1973), 447.
22. *Ibid.,* 448.
23. Fromm, *The Art of Loving,* 41–42.
24. C. L. Becker, *New Liberties for Old* (New Haven, Yale University Press, 1941), 148–50.
25. Nygren, *op. cit.,* 61–68.
26. Paul Tillich, *Systematic Theology* (Chicago, University of Chicago Press, 1951), 279.
27. Paul Ramsey, *Basic Christian Ethics* (New York, Scribners, 1950), 47.
28. Fulton J. Sheen, *The Power of Love* (New York, Beacon Press, 1964).
29. *Ibid.,* 15.
30. *Ibid.,* 33.
31. Nygren, *op. cit.,* 78.
32. *Ibid.,* 77.
33. *Ibid.,* 76.
34. Sheen, *op. cit.,* 110.
35. *Ibid.,* 115.
36. Nygren, *op. cit.,* 76–77.
37. C. S. Lewis, quoted in Nelson Rosewell, *Successful Living Day by Day* (New York, Macmillan, 1972), 112.
38. Oscar Wilde, quoted in *Colliers Year Book, 1973* (New York, Crowell Collier, 1973), 92.
39. Brian McNaught, "The Sad Dilemma of the Gay Catholic," *U.S. Catholic,* Vol. 8 (August, 1975), 6.
40. *Ibid.,* 6–7.
41. *Ibid.,* 7.
42. *Ibid.*
43. *Ibid.*
44. Benjamin Karpman, "Sex Life in Prison," *Journal of the Institute of Criminal Law,* Vol. 38 (January–February, 1948), 486.
45. John W. Dixon, Jr., "Paradigms of Sexuality," *American Theological Review,* Vol. 56 (April 1, 1974), 163.
46. *Ibid.*
47. Robert Springer, "Sermon of Sexual Freedom," *New Catholic World,* Vol. 216 (March–April, 1973), 258.
48. "The Unreal World of an NCC Meeting," *Christian Century,* Vol. 92 (March 19, 1975), 276.
49. "Methodists Face the Homosexual Issue," *Christian Century,* Vol. 12 (March 12, 1975), 243.

Notes

50. Robert H. Mayo, "Sex—Normal, Natural and Healthy," *The Presbyterian Layman* (January, 1976), 5.
51. *Ibid.*
52. *Ibid.*
53. Paul Blanshard, "Christianity and Sex: An Indictment of Orthodox Theology," *The Humanist*, Vol. 24 (March–April, 1974), 33.

CHAPTER 4

1. Emil Brunner, *The Divine Imperative: A Study of Christian Ethics*, trans. by Olive Wyon (New York, Macmillan, 1937), 350.
2. James A. Peterson, *Toward a Successful Marriage* (New York, Scribners, 1960).
3. *Ibid.*, 71.
4. Herman Alexander von Keyserling, quoted in Seldes, *op. cit.*, 644.
5. Otto Piper, *The Christian Interpretation of Sex* (New York, Scribners, 1949), 95.
6. Ruel L. Howe, "A Pastoral Theology of Sex and Marriage," *Pastoral Psychology*, Vol. 3 (September, 1952), 39.
7. Reinhold Niebuhr, *The Nature and Destiny of Man*, New York: (Scribners, 1941), 239.
8. Brunner, *The Divine Imperative*, 349.
9. *Ibid.*, 348.
10. Peterson, *op. cit.*, 37.
11. Havelock Ellis, quoted in Seldes, *op. cit.*, 861.
12. Peterson, *op. cit.*, 150.
13. Ellis, *Studies*, 860.
14. Peterson, *op. cit.*, 162.
15. Aristotle, quoted in Seldes, *op. cit.*, 34.
16. Peterson, *op. cit.*, 82.
17. *Ibid.*, 115.
18. Peterson, *op. cit.*, 165.
19. *Ibid.*, 190.
20. Robert O. Blood, Jr., *Marriage* (New York, Free Press, 1969).
21. John Dewey, quoted in Seldes, *op. cit.*, 207.
22. François La Rochefoucauld, *Maxims* (New York, Peter Pauper Press, 1961), 11.
23. Blood, *op. cit.*, 360.
24. La Rochefoucauld, *op. cit.*, 55.
25. Blood, *op. cit.*, 351.
26. *Ibid.*, 352.
27. *Ibid.*, 385.
28. Alfred Kinsey, quoted in Blood, *op. cit.*, 385.
29. Kahlil Gibran, *The Prophet* (New York, Alfred A. Knopf, 1961), 25–26.
30. Kahlil Gibran, *Sand and Foam* (New York, Alfred A. Knopf, 1961), 25–26.

A Religious Foundation of Human Relations

31. Henderson, *op. cit.*, 198.
32. Johann Wolfgang von Goethe, quoted in Seldes, *op. cit.*, 940.
33. Gibran, *Sand and Foam*, 14.
34. Blood, *op. cit.*, 326.
35. George O'Neill and Nena O'Neill, *Open Marriage* (New York, Avon Books, 1972), 29-30.
36. Donald Meyer, "Churches and Families," in McLoughlin and Bellah, *op. cit.*, 237-38.
37. C. A. Patrides (ed.), *John Milton: Selected Prose* (Baltimore, Penguin Books, 1974), 139.
38. Hans Martensen, *Christian Ethics* (New York, Scribners, 1928), III, 42.
39. Patrides, *op. cit.*, 140.
40. Allan Fromme, "Get Yourself Another Husband Before the Divorce," *Cosmopolitan*, Vol. 173 (September, 1972), 132.
41. See Andrew R. Eickhoff, *A Christian View of Sex and Marriage* (New York, Free Press, 1966).
42. Judson T. Landis and Mary G. Landis, *Building a Successful Marriage* (Englewood Cliffs, N.J., Prentice-Hall, 1958), 159.
43. Gale Greene, "Perils of the Second Wife," *Cosmopolitan*, Vol. 173 (July, 1972), 106.

CHAPTER 5

1. Christiaan Becker, "Biblical Theology Today," in Marty and Peerman, *New Theology No. 6*, 23.
2. Plato, *The Republic and Other Works*, trans. by Benjamin Jowett (Garden City, N.Y., Doubleday, 1960), 90.
3. *Ibid.*, 229.
4. Reginald D. Archambault (ed.), *John Dewey on Education: Selected Writings* (New York, Modern Library, 1964), 399.
5. John Dewey, *Reconstruction in Philosophy* (New York, Henry Holt, 1920), 176-77.
6. Archambault, *op. cit.*, 113.
7. *Ibid.*, 13.
8. John Dewey, *Democracy and Education* (New York, Macmillan, 1916), 192.
9. See J. O. Ormson (ed.), *Concise Encyclopedia of Western Philosophy and Philosophies* (New York, Hawthorn Books, 1960).
10. John Dewey, *Common Faith* (New Haven, Yale University Press, 1934), 22.
11. *Ibid.*, 42.
12. George C. Hackman, Charles W. Kegley, and Viljo K. Nikander, *Religion in Modern Life* (New York, Macmillan, 1957), 164-65.
13. See Andrew M. Greeley, *Life for a Wanderer: A New Look at Christian Spirituality* (Garden City, N.Y., Doubleday, 1969).
14. *Ibid.*

Notes

15. John Ruskin, quoted in Seldes, *op. cit.*, 308.
16. David E. Roberts, *Psychotherapy and a Christian View of Man* (New York, Scribners, 1959), 46–47.
17. Abraham H. Maslow, *Toward a Psychology of Being* (Princeton, N.J., Van Nostrand, 1968).
18. James H. Cone, *Black Theology and Black Power* (New York, Seabury Press, 1969), 52. For a discussion of "cheap grace," *see* Dietrich Bonhoeffer, *The Cost of Discipleship* (New York, Macmillan, 1963).
19. Albert Hofstader, "The Career Open to Personality: The Meaning of Opportunity for an Ethics of Our Time," in *Aspects of Human Equality* (New York, Conference on Science, Philosophy and Religion, 1956), 112ff.
20. Henry M. Levin, "The Coleman Report: What Difference Do Schools Make?" *Saturday Review*, Vol. 48 (January 20, 1968), 57.
21. Richard Hubert, "Class Integration: A Fundamental Break with the Past," *Saturday Review*, Vol. 55 (May 27, 1972), 58–59.
22. Godfrey Hodgson, "Do Schools Make a Difference?" *Atlantic Monthly*, Vol. 231 (March, 1973), 35–46.
23. Hubert, *loc. cit.*
24. *Ibid.*
25. Hodgson, *loc. cit.*
26. Stephen C. Rose, *The Grass Roots Church* (New York, Holt, Rinehart & Winston, 1966), 97.
27. Francisco Ferrer, quoted in Seldes, *op. cit.*, 305.
28. James S. Coleman, "How Do the Young Become Adults?" *Education Digest*, Vol. 38 (May, 1973), 51.
29. *Ibid.*
30. *Ibid.*, 52.
31. J. D. Douglas (ed.), *The New Bible Dictionary* (Grand Rapids, Mich., William B. Eerdmans, 1962), 335.
32. Ronald E. Murphy (ed.), *The Jerome Biblical Commentary* (Englewood Cliffs, N.J., Prentice-Hall, 1968), 487–94.
33. Rosemary Haughton, *Christian Responsibility* (London, Sheed and Ward, 1964), 18.
34. Roger Harrison and Richard Hopkins, "The Design of Cross-Cultural Training: An Alternative Model," in Warren G. Bennis, Kenneth D. Benne, and Robert Chin (eds.), *The Planning of Change: Readings in the Applied Behavioral Sciences* (New York, Holt, Rinehart & Winston, 1969), 375.
35. *Ibid.*, 2.
36. Harvey G. Cox, "The 'New Breed' in American Churches," in McLoughlin and Bellah, *op. cit.*, 378.
37. Bennis *et al.*, *op. cit.*, 570.
38. *Ibid.*, 576–79.

CHAPTER 6

1. William Godwin, "An Epistemological Basis for Anarchism," in Leonard I. Krimerman and Lewis Perry (eds.), *Patterns of Anarchy: A Col-*

A Religious Foundation of Human Relations

lection of *Writings in the Anarchist Tradition* (Garden City, N.Y., Doubleday, 1966), 187.

2. St. Augustine, quoted in Seldes, *op. cit.,* 536.
3. James Madison, quoted in Seldes, *op. cit.,* 538.
4. Reinhold Niebuhr, "Limits of Liberty," *The Nation,* Vol. 154 (January 29, 1942), 87.
5. Joseph C. Hough, Jr., *Black Power and White Protestants: A Christian Response to the New Negro Pluralism* (New York, Oxford University Press, 1968), 133.
6. Plato, *The Republic,* 552.
7. *Ibid.,* 31.
8. *Ibid.,* 36–37.
9. *Ibid.,* 52.
10. *Ibid.,* 107.
11. John C. Bennett, *The Christian As Citizen* (New York, Association Press, 1955), 58.
12. Plato, *The Republic,* 109.
13. *Ibid.,* 166.
14. Gregory Vlastos (ed.), *Plato: A Collection of Critical Essays* (Garden City, N.Y., Doubleday, 1971), II, 79.
15. *Ibid.,* 133.
16. *Ibid.,* 134–35.
17. *Ibid.,* 82.
18. Plato, *The Republic,* 422.
19. Tillich, *Systematic Theology,* 282.
20. Plato, *The Republic,* 423.
21. *Ibid.*
22. Alexandre Koyre, *Discovering Plato* (New York, Columbia University Press, 1945), 107.
23. Plato, *The Republic,* 422.
24. Joseph Wood Krutch (ed.), *Thoreau: Walden and Other Writings* (New York, Bantam Books, 1971), 100.
25. *Ibid.*
26. *Ibid.,* 103.
27. *Ibid.,* 91.
28. Letter to Harrison Blake From Henry David Thoreau, August 9, 1850, quoted in Seldes, *op. cit.,* 211.
29. Krutch, *op. cit.,* 94.
30. *Ibid.,* 95.
31. See Jean-Jacques Rousseau, *First and Second Discourses,* trans. by Roger D. Masters and Judith Masters (New York, St. Martin's Press, 1964).
32. Cone, *op. cit.,* 35.
33. Paul Tillich, *Love, Power, and Justice* (New York, Oxford University Press, 1960), 11.
34. Joseph Fletcher, *Situation Ethics: The New Morality* (Philadelphia, Westminster Press, 1966), 92–93.
35. Martin Luther King, Jr., *Stride Toward Freedom* (New York, Harper & Row, 1968), 212.
36. Plato, *The Republic,* 480.

Notes

37. *Ibid.*, 484.
38. King, *Why We Can't Wait*, 81.
39. *Ibid.*, 83.
40. *Ibid.*, 84.
41. Thomas W. Ogletree, "From Anxiety to Responsibility: The Shifting Focus of Theological Reflection," in Marty and Peerman, *New Theology No. 6*, 52.
42. William O. Douglas, quoted in Seldes, *op. cit.*, 697.
43. William O. Douglas, *An Almanac of Liberty* (Garden City, N.Y., Doubleday, 1954), vii.
44. William O. Douglas, quoted in Seldes, *op. cit.*, 134.
45. Charles de Montesquieu, quoted in Seldes, *op. cit.*, 596.
46. William O. Douglas, quoted in Seldes, *op. cit.*, 986.
47. William O. Douglas, *Being an American* (New York, John Day, 1948), 208.
48. William O. Douglas, quoted in Seldes, *op. cit.*, 758.
49. Douglas, *Being an American*, 209.
50. William O. Douglas, *The Three Hundred Year War* (New York, Random House, 1972), 179.
51. William O. Douglas, *Points of Rebellion* (New York, Random House, 1970), 95.
52. *Ibid.*, 16.
53. *Ibid.*, 53–54.
54. *Ibid.*, 44.
55. *Ibid.*, 93–94.
56. *Ibid.*, 32–33.
57. Douglas, *Being an American*, 119.

CHAPTER 7

1. Joseph Julian (ed.), *Social Problems* (New York, Meredith Press, 1973), 4–5.
2. Lynn White, Jr., "The Historical Roots of Our Ecological Crisis," *Science*, Vol. 155 (1967), 1203–1207.
3. See C. F. D. Moule, *Man and Nature in the New Testament: Some Reflections on Biblical Ecology* (Philadelphia, Fortress Press, 1967), *and* Eric Rust, *Nature and Man in Biblical Thought* (London, Lutterworth, 1953).
4. *Responsibility of Christians in an Interdependent Economic World* (Detroit, National Study Conference on Church and Economic Life, February 16–19, 1950).
5. Melvin A. Benarde, *Our Precarious Habitat* (New York, W. W. Norton, 1970), 132.
6. Donald E. Carr, *Death of the Sweet Water* (New York, W. W. Norton, 1966), 139.
7. Thomas G. Aylesworth, *This Vital Air, This Vital Water* (New York, Rand McNally, 1968), 115–22.
8. Carr, *op. cit.*, 48–50.

9. *Ibid.*, 166.
10. *Ibid.*, 177-78.
11. Grant S. McClellan, *Protecting Our Environment* (New York, H. W. Wilson, 1970), 100.
12. Joseph Fletcher, *Moral Responsibility: Situation Ethics at Work* (Philadelphia, Westminster Press, 1966), 89.
13. Paul Ehrlich, *The Population Bomb* (New York, Ballantine Books, 1968).
14. *Ibid.*, 152.
15. Paul Ehrlich, *The End of Affluence* (New York, Ballantine Books, 1974), 146.
16. *Ibid.*, 31.
17. Gordon R. Taylor, *The Doomsday Book* (New York, World, 1970).
18. *Ibid.*, 255.
19. *Ibid.*, 306.
20. Richard A. Falk, *This Endangered Planet* (New York, Random House, 1971).
21. Barbara Ward and Rene Dubos, *Only One Earth* (New York, W. W. Norton, 1972).
22. Edward T. Hall, *The Hidden Dimension* (Garden City, N.Y., Doubleday, 1966), 2.
23. *Ibid.*, 5.
24. *Ibid.*, 15.
25. Howard Moody, "Abortion Revisited," *Christianity and Crisis*, Vol. 36 (July 21, 1975), 167.
26. Roe v. Wade, 410 U.S. 113 (1973). See also Wesley D. H. Teo, "Abortion: The Husband's Constitutional Rights," *Ethics*, Vol. 83 (July, 1975), 337.
27. Teo, *loc. cit.*, 337.
28. Willis E. Wygant, Jr., "A Protestant Minister's View of Abortion," *Journal of Religion and Health*, Vol. II (July, 1972), 274.
29. Patrick J. O'Mahony, "The Beginning of Human Life: Reflections on Recent Writings," *The Month*, Vol. 7 (May, 1974), 572.
30. Pope Pius XII, quoted in Joseph Margolis, "Abortion," *Ethics*, Vol. 84 (October, 1973), 56.
31. Pope Pius XI, quoted in James Greenwell, "Catholic Inconsistency on International Killing," *The Humanist*, Vol. 26 (January-February, 1976), 20-21.
32. O'Mahony, *loc. cit.*, 574.
33. *Ibid.*, 537-74.
34. Raymond Schroth, "Recovering American Catholic Culture," *New Catholic World*, Vol. 215 (January-February, 1972), 88.
35. Walter W. Curtis, "We Need a Right to Life Amendment," *U.S. Catholic*, Vol. 39 (June, 1974), 14.
36. "Politics and Abortion," *Commonweal*, Vol. 103 (February 27, 1976), 131.
37. Robert N. Lynch, "'Abortion' and 1976 Politics," *America*, Vol. 134 (March 6, 1976), 178.
38. Gary L. Chamberlain, "The Abortion Debate Revealing Our Values," *New Catholic World*, Vol. 215 (January-February, 1972), 208.

Notes

39. *Ibid.*
40. Wygant, *loc. cit.*, 271.
41. *Ibid.*, 272.
42. *Ibid.*, 273.
43. *Ibid.*
44. Joseph Fletcher, "Abortion and the True Believer," *Christian Century*, Vol. 91 (November 27, 1974), 1126.
45. *Ibid.*, 1127.
46. *Tulsa World*, March 25, 1976, p. 2.
47. H. Tristram Engelhardt, Jr., "The Ontology of Abortion," *Ethics*, Vol. 84 (April, 1974), 229.
48. *Ibid.*, 226.
49. *Ibid.*, 231.
50. Aristotle, *Politics*.
51. Seneca, *Epistolae Morales*, LXX.
52. Dahlstrom, *op. cit.*, 291.
53. See Thomas C. Oden, "A Cautious View of Treatment Termination," *Christian Century*, Vol. 93 (January 21, 1976), 40.
54. *Ibid.*
55. "Empowerment, Oppression and Social Justice," *Church and Society*, Vol. 66 (September–October, 1975), 46.
56. Joseph Margolis and Clorinda Margolis, "On Being Allowed to Die," *The Humanist*, Vol. 26 (January–February, 1976), 17.
57. Bryon L. Sherwin, "Jewish Views on Euthanasia," *The Humanist*, Vol. 24 (July–August, 1974), 20.
58. *Ibid.*
59. Daniel C. Maguire, "A Catholic View of Mercy Killing," *The Humanist*, Vol. 24 (July–August, 1974), 16.
60. *Ibid.*
61. Merle Longworth, "Karen Quinlan's Coma," *Christian Century*, Vol. 92 (October 22, 1975), 917.
62. Cardinal Jean Villot, quoted in Manguire, *loc. cit.*
63. Thomas C. Oden, "Judicial Restraint in the Quinlan Decision," *Christian Century*, Vol. 92 (November 26, 1975), 1069.
64. Joseph Fletcher, "The 'Right' to Live and the 'Right' to Die, A Protestant View of Euthanasia," *The Humanist*, Vol. 24 (July–August, 1974), 13.
65. R. G. Twycross, "A Plea for 'Euthanatos,'" *The Month*, Vol. 8 (February, 1975), 39.
66. Anonymous, quoted in *Nursing Mirror* (August 9, 1968).
68. Kenneth Vaux, "The Giving and Taking of Life: New Power at Life's Thresholds," *Christian Century*, Vol. 92 (April 16, 1975), 44.
68. Jeanne Richie, "Church, Caste, and Women," in Martin E. Marty and Dean G. Peerman (eds.), *New Theology No. 8: Our Cultural Revolution* (New York, Macmillan, 1971), 258.
69. Kate Millett, *Sexual Politics* (New York, Avon, 1970), 51.
70. Haughton, *op. cit.*, 77–78.
71. Judy Syfers, quoted in Francine Klagsbrun (ed.), *The First Ms. Reader* (New York, Warner, 1973), 23–25.
72. Millett, *op. cit.*

A Religious Foundation of Human Relations

73. David Riesman, quoted in Caroline Bird, *Born Female* (New York, Simon & Schuster, 1968), xiii.
74. *Ibid.*, 127.
75. Richie, *loc. cit.*, 259-60.
76. Margaret N. Maxey, "Beyond Eve and Mary," in Marty and Peerman, *New Theology No. 9,* 224.
77. Phyllis Bird, "Images of Women in the New Testament," in Rosemary R. Ruether (ed.), *Religion and Sexism: Images of Women in the Jewish and Christian Traditions* (New York, Simon & Schuster, 1974), 65.
78. Caroline Bird, *op. cit.*, 49.
79. *Ibid.*, 209.

CHAPTER 8

1. Barth, *op. cit.*, III, 250ff.
2. Troeltsch, *op. cit.*, I, 57.
3. Martin Buber, *I and Thou* (New York, Scribners, 1958), iii.
4. Martin Buber, *Pointing the Way* (New York, Harper & Row, 1957), 27.
5. Buber, *I and Thou*, 8.
6. Martin Buber, *The Way of Response* (New York, Schocken Books, 1966), 132.
7. Buber, *I and Thou*, 6.
8. Buber, *Pointing the Way*, 30.
9. Buber, *I and Thou*, 43.
10. Buber, *Pointing the Way*, 110.
11. Buber, quoted in Lowell D. Streiker, *The Promise of Buber* (Philadelphia, J. B. Lippincott, 1969), 42.
12. Karl Heim, *God Transcendent* (New York, Scribners, 1936).
13. Barth, *op. cit.*, III.
14. Brunner, *The Divine Imperative*.
15. *Ibid.*, 175-76.
16. Streiker, *op. cit.*, 66.
17. Franz Kafka, quoted in Seldes, *op. cit.*, 546.
18. Buber, *I and Thou*, 51.
19. Abraham H. Maslow, *The Farther Reaches of Human Nature* (New York, Viking Press, 1971), 4.
20. Abraham H. Maslow, *Motivation and Personality* (New York, Harper & Row, 1970), 46.
21. Albert Einstein, quoted in Seldes, *op. cit.*, 683.
22. Maslow, *Farther Reaches*, 43.
23. Maslow, *Motivation and Personality*, 242.
24. Archibald MacLeish, quoted in Seldes, *op. cit.*, 619.
25. Robert R. Carkhuff, *Helping and Human Relations*, Vol. I, *Selection and Training* (New York, Holt, Rinehart & Winston, 1969), 31.
26. Maslow, *Motivation and Personality*, 155.
27. Carl R. Rogers, *On Becoming a Person* (Boston, Houghton Mifflin, 1961), vi.

Notes

28. *Ibid.*
29. *Ibid.*, 31.
30. *Ibid.*, 186-87.
31. *Ibid.*, 191-92.
32. *Ibid.*, 16-26.
33. *Ibid.*, 34.
34. *Ibid.*, 56.
35. Fulton J. Sheen, *Theology and Sanity* (New York, Sheed and Ward, 1964), 347.
36. Bonhoeffer, *op. cit.*, 60.
37. J. Schoneberg Setzer, *What's Left to Believe?* (New York, Abington Press, 1968), 63.
38. Joseph A. Leighton, *The Individual and the Social Order* (New York, D. Appleton, 1930), 288.
39. Carl G. Jung, *Modern Man in Search of a Soul* (London, Kegan Paul, Trench, Trubner, 1933), 270-71.
40. Howard J. Clinebell, Jr., *The Pastor and Drug Dependancy* (New York, Council Press, 1968), 11-12.
41. Kenneth W. Mann, "The Mission of the Church in a Drug Culture," *Journal of Religion and Health*, Vol. 11 (October, 1972), 330-31.
42. See Edward Wakin, "Pity Not the Junkies," *U.S. Catholic*, Vol. 39 (May, 1974), 7.
43. Clinebell, *op. cit.*, 13-14.
44. William B. O'Brien, "Where the Drug Scene Is," *America*, Vol. 126 (March 11, 1972), 252.
45. Wakin, *loc. cit.*, 8.
46. Huston Smith, "Do Drugs Have Religious Import?" *Journal of Philosophy*, Vol 61 (October, 1964), 529.
47. Wakin, *loc. cit.*, 8.
48. Joseph H. Fichter, "Parallel Conversions: Charismatics and Recovered Alcoholics," *Christian Century*, Vol. 93 (February 18, 1976), 148.
49. See Thomas E. Price and Ruth Hargraves, "Decriminalization of Marijuana: Dealing with the Reality, Not the Symbol," *Christian Century*, Vol. 91 (September 4, 1974), 822.
50. Timothy Miller, "Heroin and Realism," *Christian Century*, Vol. 92 (November 19, 1975), 1045.
51. Ralph Waldo Emerson, Divinity School Speech, 1838.
52. Menninger, *Love Against Hate*, 114.
53. Henry Guntrip, *Mental Pain and the Curse of Souls* (London, Independent Press, 1964), 65-66.
54. Leon Festinger, *Theory of Cognitive Dissonance* (Stanford, Calif., Stanford University Press, 1957), 2-8.
55. Ogletree, *loc. cit.*, 57.
56. Festinger, *op. cit.*, 13-15.
57. *Ibid.*, 16-17.
58. Leon Festinger, *Conflict, Decision and Dissonance* (Stanford, Calif., Stanford University Press, 1964), 5-6.
59. "Thinking: Cognitive Organization and Processes," in Vol. 15 of *The International Encyclopedia of the Social Sciences* (New York, Macmillan, 1968), 619-20.

A Religious Foundation of Human Relations

60. Leon Festinger and James M. Carlsmith, "Cognitive Consequences of Forced Compliance," *Journal of Abnormal Social Psychology*, Vol. 58 (1959), 203-210.

CHAPTER 9

1. Bertrand Russell, *Has Man a Future?* (New York, Simon & Schuster, 1962), 18.
2. *Ibid.*, 69.
3. *Ibid.*, 21.
4. *Ibid.*, 56-57.
5. *Ibid.*, 87-94.
6. *Ibid.*, 119.
7. *Ibid.*, 126.
8. Tournier, *op. cit.*, 15-16.
9. Arnold Toynbee, "Higher Education in a Time of Accelerating Change," in Alvin C. Eurich (ed.), *Campus 1980* (New York, Dell, 1968), xx.
10. Nathan M. Pusey, "Religion's Role in Liberal Education," *Christian Century*, Vol. 71 (July 14, 1954), 850.
11. Christopher Jenks and David Riesman, "The Triumph of Academic Man," in Eurich, *op. cit.*, 113.
12. Nevitt Sanford, "The College Student of 1980," in Eurich, *op. cit. passim.*
13. *The Letters to the Corinthians*, trans. by William Barclay (Philadelphia, Westminster Press, 1957), 95-96.
14. William Birenbaum, "Cities and Universities: Collision of Crisis," in Eurich, *op. cit.*, 59.
15. C. R. Carpenter, "Toward a Developed Technology of Instruction," in Eurich, *op. cit., passim.*
16. James H. Robinson, "Social Practices and the Christian Way," in William S. Nelson (ed.), *The Christian Way in Race Relations* (New York, Harper & Row, 1948), 107.
17. Howard Omhart and Vincent O'Leary, *The Challenge of Crime in a Free Society* (Washington, D.C., U.S. Government Printing Office, 1967), 159.
18. *Ibid.*, 162.
19. *Ibid.*, 171.
20. Bruce C. Birch, "Hunger, Poverty and Biblical Religion," *Christian Century*, Vol. 92 (June 11, 1975), 593.
21. Norman Faramelli, "The Role of the Church in Eco-Justice," *Church and Society*, Vol. 64 (September-October, 1973), 6.
22. J. Oscar McCloud, "Lifestyle Covenants: A Proposal for Action," *Church and Society*, Vol. 66 (March-April, 1975), 5.
23. Confucius, quoted in Seldes, *op. cit.*, 743.
24. Edward M. Huenemann, "Theological Perspective on the Hunger Issue," *Church and Society*, Vol. 66 (November-December, 1975), 6.
25. Charles W. Maynes, "Can We Build on Fear? A New International

Notes

Economic Order," *New Catholic World*, Vol. 218 (September–October, 1975), 227.

26. Denis Goulet, "World Hunger: Putting Development Ethics to the Test," *Christianity and Crisis* (May 26, 1975), 126.

27. Frederick J. Perella, "Value Dilemma: Our Need for Equality Sharing," *New Catholic World*, Vol. 218 (September–October, 1975), 236.

28. Richard A. Hoehn, "A Hunger Exercise," *Christian Century*, Vol. 92 (January 22, 1975), 60–61.

29. Stewart Hilther, "Starving the Future's Children," *Christian Century*, Vol. 93 (January 21, 1976), 38.

30. George R. Lucas, Jr., "Famine and Global Policy," *Christian Century*, Vol. 92 (September 3, 1975), 753.

31. Desmond O'Grady, "When I was Hungry, You Gave Me . . . ," *U.S. Catholic*, Vol. 40 (May, 1975), 24.

32. Lincoln Richardson, "Pride and Poverty," *Presbyterian Life*, Vol. 25 (January, 1972), 20–21.

33. *Ibid.*

34. Birch, *loc. cit.*

35. *Ibid.*, 595.

36. *Ibid.*, 597.

37. Robert A. Bennett, "Black Experience and the Bible," in Marty and Peerman, *New Theology No. 9*, 177–78.

39. Acklyn Lynch and Alma Lynch, "Images of the 21st Century . . . Blackness," in Floyd B. Barbour (ed.), *The Black 70's* (Boston, Porter Sargent, 1970), 206.

39. George D. Kelsey, *Racism and the Christian Understanding of Man* (New York, Scribners, 1965), 26.

40. *See* Matthew Holden, Jr., *The Divisible Republic* (New York, Abelard-Schuman, 1973), xiv.

41. *Ibid.*

42. Lynch and Lynch, *loc. cit.*, 207.

43. *Ibid.*

44. *Ibid.*, 227.

45. *Ibid.*, 211.

46. *Ibid.*, 212.

47. Emil Brunner, *Justice and Social Order* (New York, Harper & Row, 1945), 60.

48. W. E. B. Dubois, quoted in Gladys Curry (ed.), *Viewpoints from Black America* (Englewood Cliffs, N.J., Prentice-Hall, 1970), 1.

49. John G. Kemeny, *Man and the Computer* (New York, Scribners, 1972), 16.

50. *Ibid.*, 145.

51. *Ibid.*, 144.

52. *Ibid.*, 10.

53. *Ibid.*

54. *Ibid.*, 11.

55. *Ibid.*

56. Thomas W. Ogletree, *loc. cit.*, 61–62.

57. Kemeny, *op. cit.*, 12.

INDEX

Abortion: 29, 33, 173; problem of, 189–90; U.S. Supreme court decision of 1973, 190–91; and decision of 1976, 191; constitutional amendment sought on, 191, 197; church views of, 191–97; defenders, 195–98
Adjustments, marriage: 98–109
Adler, Alfred: 60–61
Agape and Eros: 83
Ahlstrom, Sydney: 58
Alcoholics: 135
Alcoholics Anonymous: 28, 235
Alcoholics Anonymous: 28
Alinsky, Saul: 60
Anger: 101, 104
Antiabortionists: 192
Aquinas, St. Thomas: 159, 191–92, 198
Aristotle: theories of love, 69–73; on anger, 101; on euthanasia, 198; on poverty, 265
Ashforeth: 91
Asian Americans: 55, 60, 136
Atomic bomb: 248–49
Aylesworth, Thomas G.: 175

Baal: 91
Bahm, Archie J.: 5
Balance in human relations: 237
Barth, Karl: 74, 212, 215
Becker, C. L.: 82
Becker, J. Christiaan: 118–19
Beckett, Samuel: 4
Beebe, the Reverend L. Peter: 208
Being values (B-values): 219–20
Bellah, Robert N.: 3
Benarde, Melvin A.: on definition of water pollution: 175
Benne, Kenneth D.: 142
Bennett, John C.: 150
Bennett, Robert A.: 270
Bennis, Warren G.: 119, 142–46
Berger, Peter: 58
Bergson, Henri: 35
Berne, Eric: 27
Beyond Racism: 37, 55
Bhavagad-Gita: 45
Bible, the: 11, 33–34, 36, 45, 52, 52ff., 117, 122, 132–35, 206, 275; King James Version, 34; interpretations, 34; and love, 72–73, 85; on marriage, 115–16; Revised

Standard Version, 211; on helping others, 212–13; concept of warless world, 246; and blacks, 270–71
Biestek, Felix P.: 27–28
Bill of Rights: 166
Birch, Bruce C.: 268
Bird, Caroline: 207, 211
Birmingham, Ala.: 51–52, 164
Black Americans: see Racism
Black power: 54
Blake, Harrison: 155
Blanshard, Paul: 96
Blood, Robert O., Jr.: 103, 105, 108–109, 115–116
Bonhoeffer, Dietrich: 228, 238
Bowman, Gard: 210
Boycott, Montgomery, Ala.: 51, 159
Brahmacharya: 45
Brave New World: 153
Brickner, Rabbi Balfour: 197
Brill, Naomi: 27
British Broadcasting Corporation film: 27
Brotherhood, universal: 13, 35, 127, 274; defined, 35–36, 148–49; and Mohandas K. Gandhi, 36, 38–49, 52; and Martin Luther King, Jr., 36, 39–41, 49–55; and Whitney M. Young, Jr., 37, 39–41, 55–60; and Rudolf Dreikurs, 37, 39, 42, 60–65; and passive resistance, 41–49; nonviolence, 49–55; and open society, 37, 55–60; and individual initiative, 60–65
Brown, H. Rap: 54–55
Brown case, U.S. Supreme Court decision in: 158
Brunner, Emil: 97–98, 100, 215–16, 273
Buber, Martin: 18; and I-Thou relationship, 160, 213–17
Buckley, Senator James: 191

Carkhuff, Robert R.: 220
Carlsmith, James M.: 239–40
Carlyle, Thomas: 13
Carmichael, Stokely: 54–55
Carr, Donald E.: 175
Catholics: 11, 13, 30, 96, 117, 235; Bible of, 33; church positions on abortion, 191–94; and euthanasia, 202–205
Catholicism: 30
Celestin, George: 53–54
Censorship: 153–54
Chamberlain, Gary L.: 194
Cheek, the Reverend Allison: 208
Chicago, University of: 120, 125
Chin, Robert: 142
Choices: in helping relationship: 21–22
Christ: see Jesus
Christ Episcopal Church, Oberlin, Ohio: 208
Christian, John: 188
Christian Century: 202
Christianity: 4, 10, 23, 30, 33–35, 52, 91, 124, 249; contribution to human relations, 11–12; values, 31–32
Christians: 29–31, 53, 92, 116–17, 125–26, 199, 228–29, 238–39, 241, 249; focus on compassion, 31; denominations of, 34; early, 161, 164
Church: 8–9, 19, 33, 228, 234; role of, 12, 163–64, 207, 263; do-good activities of, 13; and human relations training, 14–15; criticized by Whitney Young, Jr., 37, 57–58; in Dark Ages, 92; in Middle Ages, 92
Church Dogmatics: 212
Cincinnati, University of: 142
Civil rights: 12–13, 38, 50–51, 53, 157, 207; homosexual, 94; and Martin Luther King, Jr., 157–65; impact of, 165; of blacks, 274
Civil Rights Act of 1964: 135
Claudel, Paul: 109
Clinebell, Howard J., Jr.: 231
Code of Hammurabi: 147
Code of Justinian: 147
Cognition: 238–39
Coleman, James S.: 119, 135–40
Coleman Report: 136–40
Colleges: 252
Colossians quoted: 116
Commissioner of Education: 135
Commission on Interfaith Activities

300

Index

of the Union of American Hebrew Congregations: 197
Common law, English: 147, 168
Commonweal: 193
Computers: 274-79
Cone, James H.: 157-58
Conscience: 154-57
Conservation: 178
Conservationists: 174
Constantine: 91
Constitution, U.S.: 166
Consumer-credit practices: 170
I Corinthians quoted: 73, 85, 115-17, 181, 210
Correctional institutions: 255-62
Council of Elvira: 91
Council of Youth Ministry: 95
Counselors, marriage: 104
Cox, Harvey G.: 54, 58, 143
Curtis, Bishop Walter W.: 193

Dahlstrom, Earl C.: 32-33, 199
Daniel: 140
Death of the Sweet Water: 175
Democracy: 150
Democracy and Education: 126
Demonstrations: 158
Department of Agriculture, U.S.: 263-64
Desegregation: 56
Deutero-Isaiah: 247-48
Deuteronomy: 122, 134, 180-81, 211, 268
Dewey, John: 103-104; on education, 119-28
Discrimination, racial: 167
Dissonance: 237-41
Divorce: 98, 111-17, 207
Dixon, John W., Jr.: 93-94
Donne, John: 65
Douglas, J. D.: 139-40
Douglas, Justice William O.: 148, 165-72
Dreikurs, Rudolf: views of brotherhood, 37, 42; on social equality, 39-40; on nonviolence, 42; on individual initiative, 60-65
Drug abuse: 29, 33
Drug addicts, addiction: 135, 230-37
DuBois, W. E. B.: 274

Dubos, Rene: 186
Due Process: 167

Ecclesiastes: 134, 143, 180, 239
Edicts of Solon: 147
Education, higher: 13; human relations in, 141-47; of future, 249-55
Education, progressive: 119-28
Egypt: 6-7
Ehrlich, Paul: 179
Eliot, T. S.: 164
Ellis, Havelock: 66, 100
Ellis, John Tracy: 58
Emerson, Ralph Waldo: 156, 267
Employment opportunities: 13
Encounter groups: 14, 28
Engelhardt, H. Tristram, Jr.: 197-98
Environment, the: and conservationists, 174; protection of, 174; pollution of, 175-77, 182; and public recreation, 176; *see also* water pollution
Environmental control: 12
Ephesians quoted: 115, 122, 209
Episcopal Church: 96; women ordained to priesthood, 208; women permitted to be bishops, 208
Equality of Educational Opportunity: 136
Equal rights: *see* civil rights
Escobedo case (Escobedo v. Illinois): 167
Establishment, the: 63, 169
Ethics, Christian: 32-33
Euthanasia: 29, 173, 198-205
Existentialism: 26
Exodus: 79, 197, 276
Ezekiel: 180

Fagone, Father: 193
Falk, Richard A.: 182-84
Festinger, Leon: 237-39
Feuerbach, Ludwig A.: 18
Fichter, Joseph H.: 235
Fleishner, Eva: 30
Fletcher, Joseph: 158, 186-97, 203-204, 266
Fourteenth Amendment: 190
Freud, Sigmund: theories on love, 75-82; on self-actualization, 217-18

301

Fromm, Erich: theories on love, 75–82
Futurology: 243–49
Future Shock: 60

Galatians: 210
Gallup poll on euthanasia: 199
Gamblers Anonymous: 28
Games: 26–27
Gandhi, Mohandas K.: belief in brotherhood, 36, 40, 52; philosophy, 38–39, 54; and nonviolent idealism, 40, 46, 164; and Satyagraha movement, 40, 45–47; and passive resistance, 40–41, 156; accomplishments for India, 42–43; beliefs regarding God, 43–45; on love, 46–47
Garton, Jean: 197
GATT-Fly: 266–67
General Assembly of the United Presbyterian Church: 200
Genesis: 130, 177, 181, 205–206, 246, 271, 275
Gestapo, the: 153
Gibran, Kahlil: 106, 108
Gideon case: 167
Gilkey, Langdon: 12
Glasser, William: 25–26
God: 7, 10, 43–45, 124, 128, 134–35, 143, 157, 164, 195, 213, 215–16, 223, 228–30, 275–76, 278; of love, 66–68, 74, 77, 84, 152, 268–69; author of life, 199
Godwin, William: 147–48
Goethe: 108
Goldstein, Kurt: 21–22, 24
Good News: 95
Goulet, Denis: 264
Great Powers, leaders of: 244
Greeks: and mythology, 10; Bible of, 34
Greeley, Andrew: 127
Guntrip, Henry: 236–37

Hall, Edward T.: thesis on area population, 188–89
Ham: 271
Hamilton, Edith: 8–9
Häring, Bernhard: 74

Harrison, Roger: 141–42
Haughton, Rosemary: 140–41, 206
Head Start programs: 13
Hebrews: 7, 77; Bible of, 33
Heidegger, Martin: 238
Heim, Karl: 215
Helper-client relationship: 223–30
Helping relationship: 15–29
Henry VIII: 93
Heraclitus: 118
Herberg, Will: 58
Heywood, the Reverend Carter: 208
Hillel, Rabbi: 30
Hiltner, Stewart: 265
Hitler, Adolph: 93, 161
Hodgson, Godfrey: 136
Hoehn, Richard A.: 265
Hofstader, Albert: 135
Hogan, Representative Lawrence: 191
Holden, Matthew, Jr.: 271–72
Holmes, John H.: 38, 40
Homosexuality: 29, 33, 73, 89–96
Hopkins, Richard: 141–42
Hough, Joseph C., Jr.: 148
Housing: 13, 207
Howe, Ruel L.: 99
Huenemann, Edward M.: 264
Humanist Manifesto of 1933: 32
Human relations: 8, 120; and Christian concept of love, 10–11; Christianity contribution to, 11–12; training in churches, 14–15; helping relationship in, 15–22; workshops, 73; in higher education, 141–46; I-Thou relationship, 160, 213–17; self-actualization, 217–23; nature of helping relationship, 223–30; and drug addiction, 230–37; and balance, 237–41; religious foundation of, 279
Hungarian Freedom Fighters: 161
Huxley, Aldous: 153

Imbalance, psychological: 237
Inaugural address, President Kennedy's: 3
India: 42–43, 46–47
Indians, American: 55, 60, 90, 136
Inflation: 62
Initiative: 60–65

Index

Injustice: 149, 153
Intimate Behavior: 20
Isaiah quoted: 134–35, 176, 246, 268
I-Thou relationship: 160, 213–17

Jalee, Pierre: 272
James, epistle of: 131, 222
Japheth: 271
Jeremiah: 197, 243
Jesus: 45–46, 48, 52, 85, 116, 123–27, 131–32, 159, 164–65, 195–96, 221–22, 232, 248–49; teachings of, 10, 32; as psychiatrist, 11; and values, 30; ministry, 31; and liberation, 157
Jews: 8, 13, 96, 139–40, 247; esteem for judgment, 31; and euthanasia, 199–201
Job quoted: 132, 256
John quoted: 62, 87–88, 122, 248, 278–79
Judaeo-Christian values: 29–33, 93, 119, 128, 130, 163, 187, 241; perspective on hunger, 262–63
Judaism: 8; contribution to Christianity, 30; values, 31–32; on abortion, 197
Judgment: 13; Jewish esteem for, 31
Jung, Carl G.: 17–20, 231
Justice, democratic: *see* Justice William O. Douglas
Justice, social and legal: 147–48; Platonic, 148–54; Henry David Thoreau views of, 148, 154–57; and Martin Luther King, Jr., 148, 157–65; and Justice William O. Douglas, 148, 165–72
Justinian: 92

Kafka, Franz: 216
Karpman, Benjamin: 93
Kemeny, John G.: 274–75, 277–78; criteria for life, 276
Kennedy, President John F.: 3
Keyserling, Herman Alexander von: 98
Kierkegaard, Søren: 23
King, Martin Luther, Jr.: practitioner of brotherhood, 36–37, 41, 44; view of racism, 39; and nonviolence, 41, 49–55, 156; assassination, 41, 165; war on racism, 50–52; success, 55; and civil rights, 148, 157–65; and Nobel Peace Prize, 158; criticism of, 162
II Kings quoted: 177
Kinsey, Alfred: 106
Kohlberg, Lawrence: 31–32
Koyre, Alexandre: 153

Lair, Jesse: 19, 22
Lake Erie: 177
La Rochefoucald: 104
Laws, The: 152
Leighton, Joseph A.: 229
Leviticus quoted: 87, 116
Lewis, C. S.: 89
Lincoln, C. Eric: 39
Linse, Eugene W., Jr.: 197
Littell, Franklin H.: 13
Longworth, Merle: 202
Lord's Prayer: 10, 131
Love: 40, 46, 99–100, 108, 111, 125, 127, 133, 157, 159, 168, 274; Christian, 10–11, 18–19, 66, 74, 84, 163, 233; in helping relationship, 19–21, 23; self, 32–33, 69–71, 99; Greek words for, 66, 74; Plato views of, 67–69, 73; Aristotle's theories of, 69–73; and psychological perspectives, 75–82; non-sexual, 77–78; brotherly, 79–81; motherly, 80–81; and lovers, 81–82; theological perspectives, 83–89; and homosexuality, 89–96
Lovelace, Richard: 96
LSD: 12
Luke: 157, 195, 222
Lutheran Church: 197
Lynch, Acklyn and Alma: 272–73
Lynch, Robert N.: 194

Maartens, Maarten: 253
McCarthy, Senator Joseph: 91
McCauley, George C.: 29–30
McCloud, J. Oscar: 263
McKeon, Richard: 63–64
MacLeish, Archibald: 220
McNaught, Brian: 91

Madison, President James: 148
Magna Charta: 147
Malachi: 111
Malcolm X: 53-54
Mana: 6-7
Mann, Kenneth W.: 231-32
Marches, freedom: 52, 158
Marijuana: 236
Maritain, Jacques: 74
Mark: 195, 272
Marriage, Biblical view of: 115-17
Martensen, Hans: 111
Marty, Martin: 58
Maslow, Abraham H.: 19, 119, 218-23; on basic human needs, 129-35; philosophy, 220
Mass media: 278-79
Matthew quoted: 40, 44-45, 62, 87, 117, 122, 131-33, 221
Maxey, Margaret N.: 208
May, Rollo: 22
Maynes, Charles W.: 264
Mayo, Robert H.: 95
Mead, Sidney E.: 58
Medicare: 171
Menninger, Karl: 13-14, 236
Mental health: 25
Mesopotamia: 6-7, 9
Meta-goals: 142-43
Methodists: 95
Mexican Americans: 55, 136, 188
Military-industrial complex: 171
Miller, Robert W.: 18
Millett, Kate: 205-206
Miranda case (Miranda v. Arizona): 167
Money: 102-103
Monotheism: 7, 74
Montesquieu: 166
Moody, Howard: 190
Morality, levels of: 31-32
Morris, Desmond: 20
Moses: 7
My Gandhi: 38

National Council of Churches: 94, 211, 235-36
Nazi Germany: 93, 153, 161, 213
Needs, basic: 128-29; physiological, 129-31; safety, 129, 131-32; be-longingness and love, 129, 132-33; esteem, 129, 133-34; self-actualization, 129, 134-35
Nehemiah: 269
New Catholic World: 94, 264
New Testament: 31-32, 34, 45, 73, 84, 90, 131-33, 221, 229, 268-70
Niebuhr, H. Richard: 58
Niebuhr, Reinhold: 58, 99, 148, 165, 236
Nicoll, Maurice: 19
Nicomachean Ethics: 69
Ninth Amendment: 190
Nixon, President Richard M.: 184
Noah: 271
Nonwhites: 273-74
Nonviolence: 40-41, 49-55, 162, 164-65
Northern California Conference of the United Church of Christ: 96
Novella 77: 92
Novella 141: 92
Nygren, Anders: 74; and theological study of love, 83-89

O'Brien, Monsignor William B.: 233
Oden, Thomas C.: 199; on Karen Ann Quinlan case, 203
Ogletree, Thomas W.: 165
Old Testament: 8, 34, 45, 58, 90, 123, 132-33, 140, 268-69, 278; commandments, 147; on abortion, 197
O'Mahony, Father: 192-93
On Becoming a Person: 227
O'Neill, George and Nena: 109-10, 117
Open Marriage: 109-11, 117
Open Marriage: 109
Open Society: 37; advocated by Whitney Young, Jr., 55-60; answer to racism, 55-59; guidelines for, 59-60
Opportunities, equal educational: 135-41
Organizational development: 28
Orwell, George: 153, 275

Pakistan: 43
Panentheism: 7

Index

Pantheism: 7
Parables: 10, 143
Passive resistance: 41-49
Paul: 9, 11, 73, 111, 116-17, 140, 181-82; monotheism of, 74; quoted on homosexuality, 95
Penal reform: 12
Pentecost, first: 235
Perella, Frederick J.: 264-65
Peterson, James A.: 98, 102-105, 115
Philippians quoted: 62
Pillage of Third World, The: 272
Piper, Otto: 99
Plato: philosophy of love, 67-69, 73-74; on education, 119; on justice, 148-54; critics, 153-54
Points of Rebellion: 169
Polytheism: 7, 74
Pope Pius XI: 192
Pope Pius XII: 202
Population, world: explosion, 173, 177-80, 242; control, 173, 180-87; and ecology, 179-80
Population Bomb: 178
Poverty: 11, 29, 33, 53, 170-71; future, 262-70
Prayer: 45
Prejudice: 39, 43, 59, 62
Program for justice, Douglas: 171-72
Protestants: 11-13, 96, 197, 231, 235; Bible versions of, 34; on euthanasia, 202-205
Proust: 4
Proverbs: 122, 134, 142, 144, 146, 206, 252-53, 257
Psalms: 42, 79, 122, 135, 229-30, 268
Psychotherapy: 218
Puerto Ricans: 60, 136
Pusey, Nathan M.: 250

Racism: 11, 29, 33, 37, 39, 53, 55, 57-58, 213; future, 270-74
Rahner, Karl: 54
Ramsey, Paul: 83
Recovery (self-help group); 28
Régamery, Père: 54
Religion: in political ideology, 3-4; in search of ultimate value, 4-5; and early influence on western world, 6-12; modern issues, programs, 12-29; and Judaeo-Christian perspectives, 29-33; Bible as point of reference, 33-34; in helping relationship, 22-24, 215; and drug addiction, 231, 234; in human relations, 279
Remarriage: 112-15
Republic, The: 119, 149, 153
Revelations quoted: 39
Revolution, issue of: 54
Richardson, Herbert W.: 50
Richie, Jeanne: 205, 207
Riesman, David: 207
Right to work: 166
Riverside, Calif.: 176
Robespierre: 167
Robinson, Jackie: 58
Robinson, James H.: 255
Robots: 277-79
Rogers, Carl R.: 19, 107, 224-30
Roman Catholics: *see* Catholics
Romans quoted: 41, 46-47, 144-45
Roman Twelve Tables: 147
Rose, Stephen C.: 137-38
Ross, W. Gordon: 23
Roszak, Theodore: 19, 27
Rougemont, Jean de: 16
Rousseau: 156
Rules for Radicals: 60
Ruskin, John: 128
Russell, Bertrand: on survival of mankind, 243-44, 246; world peace proposal, 244-45, 275

St. Augustine: 147-48, 158
St. Stephen and Incarnation Church, Washington, D.C.: 208
Satyagraha (soul force): 40, 45-47
Schweitzer, Albert: 33
Segregation, racial: 51, 56
Self-actualization: 134-35, 217-23
Self-help groups: 28-29
Self-knowledge: in helping relationship, 19
Seneca: 198-99
Sermon on the Mount: 10, 140
Servodidio, Father John T.: 232
Setzer, J. Schoneberg: 228-29
Sexism: 11, 33

Sexual revolution: 12
Shaull, Richard: 42
Sheen, Fulton J.: 83-89
Shem: 271
Simulation game: 14
Sit-ins: 158
Sixth Commandment: 238
Smith, Houston: 234
Social casework in helping relationship: 27-28
Socrates: 148-49, 159-60, 224
Sodom and Gomorrah: 90
Sodomy: 92
Solomon: 111
Sorokin, Pitirim A.: 21
Southern Christian Leadership Conference: 50
Spanish Americans: 55
Spanish Inquisition: 92-93
Spatial control: 187-89
Springer, Robert: 94
Stalin: 167
Steiner, Claude: 24
Stevenson, Adlai: 38, 125
Stones of Venice: 128
Storr, Anthony: 16-17
Streiker, Lowell D.: 216
Strike Toward Freedom: 159
Syfers, Judy: 206
Symposium, Plato's: 67, 73
Synanon: 28

Taylor, Gordon R.: 180, 182
Ten Commandments, the: 7-8, 23, 238, 241
T-groups: 14, 28
Theology: 12, 200; and Christian theologians, 232
Therapy in helping relationships: 22, 25
Third World, the: 262
Thomas, Dylan: 205
Thomas, George F.: 32
Thoreau, Henry David: views on conscience and justice, 148, 154-57
Thrasymachus: 149
Tillich, Paul: 22-23, 83-84, 157-58; on justice, 152
I Timothy: 131

Titus quoted: 209
Tobit quoted: 97
Toffler, Alvin: 60
Tournier, Paul: 15-16, 248-49
Transactional analysis: 14, 26
Troeltsch, Ernest: 212
Truth, divine: 44
Unemployment: 62
United Church of Christ: 195
United Nations: 50
United Nations Conference on the Human Environment, report of: 185-86
United Nations Declaration of Human Rights: 184, 267
United Nations Food and Agriculture Organization: 262
United States Commission on Civil Disorders: 271
Universities: Christian, 250; and specialization, 250; contracts, grants, 251; depersonalization, 251-52; city, 254; role in corrections, 261
Untouchability, untouchables: 20-21, 47
Urban League: 59
Usury laws: 170

Valentian, Emperor: 91-92
Values: in helping relationship, 22, 24; Christian, 29-30
Villot, Cardinal Jean: 202-203
Violence: 20, 40-41, 53-54, 56, 141, 158-59, 162
Vlastos, Gregory: 150
Vocational-technical programs: 252
Voting rights: 160

Wakin, Edward: 234-35
War: 11-12, 53; and world peace, 244-45; and prophecy, 246-48; and nuclear age, 248-49
Ward, Barbara: 186
Water, pollution of: 175-77; *see also* environment
Wedel, Theodore: 58
Weight Watchers: 28
Wendt, the Reverend William A.: 208

Index

Where Do We Go From Here: Chaos or Community?: 53
White, Lynn, Jr.: 174
Why War?: 78
Wilde, Oscar: 90
Williams, David Day: 58
Wilson, Bryan: 13
Winter, Gibson: 58
Wisdom Literature (of Old Testament): 34

Women's liberation movement: 29, 205-11
Wygant, Willis E., Jr.: 195
Wynne-Edwards, V. C.: 188

Yahweh (God): 7, 10
Young, Whitney M., Jr.: and black-oriented brotherhood, 37; on ending racism, 39; on violence, 41; and open society, 55-60